ECONOMIC THEORY OF BANK CREDIT

Economic Theory of Bank Credit

L. ALBERT HAHN

Translated by
Clemens Matt

With an Introduction by
Harald Hagemann

OXFORD
UNIVERSITY PRESS

OXFORD
UNIVERSITY PRESS

Great Clarendon Street, Oxford, OX2 6DP,
United Kingdom

Oxford University Press is a department of the University of Oxford.
It furthers the University's objective of excellence in research, scholarship,
and education by publishing worldwide. Oxford is a registered trade mark of
Oxford University Press in the UK and in certain other countries

First Edition published in 2015

Published in the United States of America by Oxford University Press 198 Madison Avenue, New York, NY 10016, United States of America

British Library Cataloguing in Publication Data
Data available

Library of Congress Control Number: 2015935255

ISBN 978–0–19–872307–3

Introduction

Harald Hagemann

Almost a century ago in 1920, L. Albert Hahn published the first edition of his *Volkswirtschaftliche Theorie des Bankkredits*.[1] Thanks to the persistent endeavours and great enthusiasm of his translator Clemens Matt the book is available to a wider English-speaking audience for the first time. The book had attracted many readers (but limited to the shrinking group able to read German) interested in the role of banks and credit in modern debates in monetary macroeconomics. An English language translation of L. Albert Hahn's *Economic Theory of Bank Credit* is therefore not only highly welcome but long overdue.[2]

Hahn wanted to overcome the orthodox view that every credit has to be financed by means of savings deposited in banks with his *Economic Theory of Bank Credit*, which remained the most important monograph among his many writings. He regarded the classical doctrine as adequate for the state of development of the economy at the time of the classical economists (of whom he gave highest praise to Ricardo) but found it most inappropriate for a modern economy with elastic money and credit supply. The central regression line of Hahn's thought is the doctrine that '*capital formation is not the consequence of savings but of granting credit; granting credit logically precedes capital accumulation*'.[3]

Hahn stuck to this view until the end of his life despite many later modifications and some fundamental changes in his economic views which for some modern historians of economic thought mutated a

[1] Lucien Albert Hahn, *Volkswirtschaftliche Theorie des Bankkredits*, 1st ed. (Tübingen: J. C. B Mohr (Paul Siebeck), 1920).

[2] So far only an Italian translation, edited by Lapo Berti, had been published in 1990, as vol. 3 in a series on Economia Monetaria (edited by Professor Augusto Graziani) where the Italian translation of Hayek's *Prices and Production* was published as vol. 2. See Lucien Albert Hahn, *Teoria economica del credito*, trans. and ed. Lapo Berti (Naples: Edizioni Scientifiche Italiane, 1990).

[3] With this priority of credit creation over capital formation Hahn starts the explanation of his own theory in contrast to the traditional doctrine. Hahn, *Volkswirtschaftliche Theorie des Bankkredits*, 1st ed., p. 120.

'precursor of Keynesianism' into one of 'the monetarist counterrevolution'.[4] He concludes the condensed autobiographical survey of his development as a theorist over half a century by pointing to the fundamental principle of his business cycle and employment theory (which, however, needs to be applied with care): '*Every credit expansion causes an increase in production, as a consequence to a shift in distribution. Credit draws the goods from a nirvana, in which they would remain without the credit expansion*'.[5]

A second edition of Hahn's book was published in completely unaltered form (in which even the many misprints of the names of famous economists were not corrected) shortly after the end of the period of hyperinflation and currency reforms in Germany and Austria in 1924.[6] The author reveals in the preface that a lack of time was the reason for publishing an unaltered reprint. Hahn also vainly refers to the fact 'that almost every economic seminar at German universities discussed my book in detail' which contributed to a quick sell-out of the first edition whilst also complaining that his contribution had been widely neglected or misunderstood by the great majority of the economics profession. Despite Hahn's dissatisfaction, his *Economic Theory of Bank Credit* had become one of the most influential and certainly the most controversial book on monetary economics in the German-speaking world of the mid and late 1920s.

In his critical but respectful review article of Hahn's book, Gottfried Haberler came to the conclusion that 'Albert Hahn undoubtedly deserves a prominent place in the history of the most recent German monetary theory' but also 'that of late a Hahn literature has developed, inasmuch as scarcely a book is published today on money and credit that does not discuss Hahn's teachings at length'.[7] Both Haberler's and

[4] Donald J. Boudreaux and George A. Selgin, 'L. Albert Hahn: a precursor of Keynesianism and the Monetarist counterrevolution', *History of Political Economy* 22, no. 2, (1990): 261–79.

[5] Lucien Albert Hahn, *Fünfzig Jahre zwischen Inflation und Deflation [Fifty Years between Inflation and Deflation]* (Tübingen: J. C. B Mohr (Paul Siebeck), 1963). p. 13 and Lucien Albert Hahn, *Volkswirtschaftliche Theorie des Bankkredits*, 3rd ed. (Tübingen: J. C. B Mohr (Paul Siebeck), 1930), pp. 125–6.

[6] Lucien Albert Hahn, *Volkswirtschaftliche Theorie des Bankkredits*, 2nd ed. (Tübingen: J. C. B Mohr (Paul Siebeck), 1924).

[7] Gottfried Haberler, 'Albert Hahns Volkswirtschaftliche Theorie des Bankkredits' [Albert Hahn's economic theory of bank credit], *Archiv für Sozialwissenschaft und Sozialpolitk 57* (1927): 803–20, p. 803. The German review article from 1927 was translated in 1949 as a substantially reduced version and printed in Lucien Albert

von Bortkiewicz's[8] reviews of the first edition are some of the most insightful contributions to the contemporary 'Hahn literature'. The proud author of the *Economic Theory of Bank Credit* himself extensively refers to this body of literature in his preface to the third and substantially revised edition, which was published in vastly different economic conditions at the beginning of the deflationary Great Depression in 1930.

HAHN'S BIOGRAPHY

Hahn's academic life and his scholarly contributions are strongly interlinked with his entrepreneurial life and his success as a practical banker.[9] One can therefore understand Hahn's *Economic Theory of Bank Credit* better with awareness of his biography. Lucien Albert Hahn was born into a family of private bankers in Frankfurt am Main on October 12, 1889.[10] After finishing high school at the Goethe-Gymnasium, Hahn began studying medicine at Freiburg before changing to law at Heidelberg and Marburg where he received his PhD in 1912. The First World War interrupted the completion of his legal education which he could only finalize at the court of justice in Berlin in 1919. In the same year he succeeded his sick father Albert (who died in 1921) on the management board of the family bank. The Bankhaus L. Albert Hahn, founded by his great-grandfather in 1821,

Hahn, *The Economics of Illusion: A Critical Analysis of Contemporary Economic Theory and Policy* (New York: Squier Publishing, 1949).

[8] Ludwig von Bortkiewicz, 'Das Wesen, die Grenzen und die Wirkungen des Bankkredits' [The Essence, Boundaries and Effects of Bank Credit], *Weltwirtschaftliches Archiv 17* (1922): 70–89.

[9] See also Jan-Otmar Hesse, 'Some Relationships between a Scholar's and an Entrepreneur's Life: The Biography of L. Albert Hahn', *History of Political Economy 39*, Annual Supplement (2007): 215–33.

[10] For details on Hahn's biography see Bernd Kulla, 'Hahn, Ludwig Albert', in *Biographisches Handbuch der deutschsprachigen wirtschaftswissenschaftlichen Emigration nach 1933*, vol. 1, edited by Harald Hagemann and Claus-Dieter Krohn (Munich: K. G. Saur, 1999); Hesse, 'Some Relationships between a Scholar's and an Entrepreneur's Life: The Biography of L. Albert Hahn' and most informative Michael Hauck, ed., *Albert Hahn. Ein verstoßener Sohn Frankfurts, Bankier und Wissenschaftler. Eine Dokumentation [Albert Hahn: A Purged Son of Frankfurt, Banker and Scholar: A Documentation]* (Frankfurt am Main: Societäts-Verlag, 2009).

had become a public company, the Deutsche Effecten- und Wechsel-Bank in 1872, in which the Hahn family held the majority of shares.

Hahn had already published journal articles on economic problems during the First World War[11] and acquired a second PhD, this time in economics from the University of Marburg in 1919. His thesis is entitled *Der Gegenstand des Geld- und Kapitalmarktes in der modernen Wirtschaft. Ein Beitrag zur Theorie des Bankgeschäfts*[12] and formed the basis of his widely expanded *Economic Theory of Bank Credit* which was published in the subsequent year. In retrospect the author considered the results of his doctoral thesis as 'extremely unorthodox'[13] and the book as 'full of youthful enthusiasm and convinced of having discovered the path to permanent prosperity'.[14]

Hahn, who aimed for a better theoretical understanding of his practical activities as a leading private banker, had now found his role as 'a theorizing practitioner'.[15] Whereas the *Economic Theory of Bank Credit* was heavily criticised by many contemporary economists as an 'apotheosis of credit creation',[16] the insights of the author into the essence and the consequences of hyperinflation helped to maintain the capital of the bank under the direction of Hahn and his uncle Ludwig. The professional banker felt a compulsion to become 'at least an avocational theoretician'[17] who published regularly in scholarly journals.[18] Furthermore, Hahn contributed frequently to economic periodicals and the best newspapers, exerting some influence on the banking community and the public policy debate.

[11] For a complete bibliography, see Hahn, *Fünfzig Jahre zwischen Inflation und Deflation,* pp. 241–7.

[12] Lucien Albert Hahn, 'Der Gegenstand des Geld- und Kapitalmarktes in der modernen Wirschaft: Ein Beitrag zur Theorie des Bankgeschäfts' [The Object of the Money and Capital Market in the Modern Economy: A Contribution to the Theory of the Banking Business], *Archiv für Sozialwissenschaft und Sozialpolitik 46* (1919): pp. 163–215.

[13] Lucien Albert Hahn, *Fünfzig Jahre zwischen Inflation und Deflation,* p. 4.

[14] Lucien Albert Hahn, 'Die Grundirrtümer in Lord Keynes' *General Theory of Employment, Interest and Money*' [The fundamental errors in Lord Keynes' *General Theory of Employment, Interest and Money*], *Ordo 2* (1949): pp. 170–90, p. 171.

[15] Lucien Albert Hahn, *Fünfzig Jahre zwischen Inflation und Deflation,* p. 1.

[16] See, for example, Howard S. Ellis, *German Monetary Theory 1905–1933* (Cambridge, MA: Harvard University Press, 1934), p. 329.

[17] Lucien Albert Hahn, *Fünfzig Jahre zwischen Inflation und Deflation,* p. 3.

[18] The collected essays comprising Hahn's most important articles are published in Lucien Albert Hahn, *Geld und Kredit [Money and Credit],* (Tübingen; J. C. B Mohr, 1924) and Lucien Albert Hahn, *Geld und Kredit: Neue Folge. [Money and Credit: New Series],* (Tübingen: J. C. B Mohr, 1929).

Business cycles became a dominant research theme in the interwar period. In 1925, a more systematic empirical analysis started with the foundation of the German Institute for Business Cycle Research, today's DIW, in Berlin. In the subsequent year Hahn initiated the foundation of the *Frankfurter Gesellschaft für Konjunkturforschung* (Frankfurt Society for Research on Business Cycles) which was financially supported by the Frankfurt Chamber of Commerce. The Frankfurt Society was chaired by Hahn's friend Eugen Altschul[19] and strongly cooperated with the faculty members of the Goethe University. The focus on the methodological foundations of empirical research on business cycles became its trademark. This is exemplified by Oskar Anderson's[20] critical assessment of the index of general business conditions like the 'barometric' approach to forecasting of the Harvard Committee on Economic Research and which launched an important publication series.[21] In 1928, Hahn received an honorary professorship from the Goethe University for his contributions to monetary economics. Hahn lectured regularly on money and credit at the Faculty of Economics and Social Sciences from spring 1929. This came to an abrupt end four years later in spring 1933 when Hahn was among the nineteen members of the Faculty of Economics and the Social Sciences of Goethe University who were dismissed for racial and/or political reasons on the basis of the Restoration of Civil Service Act, an Act promulgated by the Nazis only seven weeks after their rise to power on 7 April 1933. The list included among others such outstanding scholars as Henryk Grossmann, Carl Grünberg, Adolf Löwe, Karl Mannheim, Fritz Neumark, Franz Oppenheimer, and Karl Pribram.[22]

[19] Hahn refers twice to Altschul's work (Hahn, *Volkswirtschaftliche Theorie des Bankkredits*, 3rd ed., p. 148 and p. 152), thus when he emphasised that 'The credit volume has increased twelvefold in the period of 1870 to 1910' (footnote 1 in chapter [2.*]C).

[20] Oskar Anderson, *Zur Problematik der empirisch-statistischen Konjunkturforschung [On the Problems of the Empirical-statistical Business Cycle Research]* (Bonn: Verlag Kurt Schröder, 1929).

[21] For a more detailed analysis of the Frankfurt Society for Research on Business Cycles see Bernd Kulla, *Die Anfänge der empirischen Konjunkturforschung in Deutschland 1925–33 [The Beginning of Empirical Business Cycle Research in Germany]* (Berlin: Duncker & Humblot, 1996), pp. 163–80.

[22] For a full list see p. 443 in Jan-Otmar Hesse, 'Die Frankfurter Wirtschafts- und Sozialwissenschaftliche Fakultät zwischen 1933 und 1945' [The Faculty of Economic and Social Sciences in Frankfurt from 1933 to 1945], in *Wirtschafts und Sozialwissenschaftler in Frankfurt am Main*, ed. Bertram Schefold, 2nd ed. (Marburg: Metropolis, 2004): pp. 440–63.

The Hahn family was able to sell their shares of the bank to a consortium of Berlin banks in 1936, just in time before the 'legal' expropriation of Jews led to a rapid decline in prices. In the same year Hahn emigrated to Switzerland where he settled in Geneva. Since the Prussian annexation of Frankfurt in 1866 the Hahn family had acquired Swiss nationality as citizens of the canton Schaffhausen to avoid their sons having to undertake military service in the Prussian army.[23] In Switzerland the only son of Hahn and Nora von Girsewald (1906–1992) was born in 1936 and named Nicolaus. They had married in Vaduz (Liechtenstein) in 1933 when Hahn converted to Protestantism. In 1939, Hahn moved from Geneva to New York, where he worked as an asset manager and lectured regularly at the Graduate Faculty of Political and Social Science of the New School for Social Research which had been founded as the 'University in Exile' in fall 1933. He gained a fortune by buying shares of American oil companies just before the United States entered the war against Nazi Germany. He now followed a strongly anti-Keynesian track in the country of the New Deal as an instructor and author of economic articles, which culminated in his collected essays *The Economics of Illusion*, published in New York with an introduction by the avowed anti-Keynesian Henry Hazlitt in 1949. In the same year Hahn left the United States and returned to Europe where he settled in Zurich, Paris, and in Southern France. From there he quite often commuted to Frankfurt, where his honorary professorship was reinstated by the Goethe University in 1948. He lectured there on Keynes's *General Theory*,[24] but didn't continue to teach regularly. However, in Germany Hahn worked again as a banker and finally became a member of the supervisory board of the former family bank in 1964. Economically and politically he was now an 'extreme liberal'.[25] No wonder that Ludwig von Mises, Henry Hazlitt, Wilhelm Röpke, but also Gottfried

[23] See Hauck, *Albert Hahn*, p. 19 and p. 57.

[24] See p. 467 in Volker Caspari, 'Die Volkswirtschaftslehre an der Wirtschafts- und Sozialwissenschaftlichen Fakultät der Universität Frankfurt am Main von der Wiedereröffnung nach dem Kriege bis in die 70er Jahre', in *Wirtschafts und Sozialwissenschaftler in Frankfurt am Main*, ed. Bertram Schefold, 2nd ed. (Marburg: Metropolis, 2004): pp. 464–92.

[25] See p. 92 in Fritz Neumark, 'Erinnerungen: Schüler Gerloffs und Privatdozent: Die Zeit von 1925–1933' [Memories: Gerloff's student and Privatdozent], in *Wirtschafts und Sozialwissenschaftler in Frankfurt am Main*, ed. Bertram Schefold, 2nd ed. (Marburg: Metropolis, 2004): pp. 83–92.

Haberler, Friedrich Lutz, and the German Minister of Economics and later Chancellor Ludwig Erhard were among the key contributors to the Festschrift that Hahn received at his seventieth birthday by his friends.[26] Hahn had become an active member in the Mont Pèlerin Society. Due to Machlup in 1963, Hahn also became a member of the Bellagio Group which was engaged in the fight for flexible exchange rates in the final decade of the Bretton Woods System. Hahn died in Zurich on 4 October 1968.

HAHN'S RELATION TO WICKSELL AND SCHUMPETER

The most interesting aspects of Hahn's *Economic Theory of Bank Credit* are contained in the second part of the book where the author is concerned with the effects of credit creation and credit extension on production. From the beginning Hahn was convinced 'that bank credit can stimulate the economy'.[27] Thus a decisive function of an economic analysis of bank credit consists in a contribution to a monetary theory of the business cycle. Consequentially, Holtfrerich[28] focuses his investigation of the development of monetary business cycle theory in the German-speaking world on the main contributions made by the pioneers Wicksell and Schumpeter, the 'breakthrough with excesses' by Hahn, and the further elaboration of a monetary overinvestment theory by Mises and Hayek.

Knut Wicksell is one of the first economists to perceive the growing importance of the banking system for the money supply of the economy at the end of the nineteenth century and the elasticity or endogeneity associated with credit creation (i.e. the banks' ability to create deposits in their act of lending). He also placed it at the centre of his analysis in *Interest and Prices*. There he confronted the case of a

[26] Volkmar Muthesius, ed., *Eine Freundesgabe für Albert Hahn zum 12. Oktober 1959* (Frankfurt am Main: Fritz Knapp Verlag, 1959).

[27] Hahn, *Volkswirtschaftliche Theorie des Bankkredits*, 1st ed., p. 156.

[28] Carl-Ludwig Holtfrerich, 'Zur Entwicklung der monetären Konjunkturtheorien: Wicksell, Schumpeter, Hahn, Mises und Hayek' [On the Development of Monetary Business Cycle Theories: Wicksell, Schumpeter, Hahn, Mises, and Hayek], in *Studien zur Entwicklung der ökonomischen Theorie*, vol. 8, ed. by Bertram Schefold (Berlin: Duncker & Humblot, 1989): p. 103–40.

pure credit economy, in which every payment, and consequently every loan, is made by means of cheques or giro facilities, with the antithesis of a pure cash economy, a system of pure outside money to which the classical quantity theory applies. In an advanced economy with highly developed credit institutions which can grant loans in excess of the amount of deposited savings, the money supply is completely elastic and is 'more and more inclined to accommodate itself to the level of demand'.[29] In such an organised credit economy, price-level stability requires equality between the natural (equilibrium) rate and the money rate of interest, that is, the rate of interest charged on loans. Discrepancies between the two rates lead to cumulative processes as described by Wicksell.

In the preface to the third edition of his *Economic Theory of Bank Credit*, Hahn[30] points out his 'basic conception of a monetary business cycle theory' and that he has 'built on the basic idea of . . . the fictitious cashless economy'. Time and again he emphasizes that he is following Wicksell[31] and that his argumentation is 'in line with the monetary business cycle theory, we claim that those business cycles are nothing other than the effects of an inflationary and then deflationary credit policy of banks'.[32] However, whereas Hahn identifies the decisive cause of cyclical fluctuations in the money and credit-generating power of the banking system, it must be stated that Wicksell was *not* a proponent of a monetary business-cycle theory. David Laidler has already rightly pointed out Wicksell's unwillingness to develop such a monetary theory of the business cycle and that his emphasis on technological shocks which lead to a change in the natural rate of interest as the decisive cause of business cycles 'places him far closer to the Marx–Schumpeter tradition on cycle theory than to any monetary tradition'.[33] Wicksell's cumulative processes caused by the divergence between the money and the natural rate of interest, although being central for an understanding of changes in the general level of prices, however, are not important for the explanation of the

[29] See Knut Wicksell, *Interest and Prices*, trans. Richard F. Kahn (London: Macmillan, 1936), p. 110. The work was published first in German as Knut Wicksell, *Geldzins und Güterpreise* (Jena: Gustav Fischer, 1898).

[30] Hahn, *Volkswirtschaftliche Theorie des Bankkredits*, 3rd ed., p. xix.

[31] See in particular chapter [2.*]C 'Credit and Business Cycles'.

[32] Hahn, *Volkswirtschaftliche Theorie des Bankkredits*, 3rd ed., p. 142.

[33] David Laidler, *The Golden Age of the Quantity Theory* (New York and London: Philip Allan, 1991), p. 145.

business-cycle phenomenon, as has been made clear by Leijonhufvud.[34] Wicksell viewed the disturbance between the two rates of interest arising on the real side as due to technical advances improving profit expectations and causing an increase in the natural interest rate and in overall investment. This was demonstrated in his article 'A new theory of crises',[35] in which 'Wicksell made an attempt to bridge the gap between monetary and real theories of crises'.[36]

The idea of creative destruction by innovations and the notion that bank credit is a decisive prerequisite for pioneering entrepreneurs to finance innovating investment activities are key pillars of Schumpeter's *Theory of Economic Development.*[37] The financing of production is essentially performed by the creation and destruction of credit. Schumpeter shares Wicksell's view that the disturbance of economic equilibrium primarily emerges from an enlargement of profitable investment options due to technical progress rather than by an artificial lowering of the money rate of interest by the banks which causes a period of unsustainable expansion. The latter is also emphasised in the works of his two Austrian compatriots Mises's *Theory of Money and Credit*[38] and Hayek's *Prices and Production.*[39] There, the bust is the inevitable consequence of the credit-induced boom in

[34] Axel Leijonhufvud, 'The Wicksellian Heritage', *Economic Notes 26* (1997): pp. 1–10.

[35] Knut Wicksell, 'A New Theory of Crises', *Structural Change and Economic Dynamics 12* (2001): pp. 335–42. The article was originally written in German in 1907 (see Harald Hagemann 'Wicksell's "New Theory of Crisis": An Introduction', *Structural Change and Economic Dynamics 12* (2001) pp. 331–4).

[36] This view has gained further confirmation by Wicksell's lecture notes from Lund, provided and discussed in Mauro Boianovsky and Hans-Michael Trautwein 'Wicksell's Lecture Notes on Economic Crises', *Structural Change and Economic Dynamics 12* (2001) pp. 343–66.

[37] Joseph Alois Schumpeter, *Theorie der wirtschaftlichen Entwicklung* (Munich and Leipzig: Duncker & Humblot, 1911), 2nd rev. ed., 1926. This was published in English as Joseph Alois Schumpeter, *The Theory of Economic Development: An Inquiry into Profits, Capital, Credit, Interest and the Business Cycle* (Cambridge, MA: Harvard University Press, 1934), reprinted in 1980 by Oxford University Press in Oxford.

[38] Ludwig von Mises, *Theorie des Geldes und der Umlaufsmittel* (Munich and Leipzig: Duncker & Humblot, 1912). This was published in English as Ludwig von Mises, *The Theory of Money and Credit*, trans. Harold E. Batson (London: Jonathan Cape, 1934). The book was reprinted in 1953 by Yale University Press in New Haven. A new edition with stylistic changes and footnote corrections was published in 1981 by Liberty Press in Indianapolis.

[39] Friedrich August von Hayek, *Prices and Production* (London: Routledge & Kegan Paul, 1931).

which the reallocation of productive resources to excessively roundabout methods of production is corrected. Mises's argument of excessive credit extension by the banking sector as the decisive cause of cyclical fluctuations is most clearly stated in his *Monetary Stabilization and Cyclical Policy*,[40] in which he distances himself from views still held by Schumpeter and even from some of his own earlier views.

In his introduction to the third edition Hahn[41] claims that he had based his first edition of the *Economic Theory of Bank Credit* on the overall economic views of Schumpeter, but that otherwise a work on the creation of purchasing power by the banks had no role model in the newer German literature. The importance of credit to finance innovative investment activities is at the very centre of Schumpeter's *Theory of Economic Development*, which has been classified by Hahn as 'epoch-making'.[42] There Schumpeter defined 'the kernel of the credit phenomenon in the following manner: credit is essentially the creation of purchasing power for the purpose of transferring it to the entrepreneur, but not simply the transfer of existing purchasing power'.[43] Like Schumpeter, Hahn emphasised the power of credit to generate a contribution to the social product.[44] In the second German edition of his *Theory of Economic Development*, Schumpeter[45] reacted to Hahn's *Economic Theory of Bank Credit* with the addition of a long opening note to chapter III on 'Credit and Capital' in which he explicitly referred the reader 'to this original and meritorious book, which has essentially advanced our knowledge of the problem'.[46] Decades later in his autobiographical reflections on the history of economic thought Hahn[47] still noted that this agreement by Professor Schumpeter was 'particularly welcome'.

[40] Ludwig von Mises, *Geldwertstabilisierung und Konjunkturpolitik* (Jena: Gustav Fischer, 1928). A translation was later published in *Mises on the Manipulation of Money and Credit,* ed. by Percy L. Greaves, trans. Bettina B. Greaves (Dobbs Ferry, NY: Free Market Books, 1978): pp. 57–107.

[41] Hahn, *Volkswirtschaftliche Theorie des Bankkredits*, 3rd ed., p. xvii.

[42] Hahn, *Volkswirtschaftliche Theorie des Bankkredits*, 1st and 2nd ed., p. 4.

[43] Schumpeter, *Theory of Economic Development*, p. 107.

[44] Hahn, *Volkswirtschaftliche Theorie des Bankkredits*, 1st and 2nd ed., p. 93.

[45] Joseph Alois Schumpeter, *Theorie der wirtschaftlichen Entwicklung,* 2nd ed., (Munich and Leipzig: Duncker & Humblot, 1926), p. 140.

[46] Schumpeter, *Theory of Economic Development*, p. 95, footnote 1.

[47] Hahn, *Fünfzig Jahre zwischen Inflation und Deflation,* p. 6.

THE CRITICAL RECEPTION OF HAHN

Schumpeter[48] deals intensively in his *History of Economic Analysis* with the important developments that occurred between 1870 and 1914 in the banking systems of all advanced economies. He also exposes the great difficulties of economists in grasping that bank loans do create deposits and have a central role to play in the financing of investment, independently of previous savings. In his analysis of the effects upon prices, Schumpeter emphasizes that 'it was not until 1924 that the theoretical job was done completely in a book by Hahn'.[49] However, with regard to the definitive impact of Hahn's book in retrospect Schumpeter came to the conclusion: 'One reason why this book left so many economists unconvinced was . . . the fact that the theory of bank credit presented there was wedded to certain highly optimistic views about the possibility of achieving permanent prosperity, which prejudiced some economists against its essential achievement'.[50] Strangely, Schumpeter in the note to the text refers to the third and completely revised edition of Hahn's book in which the vision of permanent prosperity is no longer the conclusion drawn by the author's assessment of the effects of credit creation.

It was the more radical first edition of Hahn's *Economic Theory of Bank Credit* which generated an outcry when it was republished in an unchanged second edition in 1924 just after the end of German hyperinflation and the concluding currency reform. Hahn kept the *leitmotiv*, which he took from the British economist Henry Dunning Macleod, on the cover page of the more moderate third edition: 'A bank is therefore not an office for "borrowing" and "lending" money, but it is a Manufactory of Credit.'[51] Following not only Macleod, but also Wicksell and Schumpeter,[52] Hahn denies the traditional idea of

[48] Joseph Schumpeter, *History of Economic Analysis* (Cambridge, MA: Harvard University Press, 1954), chapter 8 'Money, Credit and Cycles' of part IV.

[49] Schumpeter, *History of Economic Analysis*, pp. 1115–16. It should read 1920 since the second edition of Hahn's book is a reprint of the first edition.

[50] Schumpeter, *History of Economic Analysis*, p. 1110.

[51] Henry D. Macleod, *The Theory of Credit*, 2 vols. (London and New York: Longmans, Green and Co, 1889–91), vol. 2, part 2, p. 594.

[52] Schumpeter, *History of Economic Analysis*, p. 1115, n. 7 considered Macleod as 'an economist of many merits who somehow failed to achieve recognition, or even to be taken quite seriously, owing to his inability to put his many good ideas in a professionally acceptable form'. In a typically contradictory Schumpeterian style he

the role of the banks being to function only as the mediator of credit between savers and investors. Different from Macleod, in whose writing money creation by private banks sides with that of the central bank, the money creation capacity of the private banking sector takes the key role in Hahn. 'The position of this book is that deposits are the consequence not the cause of the credit business.'[53] Even in the third and completely revised edition of *Economic Theory of Bank Credit* Hahn emphasizes that 'It is the main purpose of this book to highlight the relative independence of credit expansion from previous or current savings. Furthermore, it wants to show the important theoretical and practical consequences of a credit expansion exceeding simultaneous savings.'[54]

Hahn belonged to the exponents of the old credit view who based their analysis on the benchmark of a cash-saving credit economy in which the limits of credit are not drawn clearly.[55] Banks could determine the amount of credit granted in an autonomous and irresponsible way. Hahn's argument that capital formation in a pure credit economy differs fundamentally from capital formation in a cash economy has been a target of critique by many contemporaries.[56]

One of the most noteworthy critics was Hans Neisser who was recognised by Keynes as one of the leading neo-Wicksellians in the German-speaking world. Keynes found 'Dr. Neisser's general attitude to monetary problems particularly sympathetic' and hoped 'that he

goes on to argue that Macleod 'laid the foundations of the modern theory of the subject... though what he really succeeded in doing was to discredit this theory for quite a time'. For a modern assessment of Macleod's credit theory of money see Neil T. Skaggs, 'Henry Dunning Macleod and the Credit Theory of Money', in *Money, Financial Institutions and Macroeconomics*, ed. Avi J. Cohen, Harald Hagemann, John Smithin (Boston, Dordrecht, London: Kluwer Academic Publishers, 1997): pp. 109–23.

[53] Hahn, *Volkswirtschaftliche Theorie des Bankkredits*, 1st and 2nd ed., p. 55.

[54] Hahn, *Volkswirtschaftliche Theorie des Bankkredits*, 3rd ed., p. 41.

[55] For a detailed survey comparing old and new credit views see Hans-Michael Trautwein, 'The Credit View, Old and New', *Journal of Economic Surveys 14*, (2000): pp. 145–89.

[56] See Adolf Lampe, *Zur Theorie des Sparprozesses und der Kreditschöpfung [On the Theory of Saving and Credit]* (Jena: Gustav Fischer, 1926), pp. 134–5; Haberler, 'Albert Hahns Volkswirtschaftliche Theorie des Bankkredits', p. 814; Heinrich Mannstaedt, *Ein kritischer Beitrag zur Theorie des Bankkredits* (Jena: Gustav Fischer, 1927), pp. 13–15; Hans Neisser, *Der Tauschwert des Geldes* (Jena: Gustav Fischer, 1928), pp. 70–1); Ellis, *German Monetary Theory 1905–1933*, p. 329.

may feel the same about my work'.[57] Although he regarded Hahn's distinction between primary banks creating credit, 'the issuing bank of the modern economy'[58] and secondary banks where the deposits appear quite fruitful, Neisser nevertheless criticised Hahn for denying the difference between the granting of credit by money creation and the granting of credit from saving deposits.[59] According to Neisser, it would never be decisive whether a deposit had been generated by paying in cash or by the granting of credit but solely whether the deposit could be used for payments, that is, functioning as money. It must be clear that additional credit could be created only by those banks which keep cheque accounts, and therefore are the carrier of cashless payments, that is, exactly those deposit banks which can increase the amount of money in the economy by lending out again the cash flowing to them, by simultaneously keeping the cheque deposits.

A similar but even harsher critique had been raised by Bortkiewicz and Haberler. Bortkiewicz found fault with Hahn's classification of two types of banks, the result of ignoring the possibility that a bank could operate alternately on the active and the passive side.[60] Haberler emphasised that the primary bank must become passive against the secondary bank in the clearing process and that it therefore becomes dependent on the latter since it can give credit only up to an amount that the passive balance is granted a deferred payment.[61] Furthermore, Haberler criticised Hahn's statement that credit banks are independent from the central bank in their expansion of credit,[62] pointing to the evident contradiction with Hahn's statement on the same page that the central bank has at its disposal the drastic means to deny the rediscounting of bankable papers.

[57] John Maynard Keynes, *A Treatise on Money*, v and vi: *The Collected Writings of John Maynard Keynes* (London, Basingstoke, and New York: Cambridge University Press, 1971). The treatise was originally published by Macmillan, London in 1930.

[58] Hahn, *Volkswirtschaftliche Theorie des Bankkredits*, 1st and 2nd ed., p. 58.

[59] See Neisser, *Der Tauschwert des Geldes*, pp. 60–1.

[60] See Bortkiewicz, 'Das Wesen, die Grenzen und die Wirkungen des Bankkredits', pp. 81–2.

[61] See Haberler, 'Albert Hahns Volkswirtschaftliche Theorie des Bankkredits', pp. 811–12.

[62] See Hahn, *Volkswirtschaftliche Theorie des Bankkredits*, 1st and 2nd ed., p. 88.

THE EVOLVING ROLE OF CREDIT IN HAHN'S THOUGHTS

Haberler was also among the first fellow economists to notice that since the first publication of *Economic Theory of Bank Credit* in 1920 Hahn had considerably watered down his radical position, that in particular his 'Kredit' essay[63] bears 'conservative features'.[64] It is all the more astonishing that a year later Hahn published his book without any changes. In retrospect Hahn himself stated that the much more moderate, completely revised third edition of his *Economic Theory of Bank Credit*, published in 1930, had already been foreshadowed in his contribution on 'Kredit' to the *Handwörterbuch der Staatswissenschaften*. He attributed his modified views on money and credit to the experiences with hyperinflation in Weimar Germany in the early 1920s and summarised his new insights in retrospect as follows:[65]

1. There are limits to inflationary credit expansion in the long run, emphasised in the final section of Hahn.[66] Credit inflations which characterise the German economy since 1870 show that such developments can undermine the value of money which makes it necessary to weigh the pros and cons of credit extension. In open economies the depreciation of the domestic currency would give a clear stop signal.
2. An 'economic theory of bank credit' must be formulated as a business-cycle theory as a consequence of the autonomous credit creation power of banks which stimulates the economy.
3. Credit expansions may help to overcome depressions, but they should never be used in boom periods to perpetuate them or to make structural maladjustments (particularly excessive wages) bearable. 'A timely stabilization of the business cycle, not their stimulation on and on by inflation is desirable'.[67]
4. A failure in the limit of credit expansion results in progressive inflation and a possible ruin of state finances.

[63] Lucien Albert Hahn, 'Kredit' [Credit], in *Handwörterbuch der Staatswissenschaften*, ed. L. Elster, A. Weber, F. Wieser, v, 4 ed. (Jena: Gustav Fischer, 1923): pp. 944–53.
[64] Haberler, 'Albert Hahns Volkswirtschaftliche Theorie des Bankkredits', pp. 819.
[65] See Hahn, *Fünfzig Jahre zwischen Inflation und Deflation,* pp. 11–13.
[66] See Hahn, *Volkswirtschaftliche Theorie des Bankkredits*, 3rd ed., pp. 151–3.
[67] See Hahn, *Fünfzig Jahre zwischen Inflation und Deflation*, 3rd ed., p. 12.

Hahn's 1923 essay on credit marked the beginning of his transformation to a more moderate position. He is not talking any longer of the idea of a perpetual boom but still points to credit extension as a strong means to stimulate economic development of a country by full utilization of its factors of production, although at the price of the relative expropriation of the owners of money. He finishes his essay with the statement 'that it is the task of an aim-conscious credit policy to guide the economy through the Skylla of economic stagnation and the Charybdis of depreciation of money and crises of the economy'.[68]

In his 1923 essay Hahn also argues against Wilhelm Lexis whom he succeeded as the contributor on 'Kredit' in the fourth edition of the *Handwörterbuch der Staatswissenschaften*. Hahn criticised Lexis for sticking to the classical view to deny the capital generating power of credit.[69] Against this view Hahn argues: 'Capital formation *ceteris paribus* is *not* a question of the *production of goods but* a question of distribution, the *distribution of goods*, and that of the distribution of goods in *intertemporal* as well as *interpersonal* relation'. An intertemporal transfer of consumption into the future implies a change in the distribution of current goods. Insofar as the granting of credit is based on voluntary savings the change in distribution is temporary because current savers can consume more of those goods in future, the production of which they have made possible. In the case of inflationary credit, however, the change in distribution becomes definitive because the price increases reduce the real purchasing power of receivers of fixed incomes who now are suffering from forced savings, that is, an involuntary reduction of consumption.[70] This 'expropriation' is either temporary, as is the case for workers whose wages will be adjusted to the price increases so that they regain their earlier share in the social product, or permanent as for rentiers because inflation has eroded the basis of their real purchasing power for all times. Thus inflation has permanent consequences on the distribution of income and wealth. Whereas the owners of real assets and the debtors in industry, agriculture, and wealth are among the winners, the owners of money wealth, creditors and all receivers of income that is adjusted with a time lag are among the losers.

Hahn takes up this argument in the third edition of his *Economic Theory of Bank Credit* where he argues that 'credit expansion . . . is

[68] See Hahn, 'Kredit', p. 953.
[69] See Hahn, 'Kredit', p. 946.
[70] See Hahn, 'Kredit', p. 951.

never as irrelevant for capital creation as the classics thought' and 'capital creation is *not* a matter of goods *production*, but a matter of the *distribution* in particular the *inter- and intratemporal* distribution of goods'.[71]

Hahn's retrospective view, which is full of warnings against the inflationary dangers of excessive credit extensions, was not yet fully developed in 1923. However, it is in his article on 'Credit' that Hahn takes up Schumpeter's distinction between 'normal' and 'abnormal' credit and develops the distinction between '*non-inflationary*' credit, granted in the amount of overall savings in the economy, and '*inflationary*' credit, which transcends these savings due to the money-creating ability of the banking sector:

> The terms deflationary and non-deflationary credit contraction are used in symmetry to the terms inflationary and non-inflationary credit expansion. An inflationary credit expansion takes place, if the newly granted credits exceed new 'savings'. Non-inflationary credit expansion takes place if new savings keep up with newly granted credits. Accordingly, a deflationary credit contraction takes place if new savings exceed newly granted credits. Non-deflationary credit contraction takes place if the reduction in savings matches the reduction in credits.[72]

The early Hahn (1920/1924) unrestrictedly favoured inflationary credit expansion because it would lead to an increase in overall demand which for its part stimulates the production of goods. Against the background of German and Austrian hyperinflation in 1922/23 the favouring of 'inflationary credit' (Hahn) or 'abnormal credit' (Schumpeter) surely was not the best choice of words or marketing strategy. It is therefore no surprise that particularly Hahn, who put much more emphasis on the directly production-enhancing effects of an inflationary credit creation and who propagated a 'perpetual boom', came under severe fire by contemporary critics and was accused as an 'inflationist'. Schumpeter felt obliged to keep some distance from Hahn and pointed out in the second German edition of his *Theory of Economic Development* with regard to Hahn's 'otherwise excellent article' on 'Credit': 'Against his formulation it appears to me correct to say: although not by *existing* goods,

[71] See Hahn, *Volkswirtschaftliche Theorie des Bankkredits*, 3rd ed., pp. 128–9.
[72] See Hahn, *Volkswirtschaftliche Theorie des Bankkredits*, 3rd ed., p. 133, n. 114.

the quantity of new purchasing power that it is possible to create is supported and limited by *future* goods' (emphases added).[73]

The early Hahn was not precise in the first two editions of the *Economic Theory of Bank Credit* when considering the question of how much available resources were already utilised when credit was extended and made no clear distinction whether the credit was used for investment or consumption purposes. With his 'Credit' essay he started to distinguish between *consumptive credits*, among which the consumptive government loans are the most important ones, and *productive credits* which lead to capital formation. These productive credits play the dominant role in the modern economy and bring about a strong link between credit and capital. Hahn thus approaches the position of Schumpeter for whom the spending of credit for innovative investments always had been decisive.[74]

Hahn elaborated his more reflected view further in the third edition of his *Economic Theory of Bank Credit* where he makes clearer that he considers the economic organism as 'elastic' so that hitherto underutilised resources, that is, previously unused labour and under-utilised factories, could be activated by credit expansion.[75]

> The credit expansion . . . is never as irrelevant for capital creation as the classics thought. Daily experience demonstrates this. If credit (also *inflationary*) is granted and appropriately used, then it creates new production machines, factories, generally capital in the economic sense for the debtor.[76]

Is it justified to talk of a 'Schumpeter–Hahn type of cycle theory' as Hahn himself (who felt flattered to be classified into a category with such an authority as Schumpeter) and others believed?[77] Hahn

[73] Schumpeter, *Theorie der wirtschaftlichen Entwicklung*, 2nd ed, p. 165, footnote 18; see also Schumpeter, *Theory of Economic Development*, p. 115, footnote 2, where Schumpeter adds at the end 'and, to repeat, by *future* goods at *present* prices'.

[74] 'Capital is nothing but the lever by which the entrepreneur subjects to his control to concrete goods which he needs, nothing but a means of diverting the factors of production to new uses, or of dictating a new direction to production.' (Schumpeter, *Theory of Economic Development*, p. 116).

[75] See esp. section II. A IV. 'The effect of credit expansion on the employment rate'.

[76] See Hahn, *Volkswirtschaftliche Theorie des Bankkredits*, 3rd ed., p. 128.

[77] Ellis classifies Hahn with Schumpeter and confronts the 'Schumpeter–Hahn type of cycle theory' with the 'Mises–Hayek analysis of cycle theory' (see Ellis, *German Monetary Theory 1905–1933*).

considered 'the typical business cycle as the consequence of alternating credit inflations and deflations'.[78] In his *Economic Theory of Bank Credit* credit cycles are identified as the main cause of cyclical fluctuations. Hahn thereby contributed to the breakthrough of monetary business-cycle theory in Germany, with Mises and Hayek representing the more conservative and the early Hahn taking the radical position.[79] In remarkable contrast to Schumpeter, however, Hahn does not make innovations a central element of his argument in any of his writings. Therefore the notion of a 'Schumpeter–Hahn type of cycle theory' should be given up.

HAHN'S ROLE AS A 'PROTO-KEYNESIAN' AND 'PROTO-MONETARIST'

Whereas the early Hahn in his *Economic Theory of Bank Credit* holds radical views, propagating a permanent boom with the support of credit expansion and denouncing bourgeois virtues such as saving, he later became a fierce anti-Keynesian. Hahn's 'proto-Keynesianism' (and even his 'proto-Monetarism'[80]) has also been discussed in more recent contributions, as well as his conversion from pre-Keynesianism to anti-Keynesianism. In particular Hesse has shown convincingly 'that the question of Hahn's precursorship was strongly woven into the particular self-construction of his biography' and that 'it was Hahn himself who brought his own work into the discussion about the roots and the critics of Keynesianism'.[81]

[78] See Hahn, *Volkswirtschaftliche Theorie des Bankkredits*, 3rd ed., p. 152.

[79] See also Holtfrerich, 'Zur Entwicklung der monetären Konjunkturtheorien: Wicksell, Schumpeter, Hahn, Mises und Hayek', p. 123 and G. Hardach, 'Der lange Abschied vom Gold: Geldtheorie und Geldpolitik in Deutschland, 1905–1933', (1989: 166–7) in *Studien zur Entwicklung der ökonomischen Theorie*, viii, ed. Bertram Schefold (Berlin: Duncker & Humblot, 1989): pp. 141–70.

[80] See Boudreaux and Selgin, 'L. Albert Hahn: A Precursor of Keynesianism and the Monetarist Counterrevolution' and Robert Leeson, 'Influence (or the Lack of It) in the Economics Profession: The Case of Lucien Albert Hahn', *History of Political Economy 29*, (1998): pp. 635–8.

[81] Hesse, 'Some Relationships between a Scholar's and an Entrepreneur's Life', p. 226.

'All that is wrong and exaggerated in Keynes I said much earlier and more clearly.'[82] This is the recurrent and contradictory *leitmotiv* of Hahn's writings on Keynes ever since he wrote an early review on the *General Theory* during his Swiss exile. This self-stylization was engraved on a large part of the later Hahn literature, finding particular resonance among his liberal friends.[83]

The first edition of *Economic Theory of Bank Credit* was published at the beginning of hyperinflation in Germany and Austria after the First World War for which the author made the anti-theoretical bent of the German historical school responsible and where he located the roots of his quantity-theoretic convictions.[84] Hahn was not alone in blaming the teachings of the historical school for the inflation. He was accompanied by many fellow economists such as Eucken and Mises, but it should also be mentioned that German was the language in which Wicksell's *Interest and Prices* had been published originally in 1898. Laidler and Stadler[85] are among the very few who have recognised important contributions by Bortkiewicz, Mises, and Hahn[86] (!) in the interpretation of German hyperinflation which made use of the quantity theory supplemented by an analysis of inflation expectations.

Hahn's later self-promotion as an important precursor of Keynes, in combination with his fierce anti-Keynesianism,[87] made him a friend of Mises but undermined the lasting importance of his own *Economic*

[82] Hahn, *Fünfzig Jahre zwischen Inflation und Deflation*, p. 6. The statement first was made explicitly in Henry Hazlitt's Introduction to Hahn's *The Economics of Illusion*, p. 1.

[83] For a more detailed analysis of Hahn's self-declaration as a 'pre-Keynesian' see section VI of Harald Hagemann, 'L. Albert Hahn's Economic Theory of Bank Credit', *Journal of Post Keynesian Economics 37*, no. 2 (2014–15): pp. 309–35.

[84] See Hahn, *Fünfzig Jahre zwischen Inflation und Deflation*, pp. 8–9. However, in contrast to Schumpeter, Marschak, or Neisser, he did not recognize the importance of Fisher's *Purchasing Power of Money*. For the early impact of Fisher in Germany see Harald Hagemann, 'The Impact of Fisher's Purchasing Power of Money in the German Language Area', *The European Journal of the History of Economic Thought 20*, no. 2 (2013): pp. 323–348.

[85] David E. W. Laidler and George W. Stadler, 'Monetary Explanations of the Weimar Republic's Hyperinflation: Some Neglected Contributions in Contemporary German Literature', *Journal of Money, Credit and Banking 30* (1998): pp. 816–31.

[86] Lucien Albert Hahn, 'Zur Frage des sogenannten "Vertrauens in die Währung"', *Archiv für Sozialwissenschaft und Sozialpolitik 52*, no. 2 (1924): pp. 289–316.

[87] See also Hahn, 'Die Grundirrtümer in Lord Keynes' *General Theory of Employment, Interest and Money*'.

Theory of Bank Credit which was suffering from exaggeration as the idea of a permanent boom and almost unlimited credit expansion. On the other hand, with his theoretical training and his experience as a practical banker he was among the first who understood the importance of bank credit for a modern economy.

Translator's Notes

Translating a writing from German to English faces two challenges: a different sentence structure and the general tendency in German to use long sentences. Hahn's book is no exception to this and I did not attempt a literal translation, which meant I restructured some sentences and paragraphs. The work is therefore slightly shorter in English than in German but should nevertheless capture the spirit of Hahn's ideas.

Hahn's *Volkswirtschaftliche Theorie des Bankkredits* was published in 1920 for the first time; in 1924 an identical reprint of the first edition appeared as a second edition, and subsequently as a completely revised third edition in 1930. This translation is based on the first (second) edition and also includes the second part of the third edition. This enables the reader to follow the substantial shift in Hahn's views on the effects of credit on the goods market. The Table of Concordance shows the changes in the high level structure of the text. The chapter numbers follow the German text but are preceded by an indication of the part of the book in square brackets and in the case of chapters from the third edition with an asterisk.

The references in the first (second) edition of Hahn's *Volkswirtschaftliche Theorie des Bankkredits* are often incomplete. I completed the references throughout the text but refrained from indicating completions in every case as it would have impaired the flow for the reader. Otherwise, editorial comments or amendments are indicated in square brackets.

London, October 2014

Table of Concordance

First and second edition		**Third edition**
Part One – Credit and Banks		**Part One – Credit and Banks**
A. Forms of Credit		A. Forms of Credit Activity
I. The prevailing view of banking activity		I. The prevailing view of the function of banks
II. Credit in the modern economy		II. Credit in the modern economy
1. Credit creation		1. Granting of credit
2. Credit prolongation		2. The network of bank relationships caused by granting of credit
3. Credit closure 4. Credit consolidation	→	3. Forms of granting credit
		a) Credit accommodation
		b) Credit expansion
		α) Inflationary credit expansion
		β) Non-inflationary credit expansion
5. The essence of bank credit		4. The bank's power to create credit
B. The Extent of Credit Activities of Banks		B. The Extent of Credit Activities of Banks
I. Forms of banks		I. Forms of banks
II. Trust and liquidity considerations as determinants for the extent of means of banks		
1. The extent of means of primary banks		II. The extent of means of secondary banks
2. The extent of means of secondary banks III. Bank liquidity	→	III. The extent of means of primary banks
	→ (from 4. Economic liquidity)	1. Economic liquidity
	→ (from 4. Economic liquidity)	2. Private liquidity
1. Money liquidity		3. Money liquidity
2. Extraordinary money demand (the money crisis)		a) Extraordinary money demand (the money crisis)
α) Money demand		α) Money demand
β) Gold demand		β) Gold demand
3. Ordinary money demand		b) Ordinary money demand
4. Economic liquidity	→ (to 1. and 2.)	
		IV. The relationship between deposits and legal tender
IV. Interest as price for lost liquidity		V. Interest on credit
		VI. Bank credit and money and capital markets

Part Two – Credit and the Goods Market	**Part Two – Credit and the Goods Market**
A. The Prevailing Opinion on the Relationship between Credit and Capital Goods (the Influence of Capital on Credit)	
I. The barter perspective	
II. The monetary perspective	
B. The Influence of Credit on Capital	A. The Influence of Credit on Goods Production
I. The priority of credit over capital goods creation	
II. The effect of credit on the composition of goods	I. The effect of credit expansion on the length of the goods flow
	II. The effect of credit expansion on the width of the goods flow
III. The effect of credit on prices	III. The effect of credit expansion on prices and wages
IV. The effect of credit on the quantity of goods	IV. The effect of credit expansion on the employment rate
V. The effect of credit on capital and the wealth of nations	
	B. Credit and Capital
	I. Does credit expansion equal capital expansion?
	II. What is 'capital'?
	III. Credit and savings
C. The Effect of Credit on Savings	
D. Credit and Business Cycles	C. Credit and Business Cycles
	D. The Limit for Inflationary Credit Expansion
Part Three – International Credit	
A. Credit and Capital Export	
B. Credit and Exchange Rates	

Preface to the First Edition

The attention which my article 'Der Gegenstand des Geld- und Kapitalmarkets in der modernen Wirtschaft'[1] received was my motivation to develop the ideas at the core of that article and its implication for the theory of banking and general economics in the form of this book. This could not be done with equal attention to all parts due to other professional commitments. The theoretically trained reader will, however, not have any difficulties seeing the implications of my ideas when they are only hinted at; further, the reader will easily see the fundamental deviation from the prevailing doctrines.

I dedicate this book to my dear friend *Dr. Hermann Mauer,* an excellent researcher on the history of agricultural credit who sadly passed away far too early. I am thankful for his strong and sympathetic interest in my studies.

Frankfurt am Main, June 1920

[1] Lucien Albert Hahn, 'Der Gegenstand des Geld- und Kapitalmarkets in der modernen Wirtschaft' [The object of the money and capital market in the modern economy], *Archiv für Sozialwissenschaft und Sozialpolitik* 46, no. 1 (1918).

Preface to the Second Edition

This book is different from most others written on money, credit, or banking because it presupposes a fictitious 'credit' economy, in which all payments are made by transferring bank deposits to arrive at its results. The fact that some deposits have to be disbursed as cash is only introduced as a modifying element.

Our results are considerably different from those derived from the usual view. The differences affect primarily four important banking and credit theoretic issues:

1. In a credit economy, a credit is used (with all its consequences for the goods sphere) as soon as the debtor *buys* goods and services on the market. Analogously, 'savings' become effective (with all its consequences for the goods sphere) as soon as the holder of purchasing power does not use it *any more to buy* but to keep it as a deposit, without any deposition of physical means of payments being required or even possible. This also implies that the actual point in time at which the physical means of payments enter or exit the bank is irrelevant for the economic consequences of granting credit and savings in the actual mixed credit–cash-using economy. The economic effect of granting credit unfolds when the debtor *buys* regardless of whether or not the payment is conducted completely without cash. They do not become effective if the debtor does *not buy*, even if notes are disbursed. The economic effect of so called 'savings' become effective as soon as someone *abstains* from using his right to buy, even if no physical means of payment enter the bank (i.e. if he does not save in the sense of the word, but also when accumulating banknotes); they also do not become effective if notes are deposited with the bank, but the corresponding account balances are used to buy. In other words: if and how much *purchasing power is expended* in the economy is always the essential factor. The fact is that whether means of payment enter or exit banks does not carry the importance which is commonly attached to it by monetary theorists particularly when analysing economic policy measures.

2. In a credit economy every credit creates claims: the bank has a claim against the debtor and the person selling goods or service to the

debtor receives a claim against the same or another bank. The debtor becomes the *economic* owner of the creditor's good and the holder of the newly created deposit is the creditor. We thus take the view seriously (which is often voiced but never fully followed through) that the holder of cash (even fully metallic currency) is the 'creditor'. There can only be *one* creditor and therefore it also breaks with the view (which is incompatible with ours) that the creditor of the granted credit is the one who is entitled to a share of the 'economic reservoir' through 'advanced performances' but chooses not to exercise this right and confers it onto the debtor via the bank. He is rather the definitive creditor of another credit which was granted in the past. One can say at most that his waiver eases (not causes) the credit prolongation on the money market.

From an economic viewpoint, it cannot make any difference whether credit is disbursed in cash or as bank balances and therefore this result (with important consequences for wider theoretical considerations) also needs to hold for the currently existing economy.

3. The previous discussion shows that every time a credit is granted in a credit economy the economic creditor is also created. This also implies that any change in the capitalistic structure of the economy (e.g. whether more factories are built) caused by granting credit solely relies on whether or not credit is actually granted. Whether or not the economy saves at the same time as granting the credit is only relevant for the goods' prices, not for the if and how the capital basis is built up in the sense of the substrate for more roundabout methods of production. The factories built with 'inflationary' credit do not distinguish themselves from the factories built with 'non-inflationary' (with simultaneous savings) credit. Naturally, this result also applies to the mixed credit–cash-using economy.

4. Granting credit and the creation of money (creation of bank balances, which the debtor can use to buy) go together in a credit economy. Thus, each money creation has the effect of granting credit, where a credit is granted for the purpose of consumption. Each time credit is granted it shows the same effect as money creation, unless its effect is compensated by simultaneous 'credit consolidation' (when purchasing power created by earlier credits is not further expanded). Further it shows that there is eventually only one reason for the

creation of bank balances: the preceding credit. *Granting credit is primary to the creation of deposits.*

This result also holds for the current mixed credit–cash-using economy with the modification that central bank credit not private bank credit is primary to deposits if physical means of payments are used when granting the credit.

The previous results show how far-reaching and important it is to start from a fictional credit economy. Despite this fact, it cannot be said that this view (which is a fundamental contradiction to the prevailing view) has been recognised or accepted by its critics. Unlike the financial press, the scientific critique[1] has limited itself to stating opinions in a few announcements and reviews[2] of the first edition of this book, with one exception which misunderstands the fundamental principles. So one could be tempted to assume that the fundamental thought (from which this book departs) is not fertile.

The contrary seems to be suggested by the relevant literature which more and more often mentions thoughts about details or the basic idea similar to ours. Furthermore, I have been repeatedly told that almost every economic seminar at German universities discusses my book in detail, which is at least noteworthy. Whatever the verdict of these discussions may have been, it cannot be denied that it gave an impulse and new motivation to look at the banking theory from a new, particular angle. Actually, one cannot deny that the younger generation shows an interest for our theoretical view, which exceeds the attention works in specialist areas generally receive. This could be explained by the fact that the young generation faces more questions about practical banking and problems of the money and capital markets than the older generation. In these areas, in particular on the relationship between these markets and the goods sphere (which this book tries to elucidate), the old approach is especially unsatisfactory. One could also think that the relatively high sales of the first

[1] Adolf Weber, *Depositenbanken und Spekulationsbanken [Deposit Banks and Speculation Banks]*, 3rd ed. (Munich and Leipzig: Duncker & Humblot, 1922) treats my economic theory of bank credit in detail. I have published a detailed response in my essay Lucien Albert Hahn, 'Depositenbank und Spekulationsbanken' [Deposit Banks and Speculation Banks], *Archiv für Sozialwissenschaft und Sozialpolitik 51*, no. 1 (1923), p. 222.

[2] E.g. Bruno Moll, 'Albert Hahn, Volkswirtschaftliche Theorie des Bankkredits' [Albert Hahn, Economic Theory of Bank Credit], *Zeitschrift für Sozialwissenschaft XII* (1921), p. 219.

edition is a further indication that there is a certain demand for a book, which views these things from the perspective attempted here.

Finally, and this seems to me the most important reason, in 1919 the well-known monetary theorist R. G. Hawtrey published the book *Currency and Credit*,[3] which was well received and shows a remarkably similar basic position to my work. This fact suggests that the development of the modern payment system virtually requires this perspective and arises as a necessity. Hawtrey calls his first chapter 'Credit without Money', completely in line with the fiction used of a 'credit economy' and stresses its advantages by answering the question 'Why invent this fantastic hypothesis of a civilization without money?' with 'We may say that the justification for the hypothesis is that it provides us with an analysis of the function of credit, which would otherwise be inextricably interwoven with the functions of money.' To show the congruence of his (which is incidentally not singular in the English literature) and my view can be illustrated by one of numerous relevant sentences: 'When a banker lends, we say that he grants or creates credit or "a credit". This is a loose way of describing a double transaction. The banker assumes an immediate obligation to his customer, in exchange for the customer's obligation to him at a future date.'

To my great regret the book has to be published in a completely unaltered form because I lack the time for its revision. Hence, I am not able to weave my later work (in particular my essay 'Zur Theorie des Geldmarktes' [On the Theory of the Money Market]) into my *Volkswirtschaftliche Theorie des Bankkredits [The Economic Theory of Bank Credit]*. As a supplement, I therefore explicitly refer to the title *Geld und Kredit* which contains this and other essays and is published at the same time by J. C. B. Mohr (Paul Siebeck).

Frankfurt am Main, October 1924
A. Hahn

[3] Ralph George Hawtrey, *Currency and Credit*, 2nd ed. (London: Longmans, Green & Co, 1923).

Preface to the Third Edition

I said in the preface to the second edition that the scientific literature has only paid little attention to this book, but I cannot maintain my allegation. Like one of my critics[1] said 'in letzter Zeit [hat sich] geradezu eine *Hahnliteratur* entwickelt' [recently almost a *Hahn literature* has developed] and 'es erscheint kaum ein Buch über Geld und Kredit, das sich nicht eingehend mit den Lehren Hahns auseinandersetzte' [barely any book on money and credit is published which does not discuss Hahn's doctrine in detail].[2]

[1] Gottfried Haberler, Albert Hahns 'Volkswirtschaftliche Theorie des Bankkredits' [Albert Hahn's 'Economic Theory of Bank Credit'], *Archiv für Sozialwissenschaft und Sozialpolitik 57*, no. 3 (1927): p. 803.

[2] I shall mention following books or articles which treat my theory exclusively or in a special section in chronological order:

> Ladislaus von Bortkiewicz, 'Das Wesen, die Grenzen und die Wirkungen des Bankkredits' [The nature, boundaries and effect of bank credit'], *Weltwirtschaftliches Archiv 17*, no. 1 (1921): pp. 70–89; Bruno Moll, 'Albert Hahn, Volkswirtschaftliche Theorie des Bankkredits' [Albert Hahn, Economic Theory of Bank Credit], *Zeitschrift für Sozialwissenschaft XII* (1921): p. 219; Adolf Weber, *Depositenbanken und Spekulationsbanken [Deposit Banks and Speculation Banks]*, 3rd ed. (Munich and Leipzig: Duncker & Humblot, 1922); H. G. Haenel, 'Geld und Kredit: Ein Beitrag zur Kritik des Nominalismus' [Money and Credit: A Contribution to the Critique of Nominalism], *Zeitschriftt für die gesamte Staatswissenschaft 79*, no. 2 (1925): p. 281; Hans Honegger, 'Albert Hahn, Volkswirtschaftliche Theorie des Bankkredits' [Albert Hahn, Economic Theory of Bank Credit], *Schmollers Jahrbuch 49*, no. 2 (1925): p. 204 ff.; Adolf Lampe, *Zur Theorie des Sparprozesses und der Kreditschöpfung [On the Theory of Savings and Credit Creation]* (Jena: Gustav Fischer, 1926); Zacharij Solomonovič Kacenelenbaum, 'Nekotorye problemy teorii kredita: k voprosu o suščnosti bankovogo depozita' (PhD dissertation, Moscow, 1926) [This work is cited as S. S. Katzenellenbaum 'Einige Probleme des Bankkredits: Das Wesen der Bankdepositen' [A Few Problems with Bank Credits: The Nature of Bank Deposits], but there is no indication that this work is available in German]; Karl Diehl, 'Über neuere Kredittheorien im Lichte der Lehre von Macleod' [On Recent Credit Theories in the Light of Macleod's Doctrine], in vol. 1, *Die Kreditwirtschaft* (Leipzig: Gloeckner, 1927), p. 126; Karl Diehl, *Die Lehre von der Zirkulation [The Theory of Circulation]*, iii: *Theoretische Nationalökonomie* (Jena: Gustav Fischer, 1927); Heinrich Mannstaedt, *Ein kritischer Beitrag zur Theorie des Bankkredites [A Critical Contribution to the Theory of Bank Credit]* (Jena: Gustav Fischer, 1927); Svend Riemer, Besprechungen der Schrift Lampes [Review of Lampe's Book], *Archiv für Sozialwissenschaft und Sozialpolitik 58* (1927): p. 420–2; Friedrich August von Hayek, 'Besprechung der

When looking at the plethora of comments on my theory, one finds a number stressing the position and importance of my research

Schrift Mannstaedts' [Review of Mannstaedt's Book], *Archiv für Sozialwissenschaft und Sozialpolitik 58* (1927): p. 422–3; Hans Neisser, 'Besprechung der Bücher von Lampe und Mannstaedt' [Review of Lampe's and Mannstaedt's Books], *Magazin der Wirtschaft 3*, no. 43 (1927): p. 1663; Carl Rosch, *Kreditinflation und Wirtschaftskrise [Credit Inflation and the Economic Crisis]* (Jena: Gustav Fischer, 1927); Hans Neisser, *Der Tauschwert des Geldes [The Exchange Value of Money]* (Jena: Gustav Fischer, 1928); Fritz Burchardt, 'Entwicklungsgeschichte der monetären Konjunkturtheorie' [The Historical Development of the Monetary Business Cycle Theory], *Weltwirschaftliches Archiv 28*, no. 1 (1928): pp. 77–143; Max Muß, 'Zur Problematik der neueren Geldlehre' [On the Problems of the Recent Monetary Theory], *Weltwirschaftliches Archiv 27*, no. 1 (1928): p. 1 ff.; Walter Heinrich, *Grundlagen einer universalistischen Krisenlehre [The Foundations of a Universal Crisis Theory]* (Jena: Gustav Fischer, 1928), p. 123ff.; Hans Honegger, *Der schöpferische Kredit [The Creative Credit]* (Jena: Gustav Fischer, 1929).

From the extraordinarily many works which only contain sporadic statements I shall only mention the following:

Jakob Marschak, 'Die Verkehrsgleichung', *Archiv für Sozialwissenschaft und Sozialpolitik 52* (1924), pp. 350–2; Adolf Weber, 'Depositenbanken und Spekulationsbanken, Erwiderung auf Hahns Kritik' [Deposit Banks and Speculation Banks, a Response to Hahn's Critique] *Archiv für Sozialwissenschaft und Sozialpolitik 52*, (1924), p. 526; Joseph Schumpeter, *Theorie der wirschaftlichen Entwicklung [The Theory of Economic Development]*, 2nd ed. (Munich and Leipzig: Duncker & Humblot, 1926), p. 140 and p. 141 (footnote 5); Rudolf Stucken, *Theorie der Konjunkturschwankungen [The Theory of Business Cycle Fluctuations]* (Jena: Gustav Fischer, 1926), p. 20 (footnote 2) and p. 27 (footnote 4); Georg Halm, 'Das Zinsproblem am Geld- und Kapitalmarkt' [The Interest Rate Problem on the Money and Capital Market], *Jahrbücher für Nationalökonomie und Statistik 125* (1926): pp. 1–34, 97–121; Adolf Lampe, 'Kann die gegenwärtige Notlage der deutschen Wirtschaft als Zirkulationskrise erklärt werden?' [Can the Current Economic Crisis in Germany Be Explained as a Crisis of Circulation?], *Jahrbücher für Nationalökonomie und Statistik 124* (1926): p. 305; Wilhelm Röpke, 'Kredit und Konjunktur' [Credit and the Business Cycle], *Jahrbücher für Nationalökonomie und Statistik 124* (1926): p. 249; Arno Aron, 'Der Liquidiätsbegriff in der Inflationsperiode des deutschen Bankwesens' [Liquidity in the Inflation Period of the German Banking System], *Jahrbücher für Nationalökonomie und Statistik 124* (1926): p. 316; Werner Sombart, *Das Wirtschaftsleben im Zeitalter des Hochkapitalismus [Economic Life in the Age of Captalism]*, i. (Munich and Leipzig: Duncker & Humblot, 1927), p. 148, pp. 149, 179–80, 187; Alfred Müller, 'Formen der Kreditexpansion und der Kreditpolitik' [Forms of Credit Expansion and Credit Policy] in *Die Kreditwirtschaft*, i (Leipzig: Gloeckner, 1927); Georg Halm, 'Schumpeters Theorie der wirtschaftlichen Entwicklung' [Schumpeter's Theory of Economic Development], *Jahrbücher für Nationalökonomie und Statistik 127* (1927); p. 126; Adolf Weber, *Allgemeine Volkswirtschaftslehre [General Economic Theory]* (Munich and Leipzig; Duncker & Humblot, 1928); C. Bresciani-Turroni, *Considerazioni sui 'Barometri' Economici [Considerations on the Economic*

question and answer in the recent monetary theoretic literature.[3] And if the comments even go so far as to claim that without a doubt

'Barometer'] (Città di Castello: Società Tipografica Leonardo Da Vinci, 1928), p. 86; Franz Xaver Weiß, 'Zins' [Interest], in *Handwörterbuch der Staatswissenschaften*, viii, edited by Ludwig Elster, Adolf Weber, Frierich Wieser (Jena: Gustav Fischer, 1928), p. 1152, p. 1155 and footnote 1; Alfred Michaelis, *Die Quanitätstheorie als Grundlage der Konjunkturforschung [The Quantity Theory as the Basis for Business Cycle Research]* (Jena: Gustav Fischer, 1929); Friedrich August von Hayek, *Geldtheorie und Konjunkturtheorie [Monetary Theory and the Trade Cycle]* (Vienna and Leipzig: Hölder-Pichler-Tempsky, 1929), pp. 58, 84, 93, 104; B. W. Szigal, 'Bargeldloser Zahlungsverkehr im ukrainischen Kreditsystem' [Cashless payment in the Ukrainian credit system], in *Travaux de la commission pour l'étude des finances*, edited by L. N. Jasnopolsky (Kiev: unknown publisher, 1929).

Also a number of dissertations assess my theory, of which only the following shall be mentioned:

Zumer Djelal, 'Kritik der Hahnschen Banktheorie' [A Critique of Hahn's Banking Theory] (PhD dissertation, Berlin, 1925); J. Männer, 'Die Theorien des Geldmarktes' [The Theories of the Money Market] (PhD dissertation, Freiburg, 1925), p. 9, 14, 17, 23–5, 49, 68; Carl Kühne, 'Geld und Kapital im Konjunkturverlauf' [Money and Capital over the Business Cycle] (PhD disseration, Frankfurt, 1928), p. 15 and in particular p. 48 ff.; P. N. M. Koolen, 'Het Crediet in de Volkshuishouding' [The Credit in the National Economy] (PhD dissertation, Nijmegen, 1928).

Also non-scientific journals and the daily press voiced their positions in more or less detailed reports and reviews, for example:

'unknown title', *Frankfurter Zeitung*, Evening issue, 27 September 1920; 'unknown title', *Berliner Tageblatt*, no. 479, 19 October 1920; 'unknown title', *Schwäbische Kronik*, 3 November 1920; 'unknown title', *Finanzherold*, 23 December 1920; 'unknown title', *Breslauer Zeitung*, 27 December 1920; 'unknown title', *Literatisches Zentralblatt*, no. 41, 1921; 'unknown title', *Literatische Rundschau*, Supplement to *Berliner Tagblatt*, 11 March 1923; 'unknown title', *Kölnische Volkszeitung*, 1 January 1925; 'unknown title', *Bankwissenschaft 1*, no. 21, 1 February 1925; 'unknown title', *Soziale Praxis 35*, no. 6, 1926.

[3] E.g. Haberler, 'Albert Hahns *Volkswirtschaftliche Theorie des Bankkredits*' [Albert Hahn's *Economic Theory of Bank Credit*'], Hayek, 'Besprechung der Schrift Mannstaedts' [Review of Mannstaedt's Book], or Hayek, *Geldtheorie und Konjunkturtheorie [Monetary Theory and the Trade Cycle]*. Joseph Schumpeter, *Theorie der wirschaftlichen Entwicklung [Theory of Economic Development]*, p.140, footnote 1: 'Der Gedankengang, der im folgenden im Wesen unverändert vorgetragen wird, hat inzwischen durch die Untersuchungen von A. Hahn (*Volkswirtschaftliche Theorie des Bankkredits*, 1. Auflage, 1920) eine wertvolle Bestätigung und Verbesserung erfahren. Der Leser sei auf dieses originelle und verdienstliche Buch, das die Erkenntnis des Problems wesentlich gefördert hat, nachdrücklich verwiesen.' [The train of thought, which is presented without any changes, has meanwhile experienced a valuable confirmation and improvement through the analysis in A. Hahn (*The Economic Theory of Bank Credit*, 1st edition, 1920). The reader is explicitly referred to this original and meritorious book, which has considerably improved the understanding of the problem.]

I deserve a place of excellence in the most recent German monetary theory,[4] then I could be tempted to draw the conclusion of all critics with a certain sense of complacency. I can only resist the temptation though, when I read the comments of the critics regarding each of my hypotheses. It shows that virtually no hypothesis remained without objection, apart from those which were conceded to be good because they were not new (a typical trait of the critics).

It has become a commonplace in the recent economic literature to shield oneself from criticism by contesting the expertise of the critic and the legitimacy of their critique. I cannot take this route. I rather have to honestly admit that all my opponents (except from maybe one author)[5] have fought with expertise and clarity and that I have learnt many important things from their objections. I hope that the changes in this third edition (compared to the previous editions) are proof of this. At this point, I want to say in my favour that the weapons with which my opponents fought me, were only forged because and with the help of my theory. Although I am aware that my theories contained some erroneous exaggerations and that its core is ultimately not original but originates from what people have often said over the last centuries, it was acknowledged by many of my opponents that the main factor for their motivation to consider the relevant problems was my writing. When one returns from the town hall, one is always more knowledgeable than before. When one reviews a piece of writing on the creation of purchasing power by banks in the year 1927 or 1928, after extensive theoretical consideration and practical experiences, one has an advantage over someone in the year 1920 who is equipped with nothing other than Schumpeter's general economic framework (and without any guidance from the recent German literature) and who attempts to expose the unsatisfactory elements of the economic framework and to find a solution

[4] Haberler, 'Albert Hahn's *Volkswirtschaftliche Theorie des Bankkredits*' [Albert Hahn's *Economic Theory of Bank Credit*], p. 803: 'zweifellos ein hervorragender Platz in der Geschichte der neuesten deutschen Geldtheorie gebührt' [[he] deserves without a doubt a place of excellence in the most recent German monetary theory].

[5] I think of Lampe, *Zur Theorie des Sparprozesses und der Kreditschöpfung [On the Theory of Savings and Credit Creation]*. Apart from what needs to be criticised from a factual point of view (cf. the comments of Neisser, 'unknown title', *Magazin der Wirtschaft* 43, 27 October 1927, p. 1663 ff.), it also has the potential to generate mistrust of economic theorists amongst practitioners. This is also due to the presentation, which is in stark contrast to the simple and lucid way one can find in the English–American literature even for the most complex problems.

with nothing other than the general economic framework. Ultimately writing like mine is not judged by the complete truth of every hypothesis in detail, but rather by the fact of whether or not the theory as a whole can progress economic knowledge. I believe I can conclude that is the case based on the fact that the terminology of the financial press[6] (as long as it is edited by younger forces) and its understanding of financial markets are heavily influenced by my view. I cannot deny that this fills me with a certain satisfaction. Particularly since in the financial press (as well as in my own occupation), one is forced by practical events on the money and capital markets to check the theoretical basis. To make the journalist's work easier is not the ultimate purpose of my writing.

Now that I am handing this third edition of my book over to the public, I am aware that this carries a certain risk. On the one hand, I have moderated my claims under the influence of my critics and also as a result of my continued work. On the other hand, some claims which were known in recent years but not sufficiently widespread are now part of the general consciousness, such that it does not require writing alone to work out the relevant relationships. My own view and that of *communis opinio*, if one can talk of one, have met each other effectively half way. My decision to nonetheless publish (also under the pressure of my publisher and a number of friends) a completely revised third edition is for the following reasons. First, I thought that it would be inappropriate for a work which is often referred to and which knowledge of is often taken for granted to disappear from the market; it is particularly in the interest of all those who want to know more about the post-war development of the German theory on money and credit. Second, the *communis opinio* in Germany, which, for example, expresses itself in many textbooks, diverges largely from my view, such that a work clearly exposing the creation of purchasing powers by banks is necessary as a counterweight to all those works seeing it as an abnormal, ancillary, or transitory effect. Third, even nowadays there are many different diverging opinions on

[6] Less credit was granted after 13 May 1927 when loans with stocks and precious items as collateral were artificially restricted. It is a characteristic example that the *Frankfurter Zeitung* described the decline in debtors as completely natural. That is how far this view, which is completely at odds with older theories cf. Paul Mombert, *Einführung in das Studium der Konjunktur [Introduction to Business Cycle Theory]* (Leipzig: G. A. Gloeckner, 1926), has diffused into the general conscious.

detailed issues amongst those whose basic conception is close to mine[7] (these are mainly proponents of a monetary business cycle theory); it therefore does not seem superfluous (even if not as necessary as nine years ago) to present the economic theory of bank credit in a monograph. Finally, I have built on the basic idea of this work[8]—the fictitious cashless economy—which gives insight into the workings of the money market, which is secondary for the general economic theory but of utmost importance in practice; given the hopeless state of the theory of money markets, this will be a welcome contribution.

If my economic theory of bank credit in its new form still has the ability to challenge the absolute belief in the correctness of some dated theories and to encourage some deep thought about the problems looked at, then I consider it to have fulfilled its purpose (regardless of whether or not my view is accepted).

I hand this book over to the public with an appeal to the reader to excuse any incoherence in the presentation of some parts. It is caused by the desire to maintain the original edition where possible but also to change what needs to be changed.

I am very grateful to Dr. J. Soudek for his invaluable help, in particular his work on the literature.

Frankfurt am Main, March 1930
Albert Hahn

[7] E.g. von Hayek, Stucken, and others.

[8] I have built on this notion in Lucien Albert Hahn, 'Zur Theorie des Geldmarktes' [On the Theory of the Money Market], *Archiv für Sozialwissenschaft und Sozialpolitik 51*, no. 2 (1923): p. 289. The article is reprinted in Lucien Albert Hahn, *Geld und Kredit, Gesammelte Aufsätze [Money and Credit: Collected Essays]* (Tübingen: J. C. B Mohr (Paul Siebeck), 1924), p. 87.

Contents

Part Three: International Credit

Economic Theory of Bank Credit (Third Edition)

Part One: Credit and Banks

Part Two: Credit and the Goods Markets

Economic Theory of Bank Credit
(First Edition)

Introduction

It has become a commonplace that money, like the veil of the Maya, conceals the movement and appearances of the goods market. Almost nobody mentions, though, that all activity involved in banking is a veil of the same kind. And it might even be that the veil of modern banking and credit, hiding the economy, is even denser. It is of such density that the picture offered by the veil is often seen as the depiction of reality and any further investigation is neglected. It is the only way to explain why a plethora of theories of money can be found in the current literature, but almost no theory of banking and credit (leaving aside the literature on central banks). A problem can only be analysed and solved if it is perceived as such.

This book is an attempt to sketch an economic theory of banking and credit. This means first, that it does not continue the long list of works describing the workings of banks, or textbooks for both bank clerks[1] and managers.[2] They all share the view of banking from the private business perspective of the bank, even if they try to evoke the appearance of a social, economic perspective. They all are guided by the same question: how to organize banking activity to obtain certain objectives of private interest. The 'economic assessment' they occasionally insert, solely occupies itself with the consequences of banking on the prosperity of other business sectors.[3] The essence of an

[1] Typical for this strand of work are, amongst others, the writings of Buchwald, Leitner, and Obst.

[2] See especially Felix Somary, *Bankpolitik [Banking Policy]*, (Tübingen: J. C. B Mohr (Paul Siebeck), 1915).

[3] A typical example for this approach is Gerhart von Schulze-Gaevernitz, *Die moderne Kreditbank [The Modern Credit Bank]* (Tübingen: J. C. B Mohr (Paul Siebeck), 1922), p. 47, where the 'economic assessment' of bank deposits shows that it imposes discipline on payments and bookkeeping and combats credit. The actual

economic assessment, though, is not just the simple sum of private (business) activities.

Economics, as we understand it, has to occupy itself with the production and distribution of goods. Accordingly, the following sketch of an economic theory of banking and credit should be interpreted as follows: it should investigate how the stock and distribution of goods are changed as a consequence of banks granting credit and, conversely, how such a change in the sphere of goods expresses itself in the banks' accounts. To name a simple example, changes in a country's means of production caused by increased bank lending, as well as the changes in balance sheets for both producers and banks that this causes, will be subject to scrutiny. Put differently: we shall investigate the economic consequences of financial activity and the financial symptoms of economic change.

The importance of such an investigation is obvious.

First, if it succeeds, it will expose the connection between the goods markets and capital and money markets. Furthermore, and of utmost practical importance, it will illuminate the complex of questions about the mutual causes of credit and production in a country.[4] It will shed some light on the question of to what extent the granting of credit to industry is subject to the availability of the resources which will be procured by means of that credit, and conversely to what extent the processing of available resources is subject to the availability of credit to industry. Finally, and closely connected to this, it will enable us to get a firmer grasp on the 'protean creature' of 'capital' that has such a versatile life in scientific and popular accounts of banking.

The importance of clarifying the term 'capital' will be readily acknowledged by everyone conscious of the frequent and loose

economic consequences, i.e. on production, are not included in this private business perspective.

[4] Despite the importance of this question, there is only one—and inaccurate—analysis in the recent literature: Arthur Spiethoff, 'Die äußere Ordnung des Kapital- und Geldmarktes' [The Organization of the Capital and Money Market], *Schmollers Jahrbuch 33*, no. 2 (1909). The analysis by Herbert von Beckerath, *Kapitalmarkt und Geldmarkt [Capital and Money Markets]* (Jena: Gustav Fischer, 1916), p. 89 is largely based on Spiethoff and too vague to resolve the issue. Johann von Komorzinsky, *Die nationalökonomische Lehre vom Kredit [The Economic Theory of Credit]* (Innsbruck: Wagner, 1903) treats this central question only marginally. His doctrine is rather a 'legal' than an 'economic' theory of credit.

usage of 'capital' in the literature on banking and stock markets. It appears in numerous phrases, is used to construct all sorts of theories, and from it also derives a vast number of value judgements and demands. Here it is said capital is abundant; here that it is too scarce. Here it is said that capital is too liquid; here that it lacks liquidity. Here it is said that there is too much, here that too little capital is invested; here that it should be exported and here that it should be imported. And yet, in almost every case, there is not the slightest attempt to interpret the term 'capital' in an economic sense or discuss which goods it is thought to comprise. How else, to name a few examples, could a complaint be made in times of crisis of a shortage of 'capital', even though especially in such times not only no shortage, but even an abundance of goods prevails. How could a campaign against capital exports be led, if at the same time it is lamented that industry exports too little; and how could, as occasionally happens, a reduction in lending be advocated by arguing that a decrease in production is necessary because otherwise 'capital creation' could not keep up.

This lack of clarity, affecting all questions related to the term 'capital' in the banking literature, is on first glance astonishing, especially since the problem of capital might well be the most central problem of the economics literature and has been thoroughly explored. The origin of this discrepancy could lie in the following: the older, classical literature has derived its results from an abstraction of an economic state completely different from the highly capitalistic state of the present, with its progressive money, credit, and banking sector, so that its results cannot be directly used any longer. The more recent literature is not only, in its dogmatic relationship, heavily dependent on the classics, but also uses the same economic state of the past to draw its conclusions. As a consequence, the modern banking literature does not receive any substantial support from current writing on general economics.[5]

This has gradually developed into a serious danger, not only for theory, but also for practical economic life. These circumstances have

[5] One of the few exceptions to this is Joseph Schumpeter, *Theorie der wirtschaftlichen Entwicklung [The Theory of Economic Development]* (Leipzig: Duncker & Humblot, 1912). This alone earns the book a place in the economic canon. On the contrary, the otherwise astute work of Emil Sax, *Der Kapitalzins [Interest on capital]* (Berlin and Heidelberg: Springer, 1916) seems useless at resolving this problem.

enabled the development of plenty of claims, views, and idioms in relation to banking. They all bear the label of economic science and are used in the assessment of the economic state, especially in reports on the business cycle, without carrying any insight of an economic nature that goes beyond that of private business. Due to the lack of a suitable theory it has not been possible to examine their economic content, therefore they steadily become axioms which one author uncritically adopts from another in order to operate with them ever more ferociously the less he is tortured by economic-scientific scruple. The damaging consequences thereof are readily appreciated if one considers how strong the modern highly capitalistic economy is reacting to imponderabilia and how general moods influence its development.

The highest practical value inherent in economic theory in general, and this sketch of a banking theory in particular, is in its defence against these imminent dangers.

Part One

Credit and Banks

[1.]A. Forms of Credit

I. THE PREVAILING VIEW OF BANKING ACTIVITIES

Every credit enables a certain individual to buy goods and services from other individuals beyond that which his or her wealth would permit.[1] The granting of credit in that sense is (without much doubt) the activity of the modern economic institutions called 'banks'.

Where, though, do banks get the 'means' to grant credit? The response of almost everyone, in particular in the recent German[2] definitions of banks, shows one commonality: they are all founded in the view that the banks' customers deposit their savings or temporarily dispensable 'means' which are then 'invested' by the banks.[3] This idea of a certain stock of investable means is the basis for all

[1] Cf. Johann von Komorzinsky, *Die nationalökonomische Lehre vom Kredit [The Economic Theory of Credit]* (Innsbruck: Wagner, 1903), p. 18 ff.

[2] Less so in the English definitions, which have a stronger orientation towards central banks. That is why these definitions are not applicable to banks in general though.

[3] A plethora of quotations document this. I only mention the most recent: Gerhart von Schulze-Gaevernitz, *Die moderne Kreditbank [The Modern Credit Bank]* (Tübingen: J. C. B Mohr (Paul Siebeck), 1922), p. 38: 'Deutschland leitet die Einlagen je nach ihrer Herkunft bald in die Kreditbanken' [Germany channels sooner or later the deposits according to their source into credit banks] and p. 10: 'Seitdem besteht das Wesen der Bank in Kreditvermittlungen' [Ever since the nature of a bank lies in the intermediation of credit] (this alludes to the actual interpersonal transfer, as shown by the juxtaposition with the intermediation of goods). Further Felix Somary, *Bankpolitik [Banking Policy]*, (Tübingen: J. C. B Mohr (Paul Siebeck), 1915), p. 3: 'Was sie (die Banken) mit den ihnen so zuströmenden Mitteln beginnen, usw.' [What they (the banks) do with the means they receive, etc.] and p. 60: 'Eine Kreditbank kann nur soweit Kredit geben, als sie Einlagen erhält, usw' [A credit bank can only grant credit to the extent of the deposits it receives, etc.].

current conceptions of the nature of credit. It also dominates the terminology on banking and credit used both in the scientific literature and in the financial press; the significance of this status should not be underestimated.

Whether this notion is true or false is of utmost importance as all explanations of the tensions between money and capital markets are rooted in this view. Similarly, all the reasons determining the liquidity of credit markets are only correct if indeed banks obtain the means to grant credit by receiving a flow of deposited 'money'. Consequentially, the validity of the widespread view that the population's savings are the actual and primary cause of the ability to grant credit is also conditional on the validity of this notion. If the means accrued by the bank in fact determine the extent of credit, then the available 'assets' can only exist if the individuals in an economy spend less than they earn. The creation of capital is according to this view a historical process. The 'newly created' capital, when projected into the sphere of goods, is identical to the good to which the saving individual is entitled by 'making an advance'; however, the very act of saving foregoes this claim in favour of the bank and its debtor respectively.

The main task of the following exposition is to show that this group of related concepts are not only exceptionally[4] wrong, but generally and fundamentally so. Further, that their assumptions are inapplicable and as such are not useful tools for analysing the credit process. It is our first and foremost task to investigate the type of 'means' the bank can use to grant credit, because only then we can draw an accurate picture of the nature of banking activities and their influence on money and capital markets.

What are the 'means' which banks, in particular credit banks, use to grant credit?

First, there is a virtual theoretical consensus that whatever it is that banks use to grant credit it is the same whether those means are invested in the capital market or the money market.[5] These markets

[4] Compare my remarks on these assumptions in footnote 38 in this chapter.

[5] To quote a few: Arthur Spiethoff, Die äußere Ordnung des Kapital- und Geldmarktes [The organization of the capital and money market], *Schmollers Jahrbuch 33*, no. 2 (1909), p. 27: 'Der Geldmarkt hat keine innigeren Beziehungen zum Gelde . . . als der Kapitalmarkt' [The money market does not have a more intimate relationship with money . . . than the capital market]; Joseph Schumpeter, *Theorie der wirtschaftlichen Entwicklung [The Theory of Economic Development]* (Leipzig: Duncker & Humblot, 1912), p. 273: 'jedenfalls ist der Kapitalmarkt dasselbe, wie das Phänomen,

do not differ in terms of what is offered, but the demand is split according to their maturity into demand for short- or long-term promises to pay.[6] The places where long-term debt like stocks, bonds, and mortgages are demanded are, in practical terms, called capital markets. Short-term debt, like credit drawn on bills of exchange, Lombard credit, and repurchase agreements, as well as so-called 'call money', is demanded from the money market. But what is given away *obligandi causa* (to use the succinct term from Roman law) is the same for all markets. There are no special 'means' of the money market or the capital market. Where this differentiation is made,[7] it can only be warranted with reference to certain differences in the person of the creditor and in particular if that person is a capitalist who prefers to grant long-term credit, or if that person is a financier, who only wants to deposit his money for the short term.

Once the question turns towards the matter of what is actually dealt on the capital and money markets, then they must be treated as one market. Hence, we will subsume both markets under the term 'credit markets' in the following. This term only implies that both markets require trust in the repayment of the loan and seems at first neutral from the viewpoint of our question. Our further analysis, however, will show the particular appropriateness of this term especially with reference to the problem at hand.

What is it though, that banks use to appear as a 'financier' on the credit markets?

If the quest for finding an answer to this question leads to the consultation of the specialist literature on banking and credit, which one would think contains explanations on these matters in abundance, we will discover that the literature leaves us in the dark. This is not restricted to the literature which exhausts itself with illustrating the technical processes of banking. The search for explanations of the question at hand in literature with a wider intention, like the work of

das die Praxis als Geldmarkt bezeichnet. Einen anderen Kapitalmarkt gibt es nicht.' [In any case, the capital market is the same as the phenomena called the money market in practice. There is no other capital market.]

6 Gerhart von Schulze-Gaevernitz, *Die moderne Kreditbank [The MODERN CREDIT BANK]*, Abteilung V, Teil II, Grundriß der Sozialökonomik (Tübingen: J. C. B Mohr (Paul Siebeck), 1915), p. 77: 'Der Unterschied beider Märkte besteht in der Verpflichtung des Schuldners auf längere oder kürzere Frist.' [The difference between both markets lies in the short- or long-term obligation of the borrower.]

7 Compare e.g. Somary, *Bankpolitik*, p. 183.

Prion[8] or Somary[9] also proves fruitless. Critical passages of these works, where one would categorically expect the authors to make a clear statement (one would almost like to say instinctively motivated by the unresolved questions), they express themselves in private-business-minded and, above all, in neutral and pallid terms, which fail to uncover the essence. In particular the term 'means', which we also use for the time being, 'liquid means' and 'invest' are not suited for drawing a clear picture of what they signify. In general, instead of using precise terms the specialist literature on banking and credit shows (obviously for the reason indicated) an increasing propensity to use a language full of pictures and metaphors, which allows the reader to make any interpretation.[10]

Nevertheless, there are certainly clues (both in the specialist literature and writing on general economics) on the authors' thoughts about the matter with which lenders in general (and banks in particular) grant loans and therefore appear as financiers on money and capital markets. It remains to be shown that all these opinions are either wrong or meaningless.

To begin with a widespread notion, which is expressed explicitly or implicitly by almost all earlier and quite a few recent authors, that 'capital' is lent to the debtor is particularly meaningless.[11]

It is not necessary to lose oneself in the jungle of definitions of 'capital', which remains as untamed as ever before, to prove this. The assertion that financiers lend '*capital*' cannot be considered an answer to our question, regardless of whether or not one concurs with this or that way of defining the term 'capital'. The question is resolved easily if one disregards the myriad of individual views and brings the three

[8] Willi Prion, *Das deutsche Wechseldiskontgeschäft [Discounting Bills of Exchange in Germany]*, (Leipzig: Duncker & Humblot, 1907).

[9] Somary, *Bankpolitik*. See also writings like Rudolph Eberstadt, *Der deutsche Kapitalmarkt [The German Capital Market]*, (Leipzig: Duncker & Humblot, 1901) in which the author includes extensive statistics on 'capital absorption' without mentioning at any point what is 'absorbed'.

[10] A characteristic example in this respect is Herbert von Beckerath, *Kapitalmarkt und Geldmarkt [Capital and Money Markets]* (Jena: Gustav Fischer, 1916). He speaks of 'Gerinnen flüssiger Vermögenssubstanz' [coagulation of liquid wealth substance] in some instances (see pp. 100, 109, 115). Hence, using four metaphors in one expression.

[11] Namely all classical economists who do not express the opinion described later in the text. More recently it was expressed e.g. by Prion, *Das deutsche Wechseldiskontgeschäft*, p. 2 ff. and also very often by Somary, *Bankpolitik* (e.g. p. 40).

main notions of capital to mind, against which no fundamental objections are raised at this point.

If one interprets 'capital' in the predominant *private business sense* as an *operating asset*, then clearly nothing is gained in terms of answering our question. Indeed the entrepreneur needs operating assets and also the money invested by banks is an operating asset from their perspective. However, capital is not an identifier for tangible goods, rights, or economic power, which are the constituents of supply and demand of any market, but a theoretical compendium of many different goods, like tools, machines, debt certificates, and so on, used by individuals to draw up their business plans.[12] Admittedly, one can say that the entrepreneur who satisfied his demand for capital on the capital market now owns capital, but one can also say that the financier who invested his asset on the capital market generates deposits which are also capital. But it is meaningless to say that the capitalist transfers capital in the private business sense to the firm. All authors claiming that banks lend 'capital' on credit markets do not say anything wrong, but in the context of our question something absolutely meaningless.[13]

It is even more meaningless to claim that banks lend capital, if it is interpreted in its *economic* sense as 'produced means of production'. This interpretation of capital is also a generalization (this time not from a private business, but from an economic perspective) as such capital cannot be subject to any demand. Capital in its economic sense as constituent of credit supply is only meaningful if certain produced means of production are demanded in their own right. This view is rendered untenable, because not only certain classes of goods but all goods, especially land, would need to be part of the demand (if at all). The notion that goods are supplied on the credit market cannot be considered seriously, as will be explained below.

Finally, 'capital' cannot be the answer to our question if one interprets it as some form of money stock, like Menger[14] and most recently

[12] Cf. Friedrich von Wieser, *Theorie der gesellschaftlichen Wirtschaft [Social Economics]*, Abteilung 1, Teil II, Grundriß der Sozialökonomik, (Tübingen: J. C. B Mohr (Paul Siebeck), 1914), p. 332 ff.

[13] This also holds for those who call 'asset' the object of credit transactions, like Johann von Komorzinsky, *Die nationalökonomische Lehre vom Kredit*, p. 24.

[14] Karl Menger, 'Zur Theorie des Kapitals' [On the Theory of Capital], *Jahrbücher für Nationalökonomie und Statistik 17* (1888), pp. 1–19.

Schumpeter[15] do. Because then 'capital' is exactly equal to the object, whose essence we are trying to determine. The word 'capital', therefore, is not an answer to the question but simply repeats it.

Therefore we are not brought any closer to the solution of the problem by all those statements in the literature which see capital (also in the form of 'liquid capital', 'fixed capital', etc.) as the constituent of credit supply. They can therefore be judged as meaningless and discarded from the outset.

The view that banks lend 'capital' has been shown to be meaningless, but the common notion that '*goods*' are supplied on credit markets, is not only wrong, but also logically indefensible.

One of the most frequent conclusions in the earlier economic literature is that borrowers do not demand money (or any similar medium of exchange) but in reality the goods which can be bought with it. It is well known why this notion developed and was often articulated. The reason is that scholars were coerced into fighting the inflationist–mercantilist opinion, which was pertinent in the popular literature at the time. It argued that the 'scarcity of money', that is, the high rate of interest, could be solved by expanding the means of payments without any consequences.[16] The classical economists, in particular Smith and Ricardo, stress time and again that only goods, not money, determine the wealth of a nation; that in truth only goods are sought by borrowers and, consequently, that only the quantity of *goods* affects the interest rate.

This is not the place to examine how strongly the classic economists linked the statement that goods are truly borrowed on credit markets with the belief that the goods themselves are in fact the object of credit demand. Such an examination is doomed to fail because the classic economists were not conscious enough of the problem to express themselves clearly and unambiguously in one way or the other. It is certain that in some passages the classics describe the goods only as indirectly demanded and the money used to buy these goods as directly demanded.[17] On the other hand, it is also certain

[15] Schumpeter, *Theorie der wirtschaftlichen Entwicklung*, p. 236.

[16] As characteristic for the recent inflationist literature cf. Walter L. Haussmann, *Der Goldwahn [The Gold Delusion]* (Berlin: Puttkammer & Mühlbrecht, 1911).

[17] Cf. e.g. chapter 27 in David Ricardo, *Grundsätze der Volkswirtschaft und Besteuerung*, trans. Edward Baumstark (Leipzig: Verlag von Wilhelm Engelmann, 1837) or 2nd edition (Leipzig: Verlag von Wilhelm Engelmann, 1877) [David Ricardo, *On the Principles of Political Economy and Taxation*, i: *The Works and Correspondences of David Ricardo*, ed. Pierro Sraffa and Maurice Dobb (London: Cambridge

that the classics associate the general term capital supply with the slightly ambiguous[18] notion of a direct supply of leasable capital goods.[19]

Even though the realization that a nation's wealth is not determined by wealth in money but by wealth in goods is undisputed, the notion derived from that that goods themselves are lent on credit markets is indefensible because it confounds reality.[20] In fact, it is not goods which are dealt on credit markets but something else. It is also of no use as an economic construct because it fails to explain the uniform interest rate as the single price for using different kinds of goods. It could also never explain why the 'financial backer' of the credit market sometimes asks for higher and sometimes lower interest. 'Financial backers' lend goods they do not know exist; in particular, they cannot recognize whether the goods are scarce or abundant and therefore lack a yardstick to guide the interest rate. The notion that goods are lent on credit markets has been called the Scylla which happened to scholarship which was trying to avoid the Charybdis of a pure monetary conception.[21] Therefore, the recent view that the goods sold underlying a bill of exchange are in fact credited when discounting a bill[22] needs to be rejected, if taken seriously, because it has the potential to add confusion to the understanding of how the credit business operates, without adding any insight into our question.[23]

The obvious and almost naïve answer is that it is 'money', that is, banknotes and coins that are passed on from banks to the borrower.

University Press, 1951), chapter 27. All subsequent English quotes from David Ricardo are based on the same edition].

[18] Ambiguous e.g. chapter 1, section 3 in Ricardo, *Grundsätze der Volkswirtschaft und Besteuerung* [Ricardo, *On the Principles of Political Economy and Taxation*, chapter 1, section 3].

[19] Ricardo calls it 'Nutzung' ['utility'] of capital (Ricardo, *Grundsätze der Volkswirtschaft und Besteuerung*, p. 41) [Ricardo, *On the Principles of Political Economy and Taxation*, pp. 11–12].

[20] Cf. section I 'The barter perspective' in chapter [2.]A. in Part Two.

[21] Cf. von Wieser, *Theorie der gesellschaftlichen Wirtschaft*, p. 307.

[22] Cf. von Schulze-Gaevernitz, *Die moderne Kreditbank*, p. 77.

[23] Highly questionable is also Herbert von Beckerath, *Kapitalmarkt und Geldmarkt* e.g. on p. 88: 'Dieser Umstand entscheidet auch darüber, wenn irgendwelche *Gütervorräte* tatsächlich dem Kapitalmarkt... zugeführt werden können' [This circumstance also decides whether any *goods stock* can actually... be supplied to the capital market]. Considering the extraordinary ambiguity of this author it is hard to tell which notion he actually leans towards.

This answer can be found in those classics economists who do not follow the above notion that goods are lent on credit markets, in passages where they clearly explain their view on what is transferred from the lender to the borrower. In particular, Mill[24] takes this view on many occasions.

In principle this notion is a consequence and expression of the quantity theory of money held by these authors, which almost fully neglects credit. Everyone needs to buy goods with 'money' and therefore the entrepreneur, who does not have any capital of his own, has to develop a demand for 'money'. He receives this money from other individuals, who have sold goods and saved some of their money and then lend it to others, whereby the lender transfers the warranted right for a service in return to the borrower. Therefore, what is 'demanded' and 'invested' is money in the narrowest sense.

One has to differentiate between the correctness, that is, the logical coherence of a theory, and the truth, that is, the correctness of assumptions, of a theory. The classical quantity theory of money has indeed the merit of being *correct* in all respects for an economy where every transaction is made with cash. It undoubtedly explains the nature of the means of granting credit for such a (conceivable) economy: eventually only an increase in savings, and therefore a reduction in consumption, can increase the supply of credit. Even an increase in production can only increase the supply of credit if it is accompanied by an increase in savings. Otherwise the increase in production causes a decline in prices, and vice versa a reduction in production, also of goods of higher order, can only cause a rise in prices not an increase in the interest rate. These are the logical consequences of the theory which are seldom drawn. The amount of money available for credit is imagined as constant and in continuous circulation; it remains per se unchanged by any variations in the sphere of production.

A theory is more destructive to the progress of any respective discipline the more complete and logically correct it is. It may sound paradoxical, but it offers an incentive to adhere to a theory even though the underlying assumptions no longer reflect reality.

[24] Cf. John Stuart Mill, *Grundsätze der politischen Ökonomie [Principles of Political Economy]*, trans. Adolph Soetbeer, 2nd ed. (Hamburg: Perthes-Besser und Mauke, 1864), p. 475 ff.

Without a doubt, the logical correctness and completeness of the quantity theory of money has curbed the scientific progress and caused stagnation. There is no other explanation for why the vast majority of authors occupied with banking and money and capital markets still base their thinking on this theory. This is evidenced by the use of terminology (e.g. the 'money' is abundant, the 'money' is scarce) introduced by the classics, which was once appropriate for the economic development of the time, but today it can only be seen as an anachronism. Further proof is given by the literature persistently using the notion that credit supply is determined by a certain stock, which will be shown to be incorrect. It was accurate for the development stage of finance and banking in the past: at that time a creditor could only use money to buy goods and services and therefore savings were the only means available to invest and lend. At that time, ideas on curtailing and directing 'capital' were right, and even the mercantile overestimation of cash might have not been as meaningless as generally assumed.

Cash does not play any role in some credit markets and only a marginal one in others; the notion that money in its narrowest definition is what banks lend is therefore wrong and does not warrant any further exposition. It is peculiar that this is given hardly any consideration. The uselessness of a strict quantity theory (whilst acknowledging its correctness) in a modern economy ever more reliant on cashless payments is only stressed in the context of the price determination of goods and not the credit business. Today it is not only those holding cash who are able to buy goods, but also those holding cheques and other forms of money substitutes. This is analogous on the credit market, where nowadays financiers not only rely on coins, notes, or paper money but to a growing extent on money substitutes such as cheques or giro accounts. This point alone proves the untenable nature of a strict quantity theory. Hence, it cannot shed light on the means used in modern banking and has to be dismissed.

The contemporary view on the determination of the 'general price level' has distanced itself from the strict quantity theory and is now dominated by the so called 'refined quantity theory'.

According to the refined quantity theory, the available quantity of money determining the 'general price level' is not solely composed of the amount of cash but also includes cheques, current account balances, and other money substitutes. Adding these to the amount of cash, they increase the demand on the goods market and can therefore cause changes in the price level.

The conception of the means of credit underlying the refined quantity theory is similar to the strict quantity theory: analogous to the usage of money substitutes in addition to cash on the goods market, financiers are not constrained by the stock of cash; rather, the inclusion of money substitutes (cheque, current account balances, etc.) 'expands' their supply beyond the available stock of cash.[25] However, authors differ about the extent to which such an expansion is possible. Occasionally, an author voices the idea that such an expansion is only possible if the economy has a certain stock of idle goods because only then can inflationary tendencies be avoided and in that way the author is confusing two distinct problems.[26] In truth, this aspect can only be considered when asking *should* the money market be expanded, not whether it *could*.

To equate the means of financiers with the expanded quantity of money (including certain money substitutes) is almost a complete reversal of the actual state of the modern economy, which makes it an indefensible position and is a typical example of the often-bemoaned lag between economic development and economic insight. Nowadays, cash does not form the basis to which money substitutes are added; on the contrary, the credit supply consists primarily (on some credit markets, even exclusively) of money substitutes, such that cash is only of minor or even of no relevance. Although cash is without doubt the *historic* origin of the money market, it is logically incorrect for a theoretical treatment to take cash as the point of departure instead of disregarding it in the first instance and introducing it only as a modification at a later point. In this context, one only has to think of the transactions on the money market for short-term money, which is generally organised such that not a single piece of cash is physically moved, supplied, or demanded. 'Money' is the last thing dealt on money and capital markets, as has been rightfully claimed.[27] It is therefore wrong to consider the means of banks as being cash plus money substitutes.

[25] Compare the essays of Arthur Spiethoff, 'Die äußere Ordnung des Kapital- und Geldmarktes' [The System of the Capital and Money Market], *Schmollers Jahrbuch für Gesetzgebung, Verwaltung und Volkswirtschaft* 33, (1909).

[26] E.g. Spiethoff, 'Die äußere Ordnung des Kapital- und Geldmarktes' and following him chapter 2, von Beckerath, *Kapital- und Geldmarkt*.

[27] von Schulze-Gaevernitz, *Die moderne Kreditbank*, p. 40.

In an attempt to account for the preponderance of money substitutes in the modern economy, some authors began to think of credit markets as the market of 'claims'. They treat cash either as secondary or as irrelevant and exclude it completely from their theory.[28]

Even this concept of 'claims' as the object of credit markets is purely quantity theoretic in nature. This is true for all notions assuming a *certain* quantity or a *well-defined, limited* stock as the object of credit markets regardless of whether this stock is made up of cash or claims.

Initially, this concept [of claims as the object of credit markets] seems to be exceptionally correct and to solve the problem.

Indeed certain concerns with the term 'claim', in the sense that it obviously refers to a claim for 'money', can be raised. This term originates from its legal meaning and not from its economic function, a mistake which is all too often committed, particularly in monetary theory. If a cheque or current account deposit is transferred to another person in order to make a payment, then this only represents a claim for money in legal terms. From an economic perspective, and as long it is not redeemed as cash, it is not a right to money, but money itself. The condition that the claim is ceded but not redeemed is true for the vast majority of cheque and current accounts. Nevertheless, to consider it as a claim for money would be a repetition of the same mistake committed for so long in the search for the nature of bank notes.[29] It is nowadays widely accepted[30] that banknotes are money as long as they are in circulation and not redeemed for cash. It is therefore only logical that some authors tried to introduce the term 'bank money' to stress the money-like nature of cheque and current account balances.[31]

[28] See Weill, 'Notenumlauf und Preisbewegung' [Note Circulation and Price Movements], *Bankarchiv 16*, no. 12 (1916/17) and also von Schulze-Gaevernitz, *Die moderne Kreditbank* with particular clarity on p. 40: 'Die Zusammenfassung von Angebot und Nachfrage nach solchen Forderungen (sc. Gegen die Banken) heißt der "Geldmarkt"' [The summary of supply and demand of such claims (i.e. against banks) is called the "money market"].

[29] Cf. in particular Adolph Wagner, *Sozialökonomische Theorie des Geldes und des Geldwesens [Socio-economic Theory of Money and Finance]* (Leipzig: C. F. Winter, 1909) and Karl Theodor Helfferich, *Das Geld [Money]* (Leipzig: C. L. Hirschfeld, 1903).

[30] Compare von Wieser, *Theorie der gesellschaftlichen Wirtschaft*, p. 308 and virtually all chartalists like Knapp, Heyn, Hertzka, Dalberg, Liefmann, and others.

[31] Compare Friedrich Bendixen, *Das Inflationsproblem [The Problem of Inflation]* (Stuttgart: Ferdinand Enke, 1917), p. 29, but also all his other writings. See also Franz Huber, 'Geldtheorie und Bankverfassung' *[Monetary Theory and the Bank Charter]*, *Bankarchiv 16*, no 15 (1916/17): pp. 275–84.

Apart from these formal concerns, and as already mentioned, it is initially quite acceptable to see a certain stock of claims as the means of banks. It is in fact true and corresponds to reality that a rather high proportion of loans are disbursed by transferring claims using cheque and current accounts. This seems to be a genuine reason to equate the stock of 'claims' with the extent to which a financier can grant credit, that is, the 'means' of the financier.[32]

Nevertheless this notion, even though it has gained popularity recently, does not hold up to close scrutiny, which reveals that it does not contribute to the solution of the problem but masks its difficulties.

In the case of private financiers, who are not banks themselves but who are their customers, it is a defensible notion that claims are their means. Apart from small loans in the normal course of business, banks play a crucial (sometimes exclusive) part in the provision of all sorts of loans. It is therefore not an exaggeration that the credit business of banks marginalizes the credit business between private individuals, of which private mortgages are probably the most important. It is banks that operate current accounts, discount bills of exchange, manage modern stock market launches and, particularly noteworthy in this context, the provision of short-term money (call money and money for monthly settlement). In all these activities a bank is at minimum involved on the asset side of the transaction. For the credit business of banks, which is our primary interest, it is indefensible or if anything only formally correct that their means are equal to their stock of claims; therefore, it is not possible to deduce the extent of means from the stock of claims.

In fact, when banks disburse a credit they often open a cheque account in the name of the debtor and therefore grant the debtor a claim against the bank. This claim is created ad hoc and comes only into existence with and because of the provision of the loan. This on its own shows that the identified view is untenable: if a claim does not constitute the potential to grant loans, but is the consequence thereof, then any effort to judge the bank's means (in particular their extent) to grant loans is based on a circular argument. Evidently, there must be something else which determines the potential to grant loans.

[32] Compare Weill, 'Notenumlauf und Preisbewegung'.

This is also shown by analysing the types of means which banks use to invest according to the prevailing doctrine. If the bank receives the means from a 'saving' customer, then these are usually held as a deposit with the bank for a certain time. This case does obviously not allow us to speak of a transfer of a claim to the bank (apart from the exceptional case where the customer received the savings in cash and not via transfer). In fact the bank might assume ownership of a claim against another bank in connection with the deposit; this claim is already invested, even if only for the short term or as call money, and hence cannot be considered a means of investment for the credit market in its *entirety*. There is, however, no transfer of claims between the customer and the bank. In fact, what happens is little else than the transformation of a short-term claim into a long-term one. If one tried to construct from this how a bank takes possession of a claim, then one will fail because the bank would simultaneously be creditor and debtor. Such a union of obligation and claim in one person would lead to the termination of the claim, so how can the assumption of a claim be both the object and the nature of banks' 'borrowing'?

The notion is also untenable if a bank, not a customer, provides the bank with the 'means'. For example, this happens if the bank borrows 'money' for a day because some payment can be expected only on the following day. In this case, the transfer of claims or bank money is out of the question. Although in practice these loans are often disbursed by transferring claims, this is solely caused by the arrangements underpinning the clearing process between banks. The transfer of claims is not relevant for the nature of lending itself and one should not be deceived by its appearance. If bank A borrows money from bank B for a day, then this could happen by exchanging cheques. Bank B passes a cheque, originating from another bank[33] and due on that day, to bank A. In exchange bank A issues a cheque due the following day to bank B. Bank A can then use the cheque due for payment in the settlement of the clearing process and in turn bank B can use the cheque drawn by bank A to settle claims in the next day's clearing process. Therefore, bank A only wanted a claim against bank B because the original claim needed to be settled. In truth, not the claim against bank B itself is part of the credit demand but the

33 In most cases the Reichsbank is the drawee of the cheque [the Reichsbank was the German central bank from 1876 until 1945].

desired continuation of the original claim by bank A; this also reveals the true motivation of bank A's behaviour. It is irrelevant for theoretical considerations, if this demand manifests itself as an exchange of claims, one due for payment and the other due at a later date. Also the notion that banks have a stock of 'claims' which enables them to grant credit seems therefore indefensible.

Our list of opinions commonly found in the literature would not be complete if we did not mention another notion, which is often found on its own[34] and sometimes alongside other notions.[35] According to this view the means of the financiers is 'purchasing power'.

'Purchasing power' is a metaphor, which gives us as a purely formal reason against using it. Also, the introduction made it already clear that such figurative expressions need to be avoided at all cost when dealing with problems like ours. 'Purchasing power', which is usually used in a very different context in English,[36] does not exist per se: 'powers' do not purchase, people do.

Apart from that, the notion does not contribute to the solution of the problem, because in fact it lacks any content. Its metaphorical character covers this emptiness initially. The assertion that borrowers need the credit only to possess purchasing power is trivial and in fact not even entirely true. There are many types of credit which in their nature prolong already existing credits. The relevant purchases were made in the past and therefore these credits certainly do not grant purchasing power. The term 'purchasing power' is therefore too narrow. On the other hand it is also too wide, because there is the possibility to 'action purchasing power', without using the credit market or owning assets. This is possible if the buyer also sells something at the same time.

Primarily the term 'purchasing power' is meaningless, even if not wrong, because it stresses only the *consequence* of credit. The question of where the transferred purchasing power originates and how it is mediated remains unanswered.[37] Therefore, the term 'purchasing power' does not get us closer to the solution of the problem, even though the wealth of possible interpretations does not rule out the right one.

[34] As can be found in the writings of almost all authors cited in footnotes 30–2.

[35] See Schumpeter, *Theorie der wirtschaftlichen Entwicklung*, p. 255.

[36] On the question of the 'general' price level cf. Irving Fisher, *Die Kaufkraft des Geldes [The Purchasing Power of Money]*, trans. Ida Stecker (Berlin: Georg Reimer, 1916).

[37] Where these considerations are irrelevant, in particular for the determination of the general price level, this term seems acceptable. It will be used by us to that extent.

II. CREDIT IN THE MODERN ECONOMY

1. Credit creation

The preceding remarks show that the literature not only contains unsatisfying opinions on the means of banks but also provides the motivation for this book. The main reason being that economic theory (maybe instinctively fearing losing the scientific results of the great authors on banking of the last decades) usually takes a cash economy as its basis and only modifies it to reflect changes that occurred over time. The theorists have certainly not been able to dispose of the notion of an underlying 'stock'.

To avoid this source of error and to resist any temptation to regress to quantity theoretic views, we will suppose the other extreme state of an economy, in which every transaction is settled cashless and no payment is made in cash. We will establish our theoretical results for this 'pure credit economy' and only then introduce cash as a modifying element to reflect the role of cash for some markets. We consciously assume an economic state that does not reflect the current situation and may only be realised in the very long term. Instead of trying to do justice to the present by fond descriptions of a *past* economic era, this method constructs and describes a *future* economy based on current trends in order to recognise the *current* state.

In a pure credit economy, as we suppose it, every credit is disbursed in the same way as certain types of credit are today: the credit amount is debited to a loan account and credited to a cheque account, or, to use a common phrase, 'made available'. Instead of being an occasional practice[38] it is the regular and fundamentally the only way to disburse a loan (apart from differences in accounting).[39]

[38] This view is very common. The older and recent literature on general economics and all writings on banking serve as evidence. The following succinct statements are from the most recent literature: Somary, *Bankpolitik*, p. 60: 'Eine Kreditbank kann nur soweit Kredit geben, als sie Einlagen erhält . . . sie kann darüber hinaus in engen Grenzen durch Girodeposit ihren Wirkungskreis erweitern' [A commercial bank can only grant loans as much as it receives deposits . . . in addition it can to a narrow extent widen its sphere through giro deposits]; Schulze-Gaevernitz, *Die moderne Kreditbank*, p. 43: 'Keine echten Depositen sind die sog. Kreditdepositen, d.h. buchmäßige Guthaben, welche durch Kredit entstanden sind' ['No real deposits are the so-called credit deposits i.e. book cash, which originate from credit']. Also see the essays by Spiethoff, *Die äußere Ordnung des Kapital- und Geldmarktes*.

[39] It is common practice to debit a loan account and book the credit amount to a cheque account only when payments are made. However, the process described here

The borrower uses the credited amount to buy those goods (which were the reason for taking out a loan) and issues a cheque or uses another way to transfer the deposit to the seller of the goods. The seller then cedes this cheque for purchases (e.g. raw materials); this second seller cedes the cheque as well and this continues until the cheque comes into possession of someone not expending it further but 'saving'.[40] In other words, the short-term bank deposit starts to circulate, no different to cash in a cash economy.

The transaction is reflected in the accounts of the banks in the economy in the following way: if and as long as all holders of the cheque have an account with the bank issuing the original loan, then only the balance sheet of that bank changes; the claim (usually long-term) against the borrower is booked as an asset of the bank, whilst the claim of the respective holder of the cheque is booked as a liability. However, if the holder of the cheque has an account with another bank, as would usually be the case, then the other bank will stand between the credit-issuing bank and the holder of the cheque: the deposit is a short term liability of the credit-issuing bank and the claim against the credit-issuing bank is held by the cheque-holder's bank not by the cheque-holder directly.[41]

This simple and fundamental banking and accounting procedure offers the answer to the negative side of our question, namely that there is no such thing as an 'investment of means' in the sense of the

of booking the amount to the recipient's account and debiting the loan account immediately is only different in terms of accounting.

[40] This is the moment we call 'credit consolidation' and which we consider in section II, subsection 4 of this chapter.

[41] Assume that A has an overdraft facility from bank I, which he uses to buy goods from B, who has a cheque account with bank II. Then the balance sheets of bank I and II are as follows:

Table 1

Bank I		Bank II	
Assets	Liabilities	Assets	Liabilities
Bill of exchange 1,000,000 Mk	Capital 1,000,000 Mk	Bill of exchange 1,000,000 Mk	Capital 1,000,000 Mk
Overdraft facility of A 10,000 Mk	Short-term claim of bank II 10,000 Mk	Short-term liability of bank I 10,000 Mk	Short-term claim of B (cheque account) 10,000 Mk

prevailing opinion—be it the bank's investment in the borrower, or a 'temporary' investment in the bank by cheque account holders.

To invest always means to expend an asset in exchange for another, that is, in accounting terms a change of an existing balance sheet item, for example, debt instead of cash. In the case of granting a credit no existing item changes on one side of the balance sheet, but seemingly enlarges it.[42] The (short-term) deposit of the cheque-account-holder appears the very moment he deposits the cheque with his bank. The bank's deposit in turn only comes into existence when it cedes the credit-issuing bank's 'money', even if it is only lent as call money. This establishes that there are no 'means' of banks in the sense of an investable stock. The means of the bank are either already invested or they do not exist at all.

One can also express this fact as: each credit granted in an economy generates a deposit and therefore the means of its own accommodation. Because the granting of credit creates a short-term deposit for another economic agent which, at least initially, does not disappear and its form and continued existence is not challenged by cash withdrawal as we are in a pure credit economy in which cash withdrawals are not possible.

The process outlined above also allows and necessitates the converse argument that every existing deposit on cheque and current accounts originates in the act of granting of credit previously. Any cheque account can only come into existence when it is instated by a

[42] An exception seems to be if e.g. in the previous example another individual C had an overdraft facility with bank II, whose supplier has a cheque account with bank I. In this case the existing short-term claim of bank II against bank I and the new claim of bank I against bank II would cancel each other and the new balance sheets would look like:

Table 2

Bank I		Bank II	
Assets	Liabilities	Assets	Liabilities
Bill of exchange 1,000,000 Mk	Capital 1,000,000 Mk	Bill of exchange 1,000,000 Mk	Capital 1,000,000 Mk
Overdraft facility of A 10,000 Mk	Short-term claim of D (cheque account) 10,000 Mk	Overdraft facility of C 10,000 Mk	Short-term claim of B (cheque account) 10,000 Mk

In truth, this case is an extension of the balance sheet. This becomes clearer if one thinks of both balance sheets merged together.

bank. The correctness of this argument can be easily verified by a short inductive consideration. One only needs to trace back one of the existing bank deposits in the economy, for example, the account of a clerk at a mutual savings bank. The clerk received his salary on the first of the quarter, let's says on an account with the Reichsbank, and was in a position to cede the claim against the Reichsbank to the mutual savings bank, which in turn deposits the amount in his savings account. If one presumes that the Reichsbank itself did not create the claim credited to the clerk, then one needs to assume that the amount was transferred by the German Reich, that a taxpayer settled a tax debt. One can further assume that the taxpayer ceded dividend payments he received on stocks. The joint stock company in turn used receipts from machines sold to an entrepreneur. This will usually be the point at which the credit is originally granted by a bank. Denying this possibility and assuming that the entrepreneur ceded a deposit received, then one will eventually trace the origin back (one can go as far back as one likes) to a point where the bank originally created the purchasing power. Otherwise, the deposit could have never come into existence and made an appearance. Even if someone calls so many goods his or her own, a *bank deposit* can only arise if a third party buys his goods. This presumes that the third party possesses purchasing power, that is, that the third party was granted credit.

We claim therefore (and in complete opposition to the entire banking and credit literature,[43,44] which has an almost unified view)

[43] Cf. citations and quotes in footnote 3 of this chapter. The predominant opinion is shown with particular clarity by Gustav Motschmann, *Das Depositengeschäft der Berliner Großbanken [The Deposit Business of Berlin's Major Banks]*, Teil 1, Band 154, Schriften des Vereins für Sozialpolitik (Leipzig and Munich: Duncker & Humblot, 1915), p. 129: 'Die Geschäfte der Banken scheiden sich in Passiv- und Aktivgeschäfte, diese sind die Grundlage, sie sind die primären Geschäfte. Erst muß eine Bank Geld aufnehmen, dann kann sie solches ausleihen oder anderweitig verwenden.' [The banking business divides into transactions of liabilities and assets, the latter are fundamental, they are the primary business. A bank first needs to collect money, which it then can lend or use it differently.]

[44] The sole exception, apart from the vague exposition by Henning Dunning Macleod, *The Theory of Credit*, 2 vols (London and New York: Longmans, Green and Company, 1889–1891), p. 599–602, is the notion of Schumpeter, *Theorie der wirtschaftlichen Entwicklung*, p. 203: 'Wer wollte auch die Tatsache leugnen, daß . . . vielleicht drei Viertel der Bankdepositen einfach auf Gutschriften beruhen' ['Who wants to deny the fact, that . . . maybe three quarters of bank deposits are created by credit']. Certainly, we maintain our claim that all deposits are created by credit.

that it is not the liabilities side of banks, particularly deposits, that is the primary business of banks. Every action on the liabilities side has been preceded by another bank's action on the asset side of the balance sheet: the deposit business is only the reflection of credit creation. The contrary view suffers from some kind of optical illusion caused by the unquestioned adoption of quantity theoretical views and widespread egocentrism, that is, from the viewpoint of the individual bank rather than from conceptualizing banking as a whole.

There will be some temptation to launch an immediate and fundamental objection: unlike what was claimed earlier, it was not necessary to leave the realm of the quantity theory because in reality payment and credit transaction would only differ formally between an economy with cash and an economy without cash. In a pure cash economy banks obtain their means from individuals saving and would lend it to someone else soon after. The same supposedly happens in the hypothetical pure credit economy, with the difference being that money takes the form of claims, that is, 'bank money'. This difference in the form of money would have the consequence, however, that banks do not obtain their means by an actual deposit of cash, but through transforming a cheque account into a savings account, which could not circulate like money. On the other hand, granting a credit would manifest itself in the creation of a new deposit instead of passing on saved money. But this newly created deposit would only be formally different to the passed-on savings, but identical in substance. Therefore the prevalent notion of a quantity theoretical circle from the saver to the bank and from the bank to the borrower could be sustained.

The objection is unconvincing, even if (despite the artificiality of the argument) one concedes that the savings accounts are identical in substance to the newly created current and cheque accounts. Under this assumption, the cheque accounts established by banks to disburse loans could not be considered newly created because of the simultaneous 'closure' and disappearance of other cheque accounts; however, the question about the origin of these closed accounts would need to be asked and answered. Following the predominant doctrine of the priority of bank's liabilities, then the answer to the question is that these accounts arise from other 'closed' accounts. This shows the notion is false. If one would continue to trace back the origin of accounts, then there will be a point (even if the construction above is maintained) after which no cheque account exists and therefore will need to be created by banks through granting credit (or alternatively through the bank purchasing assets, which is in effect the bank granting a credit to itself). If this is the case, and banks have not continuously created more cheque accounts than they have closed (because they have been transformed into savings accounts), then one would need to assume that the entirety of payment transactions, worth many billions, did not develop but had existed all the time. In reality the sum of the means of payment has developed from a state of a cash economy and only by banks first creating current accounts did this possibility arise. Without banks, there would obviously not be any cashless payments, no bank money, and all transactions would be settled in cash. The sole exception would be bank balances granted in exchange for gold and silver coins, which can at a pinch be regarded as not primarily created by banks, because they only replace and represent the coins. Unsecured accounts, as they actually exist and exceed coin-backed accounts by millions, could have never come into existence.[45] No banknotes other than those fully or partially backed would exist either because they only represent deposits and are undeniably primarily created by the central bank.

This argument shows that the usual quantity theoretical cycle where the money flows from the saver to the bank, from there back to the borrower and thus re-entering circulation cannot be sustained as a concept for the modern economy. Characteristically a cycle lacks any beginning and allows theoretical reasoning to start at any point. However, 'money' in the modern economy does not move in a cycle. The movement of modern 'bank money' reveals that an origin can be identified and therefore the moment at which the 'money' can be seen as being generated. This moment can be regularly identified as the moment a bank grants a credit to a customer. Thus it would be illogical or a misconception to maintain the notion of a cycle (as the predominant doctrine actually does) and to consider money as flowing to instead of being created by banks. Our concept outlined above, which states that the bank's asset side is primary to the liabilities side in each and every case, tries to avoid this error. In the

[45] Some authors (cf. Schulze-Gaevernitz, *Die moderne Kreditbank*, p. 48 ff. and von Beckerath, *Kapitalmarkt und Geldmarkt*, p. 89 ff.) distinguish between real and nominal purchasing power, with the latter usually understood as primarily created by credit banks. Our argument has already given sufficient reasons to render this distinction between real and nominal untenable: All purchasing power has its origin in nominal purchasing.

course of this book it will become evident that the argument is not only correct but also relevant for theoretical considerations. Our notion will give rise to conclusions, some rather different to the prevailing opinion, regarding the role of deposits in the business of banks, the function of banks in general and above all (leading to our ultimate goal) the origin and essence of capital.

The discussion so far has concerned the negative side of our question and showed that it is not possible to consider an already existing, independent stock of means to grant credit, because, in brief, the means are only created through granting a credit. What is the nature of those means in a positive sense though?

We interpret the question at first in a technical sense to be directed at the essence of those means *directly* granted by the bank lending. The answer can be easily found if one impartially considers the concept outlined above. One readily recognizes that when banks grant a credit, then two debt claims come into existence across the economy. One is the claim of the borrower against the bank and the second is the claim of the bank (or a second bank in the case illustrated in footnote 42) against the borrower.

Going beyond the legal-accounting nature of this statement and viewing it from an economic perspective, one realizes that both claims form part of a single, unitary credit agreement with the one holding deposits as the creditor and the borrower as the debtor.

This reveals the nature of credit: credit enables the borrower to consume goods and services, for which he is momentarily not in a position to offer anything in return. Therefore, the lender, from the viewpoint of economics, is the one selling goods or services whilst postponing any service in return. It is easily verified that this is whoever holds the deposit associated with the credit; he is the one who effectively divested himself of goods without receiving any service in return as long as he does not cede the deposit. If he buys goods and cedes the deposit, then he 'subrogates' the seller, who in turn will be the creditor of the original credit for as long as he holds the deposit; his goods and services end up indirectly (not effectively but according to their exchange value) with the debtor as long as he does not subrogate the 'next seller'. If he does not subrogate anyone, that is, if he does not spend but 'saves' the deposit, then he will become the permanent creditor.

The economic lender is in each and every case the holder of the deposit associated with the credit. One will readily concede that this notion is quite natural and rather unsurprising if one bears in mind that it is analogous to the common understanding of fiat money: the respective holder of fiat money is undoubtedly seen as granting a credit in the form of precious metal to the debtor. Indeed our notion differs markedly from this one, because we think that the deposit holder secures something other than precious metals.

The statement that the economic creditor is identified with the respective holder of the deposit associated with the credit also defines exactly the bank's function in credit transactions and also the nature of their means: *banks provide the levers to transfer goods from those who are willing to surrender them, permanently or temporarily, without a service in return to those who need them.* Their function is to provide the *channel for transactions of goods without service in return.* Banks fulfil this function by simultaneously creating debtors and creditors and hence constitute economic credit agreements.[46] The power of banks to fulfil this function by constituting credit agreements shall be discussed extensively below.[47] At this point, it can be stated briefly as: The one who sells a good to the borrower and the one who is eventually the economic lender are not identical, and the latter does not know the debtor. The general trustworthiness of banks enables the transaction of means to unknown debtors; claims against the banks are deemed categorically safe, are accepted by everyone and thus the 'money' circulates.

2. Credit prolongation

The ideas outlined above can be used to examine the normal credit transactions of banks in practice, and reveals that a large proportion of bank transactions can be easily classified according to our scheme and are fully explained by it, but also that there is a range of credit transactions which cannot be explained. We think of commercial borrowing (in particular at exchanges and in the form of overnight, monthly, and money for monthly settlements) as driven either by the

[46] It does not require any explanation that this notion is different to the one disputed above, according to which banks' means are identified with a certain fixed pool of claims.

[47] See section II 'Credit in the modern economy' in this chapter, subsection 5 on the 'essence of bank credit'.

bank's own or its customers' requirements, and which is supplied by other banks or even private individuals. It is particularly important to recognize the nature of the 'means' with which the 'money'-lending bank operates, because these transactions are more important than theorists would generally assume. Business papers also print regular and detailed reports on the current state of the money market and it is necessary to be clear about what is traded on these markets in order to report accurately and without error; otherwise the reports are of dubious value and risk misleading the numerous business deals arranged on the basis of the reports.

This begs the very concrete question: what is it that a bank desires and receives from another bank when borrowing, for example, 'money' from one closing of the month to the next? After our remarks in the previous section, it does not require any further reasons to show that 'money', 'capital', 'claims', or money substitutes (which are usually mentioned in the same breath) are not the answer to these questions just as they are not in the cases of granting credit described above. Also the neutral term 'purchasing power' is obviously not only meaningless but also wrong in the context of stock market transactions, because, unlike for other credits, there is no intention to purchase. More than in other areas of bank transactions, the prevailing view leaves one in the dark.

The obvious approach to this question is to analyse every method used in the lending and borrowing of money for monthly settlements, providing the basis for identifying their commonalities, their essence, and eventually the true purpose of the transaction. Such an inductive method would not work bearing in mind the wealth of seemingly different methods to disburse such monies; the most common forms of disbursement are bank transfer, drawing a cheque, ceding a cheque from other banks or the central bank. We therefore use a deductive approach and try to infer the method of transaction from the purpose of the credit.

It was shown above that granting a credit to someone in the economy gives rise to a claim of the bank against the debtor and a claim of the respective deposit-holder against his bank. If these two banks are not identical then there will also be a claim of the deposit-holder's bank against the bank of the debtor, apparently acting as a link between the two claims. This liability needs to be settled on the bank's request, as would happen if the deposit-holder's bank submitted the cheque for payment to the debtor's bank.

How are claims of one bank against another generally settled in a modern economy? As is well known, payments between banks are not settled through physically transferring money but generally through a clearing process. In a credit economy, as we assume it, there is no other way.

What does it mean to say that claims are settled in a clearing process? The clearing process is in principal nothing other than an institution to avoid physical payments either in cash or bank notes. A typical case: on a certain day bank A has to pay 1,000 marks to bank B and is due to receive 1,000 marks from bank C. The two claims involve different parties and are therefore not offset by themselves; A would have to physically pay B and C would have to physically pay A. The clearing house overcomes this and enables these claims to be offset against each other. A legal entity is created which assumes the roles of the creditor of all due liabilities and the debtor of all due claims for all banks; accordingly, the accounts of the clearing house show claims against banks with liabilities and debts to banks with claims. The unity of debtor and creditor, which is required for offsetting, is therefore achieved.[48]

The sole usage of the clearing process (in connection with other cashless payment methods) should not only be regarded as technical progress in payment methods, but also needs to be appreciated as transforming the repayment of debts: the claim against someone in the economy can be used to repay debts instead of cash, given the claims coincide in due date and are submitted for clearing.

As a result, only the appearance of the change is fixed; the financial consequences can be identified by recalling one of the possible origins of the offsetting claims. We shall assume that the first claim is due to bank A granting credit to one of its customers, who in turn draws a cheque on the associated deposit to buy some goods from a customer of bank B; bank B, therefore, obtained a due claim against bank A. The claim of bank A against bank C will result from a similar situation, with a customer of bank C drawing a cheque to buy goods from a customer of bank A. The sale of goods from A's customer to a customer of C ultimately settles the claim of B against A, because the claim of A against C is used to repay the claim of B against A. Analogously, the creation of the claim of B against A is due to a

[48] Cf. Bruno Buchwald, *Technik des Bankbetriebes [The Techniques of Banking]* (Berlin: Julius Springer, 1904). p. 76.

customer of bank A—possibly the same—buying goods from a customer of bank B. This illustrates so-called 'indirect trade': B delivers a service to A, A delivers a service in return to C. Therefore they are not exchanges of goods against money and money against goods, but goods against goods. The monetary economy is only a detour in the emergence of the 'indirect trade economy', which only distinguishes itself from the primitive barter economy by removing the latter's restricted exchange opportunities.

Banks have to pay off their debts on the due date because they would lose goodwill otherwise. If repaying debts requires that the customer of the bank (or indeed the bank itself) sells some goods, then this means that on the same day as a customer of a bank buys some goods, a customer also needs to sell some goods; the latter is effectively the service in return for the preceding purchase. Both goods transfers are in a relation of service and service in return, of course in a peculiar fashion: bank A's customer doesn't deliver to bank B's customer but instead to bank C's customer. This generates a liability for bank C in the clearing process, which needs to be repaid by offering services to, for example, bank D, which in turn needs to offer some services to someone else. The long chain of seller and buyers continues until eventually someone offers a service to bank B's customer and completes the circle.

If we assume that every bank actually arranges sales offsetting purchases every day, then there would be no reason for banks to engage with each other in credit agreements. All claims and debts would offset each other every day. This illustration points to the purpose of short-term debts between banks, which is to extend the debt relation between banks and enable customers of one bank to sell their goods later, at their convenience, to grant the customer the right to wait. In short, they are *rights to wait.* Such credit relations also translate into the goods sphere: when such credit relations exist, then the exchange value of goods owned by customers of one bank exceeds the value of the goods they deliver to others. The debt relations between banks legalize this situation. This is also why these short-term debt relations are in contrast to those explained above, which enable the individuals to consume above their means and therefore fulfil the function of economic credit. These short-term debt relations do not enable anyone to consume above their means and therefore do not classify as genuine 'credit creation'. Through postponing the payment legislation it maintains and perpetuates the pre-existing conditions in the goods sphere. They should therefore be identified as 'credit prolongations', and are only secondary financial transactions induced by the original credit transaction. This is not only a formal distinction, but can also be justified from an economic perspective. The production and distribution of goods as well as the price mechanism are clearly affected differently if the credit transaction creates new 'levers' to pull goods from one subject of the economy to another or if they simply maintain the already existing relations. The question whether a credit transaction should be classified as 'credit creation' or 'credit prolongation' is the only economic criterion to systematically distinguish between bank transactions. This claim is somewhat contrary to the usually classifications based on the form of the credit, loans, or purchases, which only seem to interest lawyers. Another classification relies on the frequency, security, and liquidity of the business, which is only relevant from the private business perspective not from an economic one.

The exposition showed the technical process banks follow to grant credit to each other, the nature of the demand on the relevant credit markets, and who can act as financier on them.

Claims need to offset liabilities exactly in the daily clearing process. If a bank does not want to meet its obligations by using its own funds or through some sales of its customers, then the liability has to be honoured in some other way. The only way is to find another bank owning a claim without a matching liability; this is the case if the bank itself or one of its customers is in possession of a claim but does not use it to buy any goods and, hence, interrupts the circular flow of goods. An agreement between the banks has to be sought, which spares both the liability of the credit-seeking bank and the claim of the second bank from the clearing process. This agreement is a deferment of payment in an economic sense not a legal sense. Of course, a deferment of payment is of a special type: the deferment is not agreed with the supplier of goods, who holds a direct claim, but with the bank which is left with a claim after the clearing process.

Which technical methods can be used to effectively defer a payment? Obviously, theoretically the easiest way is for the credit-granting bank to pass a claim against itself on to the credit-seeking bank. This claim can be put forward for clearing and cancel out the liability of the credit-seeking bank. It is important not to be enticed into the idea that such claims are part of the demand for credit. Apart from the considerations explained above,[49] it would also lose the advantage of our position: the diverse appearance of banks' 'means' could not be summarised from the same viewpoint; therefore, contrary to the aim of any investigation into the means of banks, we could not pass any verdict on the extent of the means. Thus, it has to be kept in mind that the claim is only demanded as a means of cancelling out the debtor's liability in the clearing. The same end could be reached if the bank with the original claim did not put their claim forward for clearing and therefore the credit-seeking bank would not need further credit to balance its claims and liabilities.

There must obviously be another technique for the credit-granting bank to clear the outstanding liability of the credit-seeking bank. This second way is for the credit-granting bank to cede the claim, which would result in a clearing balance in its favour, to the credit-seeking bank. When the claim is ceded this way then all clearing accounts are balanced, in particular those of the credit-seeking and credit-granting banks. This method is also used in practice and a number of different common 'money transfers' can be explained by this scheme.[50]

Finally, a third possibility is for the creditor and debtor to agree on deferring the payment of the due liability. However, explicitly agreeing a deferment of payment is only possible in cases where the debtor and creditor are already in a direct debt relation, for example, because the creditor is also the seller of those goods, which makes it necessary for the purchaser to seek credit. This possibility is also used, more often than one might think, in the regular banking business. It is, however, only possible under certain circumstances. In general only the first two techniques are feasible, which can be described as 'deferment of payment' in a wider sense. These techniques do not prolong the original credit but settle the liability and substitute it with a new liability in favour of the new creditor.

It is interesting to employ an inductive method, explore the situations in which banks seek credit from each other, in order to check whether these deductively derived results are true. What does bank A need if, for example, it borrows call money from bank B? It is obviously not money, because it does not actually receive any. It is also not goods, which could not be granted by another bank in any

[49] Compare section II 'Credit in the modern economy' in this chapter, in particular subsection 1 on 'credit creation'.

[50] Compare the concluding notes of section 2 'Credit prolongation' in this section.

case. As we repeatedly showed, bank A also does not require any 'claim'. What the bank actually requires is to be discharged from the liability which arises from receiving a service, that is, that the payment is deferred in the wider sense. The truth of this statement is shown by the only economic situation which forces bank A to borrow 'money for a day': bank A has to demand money on this day, because it has to action a payment, that is, the clearing of the day shows a negative balance and a claim has to be put forward. This would only be possible the next day, because the bank only receives 'money' on that day, for example, from selling some securities. The money for a day enables the bank and its customers respectively to wait for a day to sell securities.

The right to defer payment into the future analogously constitutes the demand for 'call money'. The only difference to money 'for a fixed short term' is due to the uncertainty about how long the payment is deferred into the future and the possibility to 'repay' the loan at any time is provided.

The truth of our notion is shown particularly well in the case of money for monthly settlements, which is traded on the stock exchange. The typical instance of such a transaction would be that bank A buys securities for its customers from bank B, payable at the end of the month. The customer speculates that the price of the securities increases and does not pay for or sell it, but prolongs his credit with bank A. Bank A in turn has to settle the liability with bank B and, if it does not receive money at the end of the month from elsewhere, bank A has to borrow money for the monthly settlement from another bank, say bank C.[51]

What is it that bank A desires from bank C? It is obviously not money or claims or even the securities themselves, which are demanded by bank A; it demands the freedom not to settle the liability through selling securities. This is the only way the bank is in a position to let its customer speculate on rising prices, that is, to wait to sell the securities until the desired price rise is realised. The borrowing of money for the monthly settlement allows the customer to defer selling the securities for one month. This is the sole purpose of the money for monthly settlement, which is also clearly indicated in the case where it is not possible or appropriate to borrow money

[51] Compare Buchwald, *Technik des Bankbetriebes*, p. 239.

for the monthly settlement. If the interest rate on money for the monthly settlement is too high and the return of the speculation is questionable, then the customer would sell the securities and would not ask to prolong the loan. The terminology used in practice is in agreement with our notion and uses the term 'offsetting'; it also serves as further evidence that in practice these relations are common and how they match the practitioners view.

Finally, the possibility that a bank grants a loan to another bank in exchange for an accepted draft on the latter's customers, shall serve as further evidence for the proposed notion. The case of granting credit in exchange for a 'bankers' acceptance' can take place the following way: bank A buys securities from bank B, but does not want to pay for them. Initially, bank A secures the necessary means by borrowing call money from bank C. Assume another bank, bank D, sells some securities and places its receipts on the money market as call money. If A would like to borrow the money for a three-month fixed term and bank D would like to carry over the call money into bankers' acceptances then bank D will discount the acceptance of A. After the trade, bank D holds a three-month fixed term bankers' acceptance from A instead of a claim due any time. Similarly, A holds a three-month fixed term loan instead of a loan which can be called at any time. The trade again has the effect of postponing bank A's sale of securities, in this case for three months.

In the situations described, how are the credits disbursed in practice? A look at credit-induced monetary transfers between banks shows that in most cases the debtor puts forward a receipt for clearing. The credit-granting bank confirms the loan value with the receipt, which constitutes a claim for the credit-seeking bank. Occasionally, the loan is also disbursed by making the 'money available' on an account, which enables the credit-seeking bank to issue a claim against it. Furthermore, it is common practice that a bank passes on a cheque issued from a third bank (possibly the Reichsbank) or that the money is made available at a third bank. If the credit is only short term, then the creditor institution will receive a cheque due on an imminent date in exchange for its cheque (the previously described practice of exchanging cheques). Finally, in some cases the credit has the form of a simple deferment of payment, for example, a provincial bank borrows money for the monthly settlement from the same bank which also sells securities to customers of the former. It does not require any further explanation that all these transactions are variations on the three fundamental forms of 'credit prolongation' explained above.

3. Credit closure

According to the prevailing opinion, the means with which banks grant credit are replenished by the annual savings of the public. We have already shown that this belief is indefensible, but also another belief can be found, which is a consequence and an extension of the former. According to this belief, the re-payments of earlier credits stock up the means of banks. This view is also not tenable in the context of a modern economy. The repayment of credits, which we call 'credit closure', does not mean a flow of 'means' back to the bank and no 'stock' in any form makes an appearance. In short, credit closure must not be seen as the primary expression of the asset side of banks.

Such a belief would only be tenable for a cash economy, in which re-payments really create the means for granting new credits disbursed in cash. However, re-payments in a pure credit economy behave very differently. Fundamentally, nothing else happens other than the disappearance of the economic credit relation (which we called the essence of every credit creation): a claim of the bank against the debtor, a claim of a cheque account holder against his bank, and also, if these banks are not identical, a claim of the latter bank against the former; all these claims are settled. Credit closure is, therefore, nothing other than the counterpart and reversal of 'credit creation' and eliminates the credit creation's consequence for the balance sheet. An examination of the technicality of a credit closure assures the truth of this claim. Generally, the debtor re-pays his debt by depositing a cheque from any bank, which he received in exchange for his goods. At this point the bank's claim against the debtor is settled. Furthermore and as our previous treatment shows, the bank of the cheque holder who used it to pay the debtor has a claim against the bank originally issuing the credit, which is also compensated. Lastly, a cheque account deposit originally created by the credit disappears.

There is further reason to see credit closure as the counterpart and reversal of credit creation. Credit creation provides the levers to transfer goods from those who are willing to surrender them without a service in return, for shorter (cheque account holders) or longer periods (savings account holders) and who are the actual creditors, to the debtor who needs those services for the purposes of production or for other reasons. The credit closure means that conversely a good from the hitherto debtor to the hitherto creditor closes the cycle of goods which was set in motion by the credit creation.

Hence, the service of the debtor needs to precede every credit closure. The necessity of closing the credit is identical to the necessity of performing a service, in particular, the sales of goods. This has consequences for the goods market as new credit increases the demand for goods and ending credit increases the supply of goods. We will have to keep this in mind when analysing the effects of different maturities of credit (e.g. short-term discounting of bills of exchange, long-term mortgages, or perpetual government bonds) on the goods market and in particular on its price formation. These relations are also fundamental for analysing the importance of a congruent maturity of the credit and its usage, for example, using long-term credits for making investments and short-term credits to ensure liquidity.

4. Credit consolidation

When credit is created it is usually disbursed in a cheque account under the control of the debtor. The borrower is using a cheque to pay for goods and services and the recipient cedes the cheque in order to pay for his expenses. The cheque starts to circulate until someone saves it either partly or fully.[52] We call this moment of saving 'credit consolidation'.[53]

'Credit consolidation', that is, saving, does not carry the importance the prevailing view attaches to it. Savings do not supply banks with means to grant credit. The term 'credit consolidation' is also not fundamental to the problem at hand because savings do not create new 'economic levers' like 'credit creation', nor do they ensure the further existence of these levers as 'credit prolongation' does, nor do

[52] Compare section II 'Credit in the modern economy' in this chapter, in particular subsection 1 on 'credit creation'.

[53] This differs slightly from the terminology used in practice, which denominates the conversion of a short-term into a long-term bank claim against its debtor. We deem this consolidation as irrelevant and therefore used the term consolidation to denominate the economically more important fact of an immobilization of the deposit against the bank.

they destroy these levers as 'credit closure' does. Credit consolidation does not alter the ownership or the composition of the stock of the goods the borrower bought. It also does not (or at least not necessarily) trigger a banking process: a cheque account deposit is consolidated (and hence becomes an economic saving) by the simple fact that it is not transferred, but rather 'left' on the account for a longer period until it is 'un-consolidated' and expanded.

The categorization of credit consolidation as one of the fundamental acts of bank credit and is motivated and justified by its importance for the economy with regard to another aspect of the economy. We will only see later in which respect credit consolidation is important.[54] We will only later be in a position to explain the conditions and laws governing credit consolidation, because its treatment is only possible when analysing the effect of credit on the goods market.

5. The essence of bank credit

Our analysis so far has centred on the changes in the economy caused by the bank's credit activity. It showed that all these activities can be exhaustively categorised as credit creation, credit prolongation, or credit closure, that is, if a credit relation is established, maintained, or severed. This taxonomy only describes the effects of banking activity but does not explain why banks can engage in them. The latter is the ultimate aim of explaining the essence of credit in the modern economy and, in particular, the role of banks in credit transactions.

The reason why banks can engage in credit transaction becomes obvious by examining whether or not credit transactions (in particular credit creation) could take place in a modern economy without banks.

In principle, one will be tempted to answer in the affirmative. As has been shown, each credit creation transfers balances from the economic creditor (the holder of short- or long-term savings) to the debtor, who can use them to buy goods and services. Therefore, there is no apparent reason why the claim of the creditor needs to be directed against a bank and not against the debtor directly; in other words: why the debtor is not able to pay by issuing 'claims against himself'. Nevertheless, the intermediation of a bank has become absolutely necessary. The seller will only be willing to give away her

[54] Cf. chapter [2.]A in Part Two of this book.

goods in exchange for a claim in the knowledge that she can cede the claim (the bank money) and buy goods herself from others. Their willingness to accept bank money hinges on the fact that they know the debtor is solvent, that is, they are sure that the debtor always meets all her obligations, in particular the punctual 'settlement' of the granted credit. This contrasts with notes as their monopolistic position renders such considerations void.[55] From this follows that a viable credit system in a pure credit economy requires all members of the economy to be publicly known as creditworthy. However, in a large economy, as modern economies typically are, an individual's creditworthiness is only known to their immediate business partners but certainly not to everyone. Consequently a claim against oneself would only be able to circulate like 'cash' amongst a small circle. Hence, there must be institutions generally recognised as being creditworthy and which are willing to confer their creditworthiness to individuals not generally known to be creditworthy. In practice, these institutions are banks, without which the modern credit system (as we know it) would be unthinkable.

The function of the banks is therefore to stand in for the actual borrower and to assume their role as debtor or better (disregarding the legal form and focusing on the economic function) to underwrite a promise to pay. They mediate the general trust, which the borrower lacks. They are therefore nothing other than intermediaries of credit in its literal meaning as intermediaries of trust.[56] *Capital and money markets are therefore markets on which credit, ergo 'trust', is traded.* They are, and herein lies also our motivation to summarize them in a single term, nothing other than credit markets.[57]

[55] Cf. Lucien Albert Hahn, *Von der Kriegs- zur Friedenswährung [From War to Peace Currency]*, xiv: *Archiv für Sozialwissenschaft und Sozialpolitik*, ed. Edgar Jaffé (Tübingen: J. C. B Mohr (Paul Siebeck), 1914), p. 11 ff. and p. 18 ff.

[56] Further comment as to why this statement is different to those by Adolf Wagner and others is not required. According to them, trust is only the motivation of each credit transaction, but according to ours it is the subject of each credit transaction.

[57] Similarly Macleod's *Theory of Credit*, p. 594 says in his idiosyncratic way: 'A bank is therefore not an office for "borrowing" and "lending" money, but it is a manufactory of credit; as Mr. Cazenove well said, it is the banking credits which are the loanable capital and as Bishop Birkeley said, "a bank is a gold mine". So we ought not to speak of the money market but the credit market.' Macleod's theory differs in all other respects from ours. He sees banks explicitly as debtors, specifically as debtors of money. We only see banks as the intermediary and see the credit value as a monetization of a credit in goods.

[1.]B. The Extent of Credit Activities of Banks

I. FORMS OF BANKS

In an economy populated by perfectly creditworthy individuals no one would ever ask a bank for a loan. Like banks, everyone could issue 'claims against themselves' and these claims would never be called into question because of the perfect creditworthiness. The abundance of newly created and prolonged credit relations would cause an interest rate of zero. The interest rate is a price, an expression of the costs, and a positive price can only form for a scarce, never an abundant good.

The economy is not populated by perfectly creditworthy individuals though. Being perfectly creditworthy is rather the exception than the rule; those who are not perfectly creditworthy have to seek credit from those who are. The fact that banks do not satisfy *any* demand but ration credit is the requirement for a positive interest rate. The amount of credit banks are willing to offer is a crucial factor in the determination of the interest rate. This is often overlooked and the literature offers only sparse assessments[1] of the determination of the *credit supply*. Yet it is as important for the level of the interest rate as the *credit demand*, which features so prominently in the literature. The credit supply can even be called the central question for banking theory in a narrow sense.

When analysing the extent of credit supply, we need to investigate whether or not we can rely on a unified treatment for all types of banks

[1] Most of the banking literature does not even mention anything on the determination of the credit supply and even if they do, they use vague terms like 'capital', 'amount of savings', 'national wealth', etc. The inadequacy of these vague terms has been discussed sufficiently.

valid across all modern developed countries. The business models of different banks like mortgage lenders, English-style deposit banks, German-style credit banks, mutual savings banks, credit co-operatives, English merchant banks, French banques d'affairs [commercial banks][2] and also central banks, which are outside the narrow frame of this assessment, vary substantially and justify this question.

The question can only be answered if the economic differences between the different types of banks are clear. Nowadays, this is certainly not the case and both early and contemporary classifications are not satisfactory, for example: the division of banks according to whether they provide long-term funding for investments or short-term liquidity.[3] The German credit bank is supposedly the prime example of a bank providing short-term liquidity. In reality it provides at least as much long-term funding for investments and its identification with the provision of short-term liquidity should be seen as a demand rather than a fact. Also the more recent categorization according to the way of gaining borrowed capital, in particular through issuing banknotes, bonds, or promissory notes[4] is not satisfactory because it compares things different to each other. Whilst issuing bankers' acceptances and promissory notes is booked on the liabilities side, issuing banknotes is not an act of gaining borrowed capital but money creation. Indeed, this distinction is identical with the traditional classification into note-issuing and non-note-issuing institutions. It does not succeed in making further distinctions in the latter class, because the term structure and the legal form of the liabilities (bonds, promissory notes, etc.) are only relevant from the private business perspective but not from an economic one; hence, they have to be ignored in this context.

We shall finally mention that contrary to the nomenclature the main difference between the two major bank types *deposit* and *credit bank* is not that one is drawing in deposits whilst the other is issuing credit. Formally such a distinction would be indefensible because it parallels a

[2] Further information on the idiosyncrasies of types of foreign banks can be found in the short but complete assessment by Edgar Jaffé, *Das Englisch-Amerikanische und das Französische Bankwesen [The English–American and the French Banking System]* (Tübingen: J. C. B Mohr (Paul Siebeck), 1915), p. 200 and p. 213.

[3] Cf. Gerhart von Schulze-Gaevernitz, *Die moderne Kreditbank [The Modern Credit Bank]* (Tübingen: J. C. B Mohr (Paul Siebeck), 1922), p. 19 and p. 23.

[4] Cf. Felix Somary, *Bankpolitik [Banking policy]* (Tübingen: J. C. B. Mohr (Paul Siebeck), 1915), p. 3 ff.

transaction on the asset side (credit bank) with a transaction on the liabilities side (deposit bank). Logically correct would be to compare only transactions either on the asset or liabilities side. Following the former, then one would discover that whilst deposit banks mainly hold claims against other banks or government bonds as their assets, credit banks mainly hold claims against industrial or commercial firms. When looking at the liabilities side of deposit banks then one discovers private deposit holders, whilst credit banks also hold deposits of other banks. But also this distinction is not useful when it comes to examining differences in the extent of their credit supply. This book's position is that deposits are the consequence not the cause of the credit business which renders the structure of the liabilities (private deposit holders or other banks) irrelevant for the extent of the 'means' of a bank. Similarly, the difference that businesses are the debtors in one case and banks and governments are in the other case does not constitute a relevant distinction.

An economically meaningful classification, which is the only meaningful distinction for each credit, can be only reached by distinguishing banks according to their role in creating 'economic credit relations'.

As extensively covered earlier,[5] the establishment of an 'economic credit relation', the 'credit creation' typically creates three claims: one of the credit-granting bank against the debtor, one of the seller of goods against his bank, and finally one of the seller's bank against the credit-granting bank. Each credit creation involves in principle two banks. This process makes it apparent that both banks have a very different role in credit creation. Whilst the first bank primarily establishes the credit relation, the second bank has a passive role and only gets involved because its customer deposits a cheque. Hence, it is only the place where the secondary effect of the credit manifests itself. It also does not (at least initially), to use the common terminology, 'invest its means' because the means it obtains from the customer's deposit are already invested with the credit-granting bank.

The deductive inference, drawn from the nature of credit creation, establishes that there exist two types of banks: those which can be called *primary banks* or *credit-creating banks* and those which are best called *secondary banks* or *credit symptom banks*.

[5] See chapter [1.]A, section II, subsection 1 on credit creation.

Banks in modern developed countries are the result of a long development process. When an inductive approach is used, one recognizes that their different types are in fact only variations of the two deduced types.

This is particularly well articulated in England and France with its two main types almost perfectly fitting into our two categories: the English (and to some extent French) deposit banks are typical secondary banks. They draw on the permanently or temporarily dispensable 'means' of the public, that is, they obtain cheques which are deposited either as savings or to make payments. They obtain claims against other banks, without actively granting credits, and which they may dispose of much later.

These secondary banks are in juxtaposition to the English merchant banks and French *banques d'affaires* [commercial banks]. These create the original claims which are deposited at deposit banks and are consequentially indebted to them. The development of primary banks is not a surprising result, but an economic necessity: those claims reaching deposit banks need to come into existence somehow. It is well known that deposit banks never disburse credit themselves by creating cheque or current accounts; to enable a sizeable credit business, primary banks have to develop as a complement to deposit banks.

These relations are not just artificial constructs, but can actually be found when comparing the balance sheets of deposit and merchant banks. The deposit bank's liabilities side shows cheque and saving deposits by the public and a large amount of banker's acceptances, that is, claims against other banks, on the asset side. On the other hand, the merchant bank's asset side shows the credits granted to industry and commerce and bills of exchange or other forms of obligations to other banks on the liabilities side. The debts of the merchant or *banques d'affaires* with deposit banks is simply another consequence of their respective roles as credit-creating banks and credit symptom banks.

Bank types in Germany differentiate themselves similarly, albeit not with such absolute clarity. Pure secondary banks are for example Sparkassen [mutual savings banks], which in addition to cash deposits obtain their 'means' through cheque deposits and therefore short-term claims against other banks. Hypothekenbanken [mortgage banks] are also pure secondary banks which obtain the means for their credits through selling their mortgage deeds to private individuals. Their 'money' comes in the form of claims against other banks which the mortgage bank can dispose of later. On the other hand, pure primary banks are represented by smaller (often provincial) banks which grant credit without receiving deposits from the public and are therefore often heavily indebted to secondary banks. The most common bank type in Germany is the Kreditbank [credit bank], with its major and also larger provincial banks, representing a mixed form of both primary and secondary banks. Their dense network of branches attract savings from the public, that is, claims against other banks, for which they act as secondary banks but also grant credit and therefore act as primary banks.

The strict distinction of primary and secondary banks allows us to gain an appropriate picture of bank types by looking at their credit business. It does not require any additional explanation to see that the different role in 'credit creation' has an influence on each bank type's possibility of granting credit. The extent of the difference becomes apparent when considering the limited credit-granting possibilities of a non-note-issuing bank compared with a note-issuing bank in an economy based on only cash and banknotes. The *'bank money'-creating primary banks,* which are more important for the credit business than the actual central bank, are nothing other than the *central bank of the modern economy*, whilst the *'bank money- retaining secondary bank*s are like the non-note-issuing banks of former ages.

II. TRUST AND LIQUIDITY CONSIDERATIONS AS DETERMINANTS FOR THE EXTENT OF MEANS OF BANKS

1. The extent of means of primary banks

Granting credit means, as repeatedly shown, in essence the creation of economic credit relations and formally creating claims. First, we consider the simplest case when the economic creditor and debtor are with the same bank and two claims are created: one (medium or long-term) claim of the bank against the borrower and one (initially short-term) claim of the one who received the cheque in exchange for goods.

The question of the extent of the means of a bank is therefore identical with the question of how many such claims (either for or against it) a bank can create. To answer this question we can use a simple but, in this context, rarely used method: the method of observing the actually prevailing conditions. Consider these conditions and in particular the reasons why a bank manager does not grant applications for credit. It is obvious to every practitioner (but not so to the theory) that the decision, given the creditworthiness of the applicant, depends solely on considerations about the bank's liquidity. The extent of the means of the bank are therefore determined by its liquidity. In fact, the only material effect of creating a claim is to extend the bank's balance sheet and to worsen its liquidity.[6]

In a way the bank manager's liquidity concerns oscillate around the objectively available liquidity or illiquidity because these concerns are highly subjective. The degree of liquidity is judged higher with a higher degree of confidence in the future prosperity of the bank and lower with a low degree of confidence. Hence, the credit supply, which by its nature means the supply of trust, is dependent on the trust in the bank.

What are the situations which reduce the credit supply of banks and impose a strain on the credit markets? It is obvious that, in general, all situations lessening the perceived liquidity of banks come into consideration. In particular, this is true for credit creation which (analogous to emptying the till in a cash economy) reduces the bank's liquidity and therefore its credit supply. This is the one and only reason. It is certainly not the case because of a depletion of a stock of investable means (as the prevailing terminology suggests). As mentioned repeatedly, each credit brings about the necessary means to accommodate itself, that is, the deposit on the cheque account. From an accounting perspective, the credit creation is not a change of the balance sheet but an extension, similarly to a guarantee which is also booked simultaneously as an asset and a liability. To underwrite a liability is also materially a form of credit (apart from the treatment on the accounts), because we see the banks as the guarantor of all those who make purchases over and above their wealth. They draw on the economy's reservoir of goods and services and become the debtor

[6] On the nature of liquidity, see subsection III 'Bank liquidity'.

to those who deliver these goods and services. Granting a credit is independent of some stock of 'means' in exactly the same way as acting as a guarantor is not dependent on some stock of 'means', but only on trust and liquidity considerations. The latter is also the channel through which granting credit and issuing a guarantee reduce the supply of credit. To this extent the credit supply is reduced *each* time a credit is granted; to avoid any misunderstanding, we refer to granting credit only in the sense of credit creation, that is, as establishing *new* debt relationships. If the credit is only granted to pay back another credit, then no new debt relationship is established and only the guaranteeing bank changes. Hence, granting such credit does not reduce the credit supply because the loss in liquidity of the new guarantor is compensated by a gain in liquidity of the old guarantor. To mention an often asserted[7], heavily contested, but never satisfactorily explained fact that *purchase-money mortgage agreements* do not influence the supply of credit. This is not because no 'new money' is needed, as can be occasionally found in the literature, or because the seller of the land automatically acts as a creditor, as has been shown to be this the case for all credit relationships. A purchase-money mortgage simply does not impact the credit markets because it does not reduce the liquidity of any bank.

These explanations already show which situations increase the credit supply of banks. Obviously these are all situations increasing the perceived liquidity of banks, which are analogous to all the situations causing a filling of the tills in a pure cash economy. In particular this is the case for a credit closure, that is, the case in which the debtor sells some goods, pays back his debt and therefore the bank's balance sheet contracts. It also includes the probably most important case in practice, when customers deposit 'savings', hence causing 'credit consolidation'. The transformation of cheque and current accounts into savings accounts is paralleled by a transformation of the bank's short-term into a long-term liability, improving the liquidity of the bank. The impact on liquidity also causes differential impacts whether, for example, an agricultural credit is granted

[7] See e.g. Herbert von Beckerath, *Kapitalmarkt und Geldmarkt [Capital and Money Market]* (Jena: Gustav Fischer, 1916), p. 74. His stilted style of writing almost obscures the explanation, which seems to be untenable in any case. Something different to 'kreditierbares substantielles Vermögen lediglich aus bisheriger eigenwirtschaftlicher Nutzung in die Kreditwirtschaft eintritt' [a shift of material wealth from own use to the credit economy] does not happen with other credits either.

to buy *property* or *for the cultivation of land*. In the former case, the seller of the property will soon 'save' its receipts at a mutual savings bank and hence the credit value manifests itself in 'consolidated' form. In the latter case, the credit value will remain on cheque and current accounts while being passed on and is saved only slowly and in small amounts by the different producers. Hence, it is at least unclear to assert that higher interest rates in Germany are explained by a higher 'capital absorption' as a consequence of higher mortgages on land and property.[8] Besides the vagueness of the notion that 'capital' is absorbed, a very large part of land mortgages are consolidated and therefore the lessening of liquidity could only be considered a temporary effect. The number of debtors and creditors for any given amount of credit can never have an impact on the interest rates, which is similar to scales which remain in balance as long as the weights on both sides are equally heavy but is not affected per se by the number of weights.

Liquidity is improved to a greater degree if the bank's indebtedness, which expresses itself in saving accounts, completely disappears. This is the case when the bank's customers use their savings to buy some of the bank's assets, for example, securities (stocks and obligations in particular). In these situations, which are best called '*credit elimination*', banks exit the nexus of debts completely and the strongest possible liquidity improvement comes into effect: the balance sheet contraction.

Above all, one has to bear in mind that liquidity improvements through credit closure, credit consolidation, and credit elimination can only be considered as a motive for extending the bank's credit business. It is not a condition in the sense that credit extension is directly dependent on credit closure, credit consolidation, and credit elimination as it would be from the cash reserves in a pure cash

[8] Rudolph Eberstadt, *Der Deutsche Kapitalmarkt [The German Capital Market]* (Leipzig: Duncker & Humblot, 1901), p. 236 says: 'Die dauernde Schwäche des deutschen Kapitalmarktes, die Unfähigkeit, zu produktiven Zwecken das nötige Kapital aufzubringen, dürfte durch die Ansprüche der Bodenverschuldung, die unbedingt erst vor allen andern befriedigt werden müssen zur Genüge erklärt sein.' [The persistent weakness of the German capital market, the inability to provide the necessary capital for productive uses, should be sufficiently explained by the high mortgages on land, which need to be absolutely met as a priority over everything else.] The writings of Eberstadt are a prime example for the limited usefulness of descriptive and statistical examinations (even if they are undertaken with the utmost care) if the theoretical relations are not fully clear.

economy. On the one hand, banks regularly grant credits of a higher value than they receive from savings and repayments. On the other hand, liquidity is only the objective basis for the subjective considerations which lead to a credit extension or credit limitation in any particular case. The crucial determinant for the extent of the credit supply is always the trust in the credit-granting bank.

So far, we have assumed that the person who ends up with the cheque deposit of the credit is with the credit-granting bank. In this case the explanations provided on the extent of the credit supply and their changes are exhaustive. In particular the explanation does need to consider any circumstances affecting the status of other banks.

This changes substantially if the eventual holder of the cheque has an account with a different bank to the original credit-granting institution, as it almost always is the case in practice. The bank creating the credit (the primary bank) and where it appears as symptom (the secondary bank) are not identical any more. The connection between the two is established through the claim of the secondary bank against the primary bank. There seems to be obviously some degree of reliance from the primary banks on the secondary bank. The sort of reliance is easily recognised by looking at the typical relationship of a pure secondary bank, for example, a pure deposit bank, with a pure primary bank, for example, a merchant bank. These show in particular clarity all those aspects which can be observed in practice in credit relations between: a credit bank (acting as a primary bank) and a deposit bank; a credit bank (acting as a secondary bank) and a pure primary bank; and two credit banks.

First of all, a dependence of primary banks on secondary banks as is postulated by prevailing opinion is not the case. According to this notion, the secondary bank (e.g. a deposit bank) grants a credit to the primary bank, which uses these 'invested' means to grant credit to its customer. Besides the point that deposits at the secondary banks result from the primary bank's credit creation, this notion is not correct, because in the very moment the secondary bank 'invests' the means in the primary bank no credit is actually granted. Even viewing the transaction from the private business perspective suggests the contrary, in fact what happens is what we called above credit prolongation; a rather irrelevant transaction, because it does not cause any substantial changes in the economy.

This is shown unambiguously in the case where a deposit bank uses its deposits to provide call 'money' or a credit for one or more months against a simple promissory note or a banker's draft to the primary bank. It is clear that this does not constitute a new credit in the economic sense of a new debt relationship.[9] In fact, the means of the secondary bank as well of its depositors have long been invested in an economic sense and the investment does not only take place with credit prolongation. A further analysis of the usual 'investments' of a secondary bank reveals that the purchase of a discounted bill of exchange or a disbursed bond from the primary bank has to be considered a credit prolongation connected with an 'elimination' of the primary bank; also in this case the number of existing economic debt relations is not increased. Finally, the case when the bank makes deposits with the central bank (in the sense of the practitioner to 'invest cash') can easily deceive. However, it is nothing other than a credit prolongation. The irrational accumulation of deposits with the central bank by discounting treasury bills is one of the most common examples of credit prolongation in Germany since the end of the war.

The regularity of this transaction in the modern economy is also the reason why liquidity does not accumulate on current accounts, but shows itself as balance sheet contractions for all credit-creating banks and for the central bank in particular.[10]

In every case: A *direct* dependence of primary banks on secondary banks in the sense of the prevailing notion is not the case. It should rather be that secondary banks are dependent on primary banks because the primary banks' activities only create the deposits which will later be invested by secondary banks. Secondary banks nevertheless do have an effect on primary banks but it is of a rather indirect nature and only shows itself ex post. Secondary banks will vary the terms and conditions, the interest rate in particular, of a credit prolongation depending on whether or not they want to grow their credit business. This does not affect the existing debt relations, but primary banks will consider the changed interest rates and change their own terms and conditions which consequentially has an effect on the their credit business. Hence, the extent of the credit business of primary banks is to some degree dependent on the credit policy of secondary banks. The latter is only governed by liquidity considerations and

[9] Compare chapter [1.]A, section II, subsection 1 'Credit prolongation'.

[10] These relations were shown in particular clarity during and shortly after the war, when immense amounts of treasury bills were bought by banks to even out the steadily growing current account balances.

therefore the existence of savings deposited at secondary banks only becomes effective through liquidity considerations.

2. The extent of means of secondary banks

The explanations above appear to fully explain the determinants of the extent of means not only of primary but also of secondary banks. Our analysis is in fact exhaustive for primary banks but not for secondary banks. They would only be exhaustive under the condition that they only act on the credit market via primary banks (through credit prolongation). In practice though, there are some cases where secondary banks are exposed directly to credit-seeking customers even if the vast majority of transactions can be classified as credit prolongations. This is the case, for example, when a mortgage bank uses the money raised by selling mortgage deeds or a mutual savings bank uses savings to fund mortgage loans. These are obviously situations where these banks grant credit; however, it is of a different form than credits granted by actual primary or even actual credit banks. The mortgage, mutual savings, and small private banks do not create any new claims but use those which the public makes available to them. Hence, it is dependent on individuals not using their bank balances for their own purposes, that is, individuals save. This means that the credit-granting activity of secondary banks is dependent on deposits,[11] which is commonly thought of being true for *all* credit transactions. This is the difference between secondary banks and other credit-granting banks; we stress this difference because it is crucial for any theoretical treatment of banking and in particular for the systematization of bank transactions.

The credit-granting secondary bank's dependence on the amount of deposits is not of a major practical relevance; the amount of credit granted by these banks remains far below the amount of credit granted by the independent primary banks. Furthermore, there is no area where secondary banks are the sole granter of credit and therefore any lack in deposits can be compensated for by the

[11] The same is true for credit-granting by private capitalists. Their activity is also dependent on their 'savings' which has some importance for some special forms of credit, like private mortgages, or certain special bank transactions, like the issuance of bonds to the public. See chapter [2.]A on the issue that the amount of savings in an economy is dependent on the amount of credit previously granted by banks.

credit activity of primary banks.[12] Credit granted directly by private capitalists (i.e. not via banks), as it still takes place for private mortgages, is analogous to credits granted by secondary banks and comparatively irrelevant for the same reasons. However, these credit-granting activities by secondary banks and private capitalists is interesting and important for the theory. It is the last rudiment of the credit business as it was conducted erstwhile and on which the contemporary theory is based. As long as only a few privileged central banks could issue notes (i.e. claims against themselves and hence create new credit), other banks were reliant on the deposits made by the public to obtain new means. The spread of cashless payment and the accompanying potential to set up cheque and current accounts enable all banks to become a credit-creating bank equal to the central bank. For such institutions a deposit by a member of the public means to receive a claim against itself and therefore savings can only be effective by transforming bank balances into long-term savings. A new credit does not need or even can be granted by using existing means but always causes the creation of new claims. Nowadays, the vast majority of credits are granted in this way and, in spite of its historical roots, is therefore the starting point for our theoretical analysis of the modern credit business.

III. BANK LIQUIDITY

The precise meaning of the *liquidity* of banks has been intentionally lacking from our explanations. There are two reasons for assessing its meaning in more detail. First, as explained earlier, liquidity considerations are central in the determination of credit supply. Second and almost more importantly, the term liquidity has readily been used in the last decades to argue for all sorts of different economic policies such that a proper economic assessment is of the utmost importance. The magnificent development of banks[13] showed the erroneousness of the movement against credit banks to everyone, apart from its originator Adolf Wagner. However, the principles he postulated are

[12] The same applies to private capitalists granting credit.

[13] More so than their extensive writing, of which we shall only refer to Adolf Weber, *Depositenbanken und Spekulationsbanken [Deposit Banks and Speculation Banks]* (Leipzig: Duncker & Humblot, 1902).

not forgotten, in particular his views on the backing of banknotes and the well-known demand of equal transactions on the asset and liabilities side to ensure liquidity. It is owing to Wagner's immense authority that these claims enter almost all popular and scientific writing on banking and reports in the financial press as axioms without any further explanation. These writings call for an increase in the *liquidity not only of individual banks but also of the 'economy'* (a term subject to further scrutiny later in the text). Of course, the economic nature of the changes demanded remain unclear. Nowadays, it is not hard to show the indefensibility of all related views tied to the alleged lack of 'liquidity of the German economy'. The First World War has shown that the liquidity of the economy was the least influential factor in Germany's economic and financial stamina. Wide circles of practitioners nowadays see the calls for improved liquidity of economies as an unnecessary disturbance of the economy, in particular in the context of a war.

To be liquid means to be able to settle claims at the right time and at the right amount. It is essential to know the form of the banks' claims. The explanations so far only showed that every act of credit intermediation creates a shorter- or longer-term claim, but deliberately avoided explaining what is given 'in obligation'. In fact, a range of entirely different things come into consideration, for example, when large bank A asks provincial bank B to settle a claim or a customer asks for disbursement of his deposits. In the former case is the expression to close the credit. The ability of the bank to close credits, which is crucial for a bank to meet its liabilities, is henceforth described as '*economic liquidity*'. In the latter case, a customer requesting his deposits in cash is obviously a different form, as a payment of 'cash' in the form of legal tender is demanded. This introduces a new element to our analysis, as our methodology was to show the relations in the realm of the abstract pure credit economy. The ability of a bank to meet demands for 'cash' shall be called '*cash liquidity*'. The introduction of cash into our system brings the analysis closer to reality and completes the picture.

1. Cash liquidity

The modern economy is, unlike previously assumed, not a pure credit economy but a *cash-saving economy*. Although cash is not used for a large amount of transactions and only used at certain times or in certain proportions for other transactions, there undeniably exists a 'cash demand' even in the best organised modern economy.

Money demand appears only in cash-saving economies; it obviously does not exist in pure credit economies as cash does not exist, but neither does it exist in pure cash economies (as is rarely appreciated). In the latter, all credit has to be made available in cash and therefore cash demand equals *credit demand.*

The *cash demand*, at least as an independent term and absolute quantity, is only possible in a cash-saving economy. Only in such an economy do both cash and other means of payments (a multiple of cash) exist simultaneously and cash assumes a certain relation to the credit demand; this is similar to the relation of divisional coins to banknotes in a pure cash economy in which there can only be a demand for certain types of cash and not for cash in general. In a cash-saving economy, there is a demand for cash in general and the amount of credit granted by banks provides the variable frame for the cash demand. The banks' ability to meet the cash demand of the economy is what we call the *cash liquidity* of banks.

To what extent does the cash liquidity govern the banks' credit transactions? The question is identical to the question: How dependent is the credit supply in an economy on the cash supply, that is, what is the relationship between the credit liquidity and the cash liquidity? The term credit liquidity should be used in the sense that in practice the term cash liquidity is inappropriately used, whilst the term cash liquidity is used to mean what is also called surplus means of payment.

When looking at cases where banks have to settle their liabilities by disbursing 'cash', then there are only two possibilities: either the demand is caused by extraordinary events (e.g. the imminent prospect of war) which is accordingly called 'extraordinary money demand'; or it is the regular cash demand in ordinary times (which is sometimes higher, sometimes lower) and accordingly called 'ordinary money demand'. The special demand for cash at the end of quarters is only a special case of the ordinary money demand.

Before examining some cases of money demand more closely, we need to assess the economic consequence (in particular its implications for the country's credit relations) and meaning of withdrawing savings or current account deposits. This is necessary to avoid any confusion, particularly since prevailing opinion views the withdrawal of cash as a decrease in their 'capital' and conversely the deposit of cash channels 'superfluous means' to the banks.[14]

From a private business perspective this view is untenable when the deposit or withdrawal affects a cheque or current account. Whenever a deposit is made on a cheque account then no one divests themselves from any means because cheques can be used instead of cash to buy goods. Similarly, if someone withdraws cash from a cheque account, then no one gains any means because the cheques could have been used as a means of payment. When adopting an economic viewpoint, this view then seems untenable regardless of whether a cheque or current account is in question. Withdrawing or depositing cash are irrelevant transactions from an economic perspective, because they do not change any credit relations between economic actors: no economic credit relations, no levers to transfer goods and services from one person to the other, are established or nullified. When cash is withdrawn then the claim against the bank is exchanged for a claim against the central bank (and vice versa in the case of a deposit). The cash deposit does not mean that the depositor grants new credit nor does the withdrawal of cash mean the withdrawal of credit on the part of the withdrawer. In the instant of receiving the cash, its new holder turns into the economic creditor of the underlying credit relations which gives rise to the banknote. Similarly, in the instant of using the notes for payment to a third party, the role of economic creditor is conferred onto the supplier of the goods or services in question. However, the holder of cash will usually assume the creditor position for a shorter time than a holder of a savings account, which has an effect on the price level and, hence, is important from an economic perspective. Yet this is not a necessary feature of holding banknotes as has been shown during the War [First World War], when large parts

[14] Countless writings could be referenced here, compare for example the following statement in Weber, *Depositenbanken und Spekulationsbanken [Deposit Banks and Speculation Banks]*, p. 44: 'Wie die Depositenbanken in ihrem lokalen Geschäftskreise die überschüssigen Kapitalien sammeln und dem kapitalbedürftigen Gewerbetreibenden zuführen.' [How the deposit banks collect the superfluous capital from their local businesses and supply it to businesses in need of capital.] or 'Geschäftsbericht der Bank für Handel und Industrie pro 1853' ['1853 annual report of the Bank für Handel und Industrie'], Bank für Handel und Industrie, p. 49: 'Sie (die Bank) hat das Recht und die Aufgabe, das Kapital, welches bei dem einen Industriellen zeitweilig disponibel, dem andern, welcher es im gleichen Augenblicke bedarf, zuzuführen.' [The bank has the right and the duty to channel the disposable capital of one industrialist to the industrialist in need of it.]

of the population withdrew from their savings accounts and 'saved' in cash. Just as no 'means' were divested from the [German] Reich in this case, it is usually not the case for any cash withdrawal. The prevailing and opposing opinion that a cash withdrawal is to withdraw 'means' and a cash deposit is to deposit 'means' is based fallaciously on the private business perspective. In particular, the fact that the deposit-holder enjoys some interest payments when depositing cash and that these payments are foregone when cash is withdrawn seems to motivate this view. This phenomenon is the result of historical development rather than a theoretical necessity. On the one hand it is easy to imagine that no interest is paid on deposits (as is the case in England for balances on cheque accounts) and on the other hand, it is a theoretical possibility to grant interest on holding cash. It is even conceivable that holders of coins (who grant 'credit' while holding the coins as has been rightfully claimed)[15] receive interest payments.

In any case: cash deposits and withdrawals do not cause, at least directly, any changes in the credit structure of the economy. It is therefore incorrect to categorize desires for withdrawals as credit or even capital demand, as they are simply cases of money demand.

2. Extraordinary money demand (the money crisis)

α Money demand

Cases of extraordinary money demand have struck almost every country, with well-known examples in England's banking history in the years 1847, 1857, and 1866. In those years, the demand for means of payment led to a suspension of Peel's Act which limited the quantity of Bank of England notes in circulation. Even stronger cases of extraordinary money demand are provided by the first and last phase of the recent World War. The mass withdrawal of deposits at banks and mutual savings banks and the subsequent hoarding of cash should be still remembered by everyone.

The case of extraordinary money demand observed during the World War shows with clarity that it is not part of the routine

[15] Already mentioned by Knut Wicksell, *Geldzins und Güterpreise* (Jena: Gustav Fischer, 1898), p. 44. [This passage can be found in Knut Wicksell, *Interest and Prices*, trans. Richard F. Kahn (London: Macmillan, 1936), p. 49].

business of an economy. They are extraordinary and disruptive forces to the normal course of the economy and such phenomena are called crises. Cases of extraordinary money demand are therefore cases of crises. In contrast to the distinct credit crises (which will be assessed later), these events are pure '*money crises*' and, thus, exclusively such events should be called '*money crises*'.

Even though the causes of other crises, in particular economic crises, are subject to disagreement, the cause of money crises is undoubted. A superficial analysis of the events preceding money crises already shows that it is the sole result of mistrust and fear, that is, a psychological phenomenon of the masses. But what is the nature of mistrust leading to a money crisis? Who is it aimed at?

The customer of a bank is used to viewing the balance on the account as cash (as long as it is not payable in future). He trusts that he will be able to exchange it for goods and services with everyone, because everyone is willing to accept a cheque just like cash. The public's mistrust that induces an exchange of deposits for cash is therefore a mistrust in the purchasing power of deposits and their means of payment character.

Such mistrust can be twofold: either the mistrust is aimed at a *single* bank or against *all* banks of a country. In the case where the public mistrusts a single bank, then the savers want to exchange their deposits at the mistrusted bank for deposits at another bank. Thus, the consequence is that many customers withdraw their deposits and transfer it to another bank. At first, this only means that the mutual credit relations between the banks are changed: the new banks assume the role of the creditor instead of the saver, which might but not necessarily cause the liquidation of the mistrusted bank. However, the mistrust against a single bank can never be the cause for an extraordinary money demand. Because the extraordinary money demand is the key feature of the money crisis, it follows that the public's mistrust against a single bank can never be the cause of money crises.

The public's mistrust against all banks will regularly lead to a money crisis. In this case the public does not have the option to exchange deposits with one bank for deposits with another. The public will feel the need to withdraw all deposits and hold other trustworthy means of payments. In the modern cash-saving economy this desire is focused on banknotes, because they are the next best money form after deposits. Their purchasing power is secured by its status as legal tender and they can also be considered for a wider range of payments from a technical perspective.[16]

If a money crisis is always caused by mistrust against *all* existing banks and there is a preference for cash over any deposits, then this implies that all banks are illiquid at the same time in the case of a money crisis. This is owing to the fact that no deposits at any bank are fully covered by banknotes and that the general mistrust inhibits a mutual support of banks. The simultaneous insolvency of all banks is precisely the reason why the central bank has to meet all cash demanded by banks to avoid chaos.

The accommodating central bank policy in the case of a money crisis is not only a necessary intervention but also a historical fact (even though most underlying bank acts do not envisage such behaviour).[17] The policy to accommodate the bank's demand for banknotes has become more and more the common central bank response to a money crisis in order to avoid its catastrophic consequences; this development is (partly) influenced by the experiences with the Bank of England's occasional adherence to the opposite policy. It is also the necessary pre-condition for cashless payment systems with the quantity of due claims on notes exceeding the number of banknotes by many multiples.

From these considerations it follows that the banking system in modern countries is protected from becoming illiquid as a consequence of extraordinary money demand. Actual permanent illiquidity is therefore turned into a permanent liquidity. Considerations about cash liquidity can therefore not play any role in the credit decisions of banks.

[16] On the reasons for the purchasing power of banknotes, in particular on nominalist and metallist theories of money, see my own Lucien Albert Hahn, *Von der Kriegs- zur Friedenswährung [From War to Peace Currency]*, vol. 14, Archiv für Sozialwissenschaft und Sozialpolitik, ed. Edgar Jaffé (Tübingen: J. C. B. Mohr (Paul Siebeck), 1914), p. 18 ff.

[17] In Lucien Albert Hahn, *Von der Kriegs- zur Friedenswährung*, p. 63, I propose the following addition, analogous to the Swedish bank act, to the German bank act governing the quantity of banknotes: 'Doch darf, wenn es mit Rücksicht auf Krieg, Kriegs- oder Krisengefahr notwendig erscheint, die Reichsbank weitere Noten ausgeben. Die auf Grund des so erweiterten Notenausgaberechts ausgegebenen Noten sind jedoch so schnell wie möglich aus dem Verkehr wieder einzuziehen.' [In the case of war, the immediate threat of war, or the threat of a crisis the Reichsbank is allowed to issue further banknotes under the proviso that these banknotes need to be removed from circulation as soon as possible.]

β Gold demand

A counter argument to the above hypothesis could be that the liquidity of the central bank imposes a limit to its ability to issue banknotes. The holder of a banknote could also demand her certified right to precious metals when desiring the next higher money form. This argument is incorrect. The conversion of banknotes into gold is similar to the exchange of deposits for banknotes and closer examination shows that the central bank's illiquidity is not possible. This is for analogous reasons: the central bank is also always latently illiquid, which means in practice an unconditional liquidity. The cogency of this argument is revealed when looking at the history of the banknote.

In the first stage of development a note-issuing bank only has a relatively small sphere of influence with its banknotes representing only a small proportion of the country's means of payments. In this arena, issuing banknotes means actually accepting an obligation which needs to be satisfied in the normal course of business; even if a bank run means a demand that all banknotes be exchanged for precious metal, then it is quite possible that all liabilities can be met. Any shortfalls in precious metal can be balanced by borrowing from other banks or by selling easily disposable assets to someone else in the economy. This is similar to what any credit bank would do nowadays. Only if the bank run affected all note-issuing banks, then meeting all obligations would not be possible because the route to other note-issuing banks would not be viable any more. A devaluation of the note against full metallic currency would be the consequence. At least this would not have any larger negative consequence for the economy, as the large amount of metallic currency in circulation would suffice to enable all transactions in the already contracting economy.

This changes substantially in the further stages of the banknote's development: as banknotes become gradually more widespread, their share as a means of payment gradually exceeds the share of cash. On the other hand, countries are forced to restrict the number of note-issuing banks to address fraudulent note issuing. This stage ends the moment a country only has *one* bank which could realistically be considered to issue notes.

The importance attached to the transformation of the note-issuing business cannot be overestimated. The situation concerning the central bank's obligation to exchange banknotes for gold changes fundamentally: the banknote is de facto (not legally) inconvertible. The requests for conversion into gold coins are met (with respect to the value of the respective banknote), but the role of metallic currency is mostly restricted to act as divisional coins. Such disbursement of gold cannot be seen as an actual conversion of the banknote into gold. If for whatever reason a large number (or in as in times of crisis a majority) of banknote-holders request to exchange their notes for gold, then every central bank needs to stop their payments (if this term can be used in this situation) in any circumstances. A central bank (the 'banks of banks') cannot cover the shortfall in gold from another actor in the economy, because it is itself the last resort and no other substantial precious metal stocks are available in the economy. In this way the situation is similar to the previously examined case, when *all* banks suspend their payments. The central bank also cannot contract the number of banknotes to bring its liabilities and reserves into equilibrium, because its notes represent the vast majority of means of payment in circulation. Apart from the fact that loans by the central bank are usually due in three months time and not daily, stripping the economy of the majority of its means of payments would cause crisis and tumbles in prices of the worst kind. This highlights substantial differences to earlier stages of development.

The fact that in practice the modern central bank cannot convert all banknotes into gold shows the formal character of convertibility (apart from the very rare case of full metallic coverage)[18] because convertibility is only possible when it is not demanded. As long as this is the case, granting the option to convert notes into some stored precious metal is superfluous. But if the conversion becomes relevant to practice then its delivery is normally suspended. It is only in earlier development stages that it is conceivable that only a small amount of banknotes will be requested to be converted because the bank issuing the notes is not deemed solvent any more. In the present stage any desire to convert banknotes into gold always affects *all* notes in circulation. Hence, it affects the vast majority of means of payments and leads regularly to a suspension of convertibility. This shows the correctness of our initial hypothesis that central banks are liquid (if we can even speak of such a concept) at all times.

[18] Even the full metallic coverage of banknotes does not guarantee convertibility, if not all deposits are also fully covered, because the deposit holders will use banknotes to demand conversion in times of crisis.

Stating these relations inevitably brings to mind the widespread agitation in pre-war Germany for higher liquidity of banks, which were part of a range of other liquidity measures suggested for the case of war. The Reichsbank was urged to increase its gold stock, not to improve the management of exchange rates, but explicitly from a private business liquidity perspective: the Reichbank's ability to issue notes under the Dritteldeckung [the rule to cover one third of banknotes].[19] Given that the Dritteldeckung is only a means to an end and needs to be suspended in every emergency, one questions the purpose of its perpetuation which was deemed to be of crucial importance. The desire to maintain the Dritteldeckung and to increase gold stocks for the domestic payment system is logically incompatible with the modern central bank's inability to maintain convertibility.

Another persistent demand on liquidity, heavily advocated by the Reichsbank, is that banks should hold larger stocks in Reichsbank notes or Reichsbank current accounts. From a private business perspective this would generate a small profit for the Reichsbank: banks would need to surrender certain interest-bearing assets (in particular bills of exchange) to the Reichsbank in exchange for the non-interest-bearing notes or current account deposits. Yet, how this measure affects the liquidity of banks or the Reichsbank is not evident. It is obviously irrelevant whether the money crisis' unavoidable withdrawal of Reichsbank notes takes place in normal times by discounting assets or through withdrawals from current accounts.

In summary: considerations about the cash liquidity in cases of extraordinary money demand do not influence the credit decision of banks.

3. Ordinary money demand

In addition, liquidity considerations for ordinary money demand are not in a position to reduce the extent of credit supply because the bank's liquidity is always sufficient to meet the ordinary money demand. This is shown by the following considerations:

[19] Even during the war some leaflets, advertising the Reichbank's gold collection, said: 'Für jedes 20-Markstück kann die Reichsbank den dreifachen Betrag an Noten ausgeben.' [For every 20 Mark coin, the Reichsbank can issue the threefold amount in notes.] This fact would lead rather to a retention of gold from the perspective that led to Peel's Act and also underlies our [Germany's] banking law.

Firstly, there is a variety of areas in which a disbursement of a loan in cash or notes is out of the question. This is the case for certain loans to wholesalers and in particular loans related to the stock market. These areas will not form part of our consideration on the grounds that physical payments are actually not used at all. As shown above, the prevailing opinion easily misleads and fails particularly in these areas. It is also the basis for the popular argument (especially in times of high-running stock market speculations) that the stock market uses up too much 'money', divesting it from other areas of the economy. In reality, the fact that loans granted for stock market speculations are usually disbursed cashless means that speculations cannot absorb 'money' in a physical sense.

Undoubtedly there are other areas where loans are actually disbursed in cash, that is, 'cash' is withdrawn from the created cheque account. As shown above, this does not mean from an economic perspective that the debtor withdraws 'capital' or his 'credit' from the bank. It rather means that the debtor is no longer satisfied with holding a claim against the bank, but instead requests exchanging the claim for banknotes as they are the only means of payment in certain situations.

Note that not all credits in question are fully disbursed in banknotes. If this was the case then cashless transactions from one account to another would be ruled out for these areas, which is not in accordance with the facts. Usually credits are rather disbursed using a horizontal split such that a certain proportion is disbursed in cash and the remainder as a deposit. For example, consider a short-term business loan intended to buy raw materials and pay wages. The part of the loan intended to buy raw materials will not be disbursed in cash, whilst the part intended to pay wages will be disbursed in banknotes. Even in the last case the banknote-holders will not want to hold their claims forever in the form of a banknote but will want to exchange it for cheque or current account deposits; so a vertical split will appear with a proportion of the total claim held in banknotes and the other in deposits. The former is usually the case for loans to pay wages as long as the worker holds the 'cash'. The latter is the case when the cash found its way from the worker via the retailer to the wholesaler.

The difference when the demand for money is induced by different credits actually causes the curious pattern of note circulation in practice. The same banknotes can be used to disburse a large number of credits because the demand for banknotes becomes effective for one credit at this time and for another credit at that time. Hence, the quantity of notes in circulation is in principle relatively steady: on the one hand an extraordinary increase in demand does not take place and on the other hand there is always a relatively large number of banknotes in circulation. Only at particular times (in particular, at the end of quarters) payments are focused on banknotes; this is the reason for the so called Quartalsanspannung [money shortage at the end of the quarter] with its distinct increase in note circulation. From this it follows that banks need a certain stock of cash in order to grant certain forms of credit, which needs sometimes to be higher, sometimes lower but always of a certain strength.

Where do banks get this stock? The contemporary view would suggest that banks build up this stock through deposits from the public, either to save or to bring their 'credit to a close, that is, when they deem it unnecessary to hold the money.

Clearly, if this was true, then our fundamental assessment which rejects the existence of any stock of investable means would be untenable and one would need to remain with the common quantity theoretic view. A credit business independent of the deposits by the saving public would not be possible.

The claims of the prevailing opinion appear unfounded because banks have the possibility of obtaining notes from central banks in addition to using their own stocks of banknotes. The central bank has the right to issue banknotes and consequently its stock of banknotes is not fixed but can be expanded practically indefinitely. In fact, central banks in all developed countries have expanded the money supply for the last few decades[20] by bringing more and more notes into circulation where they join banknotes created by the central bank earlier.[21] The central bank is nothing other than a credit-creating bank with the privilege of issuing banknotes and, therefore, banking as a whole can be seen as independent from cash deposits of the public.

Some will object that there is at least some dependence of banks on the central bank (as the officially recognised cash-creating institution)

[20] We are only thinking of the time before the war and exclude the issuing of notes for the purpose of financing public expenditures from our considerations.

[21] On the merely formal importance of regulations limiting the amount of banknotes cf. Lucien Albert Hahn, *Von der Kriegs- zur Friedenswährung.*

which imposes limits on the banks' abilities to expand credits. Nevertheless, this dependency does not exist. To justify this claim, we need to briefly assess the idiosyncratic relationship in Germany between common banks and the central bank.

Central banks are in principle nothing other than a particular type of credit-creating bank. Its distinctive feature is that first its debtors and then the 'economic creditor' possess a claim against the bank in the form of a banknote and not as a current or cheque account deposit. The payment system and the 'economic creditor' sometimes require banknotes and debtors are therefore forced to use the credit intermediation service of the central bank and not of a commercial bank. When this happens the central bank assumes the role of the non-note-issuing bank. This gives rise to the suspicion that banks are dependent on the central bank because the central bank needs to make a certain amount of banknotes available (usually against collateral) to effect the credit granted by the banks.

We readily admit that this could develop into a crucial dependency in the future. An indication for this is the Reichsbank's war-time policy to limit the amount of banknotes certain banks can draw; another area is the Konditionenkartell [a cartel agreement on terms and conditions of credits] of the banks which was initiated by the German Reichsbank. Further steps in this direction could develop a dependency of common banks on the central bank. The answer to the question of what determines the extent of means on the credit markets will simply be: the extent of the means on the credit markets and, hence, the interest rates are fixed by the government.

The development has not reached that stage yet and banks are still more or less independent of central banks: not only are they completely independent when granting credits not disbursed in cash but also when granting credits they expect to disburse partly or fully in cash.

The reason for this independence is the relative decline of cash compared to other means of payment; this reduces the impact of an increase in the bank rate (i.e. an increase in the cost of drawing banknotes) on the bank's ability to grant credit. In practice, the interest rate charged on many credits is pegged to the bank rate. However, this dependency of the bank's interest rate on the bank rate is due to tradition rather than being an economic necessity. This is particularly well highlighted by credits not pegged to the bank rate, which usually carry a much lower interest rate. The low interest rate can be explained only if the proportion of currency which has to be raised by re-discounting at the bank rate is so low compared to the total sum; this means that the cost of supplying the credit are only negligibly increased and do not need to be passed on to the debtor. They do, however, have to be passed on to the debtor in times of increased money demand (especially at the end of the quarter), when the interest rate approaches the bank rate. Even though banks have to pay higher interest rates to raise the required cash, a sustained impact on the credit decisions by banks is not necessarily the case: these expenses are only incurred for a short period such that it does not affect the profitability of expanding the credit business.

The central bank would only have a real impact on the interest rates of commercial banks and the extent of the credit supply if it set a very high bank rate. This rate would detach the central bank from the market for discounting bills of exchange and, so the central bank would not be able to set such a rate. The central and commercial banks are in direct competition to each other, both when granting credit directly to the public and for discounting bills of exchange: if the central bank's discount rate is too high then bills of exchange are only discounted at commercial banks; similarly, if the discount rate of the commercial bank exceeds the rate of the central bank, then the commercial bank has to reduce the rate to avoid losing business to the central bank.[22] It seems impossible in practice that the central bank would absolutely refuse to re-discount an eligible asset; the notion that there is a 'money demand' is too widely accepted and has displaced the idea that the money demand is only a consequence of satisfying a 'credit demand'.[23]

[22] Already Ricardo was aware of this fact and expresses himself strongly. Cf. David Ricardo, *Grundsätze der Volkswirtschaft und Besteuerung*, trans. Edward Baumstark (Leipzig: Verlag von Wilhelm Engelmann, 1837) or 2nd edition (Leipzig: Verlag von Wilhelm Engelmann, 1877), chapter 27: 'Verlangt sie (die Notenbank) weniger als den Verkehrszinsfuß, so gibt es keinen Betrag von Geld, den sie nicht anbringen könnte-- nimmt sie aber mehr Zins als den gewöhnlichen Verkehrszinsfuß, so werden sich nur Lumpen und Verschwender finden, um bei ihr Geld zu leihen' [This passage can be found in David Ricardo, *On the Principles of Political Economy and Taxation*, i: *The Works and Correspondences of David Ricardo*, ed. Pierro Sraffa and Maurice Dobb (London: Cambridge University Press, 1951), p. 364: 'If they [the central bank] charge less than the market rate of interest, there is no amount of money which they might not lend, if they charge more than that rate none but spendthrifts and prodigals would be found to borrow from them.' All subsequent English quotes from David Ricardo are based on the same edition].

[23] Compare this with the annual reports of the Reichsbank during the years of war, which always justified the increase in note circulation with an increase in money demand.

Hence, the credit banks are actually independent of the central bank in their credit business. This is not because the savings bank captured all the 'savings' in the country and built up a monopoly on credit intermediation. It is because banks can expand their credit supply independently of the saving public or the central bank. This also provides the context for why it was so often discussed before the war whether or not the 'bank rate policy' is still the 'ruler over the money market'. There was a feeling of having to negate the question, but the right consequences for the theoretical assessment of the means on credit markets were not drawn. Instead the debate fell back on obsolete quantity theoretic notions of a money and savings stock.

This assessment suggests that banks do not need to consider how they meet demands for means of payment when granting a credit. This is in accordance with practice: banks consider everything else before their stocks of payment means. They completely rely on the central bank in this respect, of which they know will always accommodate their credit expansion, and therefore commercial banks create primary purchasing power. It also follows therefore that there is no real concern for liquidity arising from the ordinary money demand as cash liquidity is always available.

This seems an appropriate point to mention the proposals voiced during the war, but also before, to expand *cashless payments.*

It is well known that the cashless payment system has supposedly the following advantages: it reduces notes in circulation and therefore strengthens the financial sector and foreign trust in the German currency; it avoids the Quartalsannspannung;[24] reduces the interest rate;[25] and therefore increases the capital base of the country.

Concerning the first argument, it certainly is correct that an increase in the use of cheques reduces the notes in circulation. However, is a decrease in the amount of notes in circulation a goal in itself? It has been shown already that a reduction is not necessary

[24] Cf. 'Allgemeine Abmachungen der Vereinigungen von Banken und Bankiers vom 16.12.1913' [The General Agreement of Bank and Bankers Federations, signed 16.12.1913].

[25] Cf. von Schulze-Gaevernitz, *Die moderne Kreditbank*, p. 46: 'Wenn in England der Zins durchschnittlich 1% niedriger sich stellt, als in Deutschland, so geht dies nicht zuletzt auf die breitere Scheck-Gewohnheit Englands zurück.' [If the interest rate in England is 1 per cent lower than in Germany then this is not least caused by a more widespread use of cheques in England.]'

with respect to the liquidity and status of the central bank. Incidentally a transition to cashless payments would not ameliorate the liquidity of the central bank. The central bank would also be the last resort for cheque deposits due to its status as 'bank of banks' and these would therefore negatively affect the central bank's liquidity (if one can even speak of one).

The amount of banknotes does not carry in itself any economic meaning. Its significance lies in its character as a symptom of previous abnormal credit expansion and the consequential inflation of prices. However, inflation will not be prevented by reducing the amount of banknotes in circulation or by camouflaging it when substituting cheques for banknotes. It is quite incomprehensible why the Reichsbank advertised cashless payment methods in its fight against inflation instead of lobbying the government for a reasonable tax policy (which would alleviate the tensions on the credit market). This behaviour seems equally as foolish as a doctor trying to fight his patient's fever by artificially pushing down the quicksilver.

If the Reichsbank tried to use the cashless payment system to conceal inflation from foreign countries, then it would commit the same error as our prestigious politicians: England, with its excellent body of literature on monetary theory reaching back a hundred years, would never have been deceived by an artificial reduction of notes in circulation. The censorship in this country, concerned about any harm to our reputation abroad prevented any factual discussion and consequently only the (in this respect) less-educated domestic population could be misled. The success of the cashless payment propaganda was, as so many things, nothing more than self-deception. It sparked a great many written words[26] suggesting policy reforms for the cashless payment system without any underlying theory. The soil on which the Reichsbank's propaganda fell was so extraordinarily fertile because in this country we think of banking exclusively in private business terms and not in economic terms.

It is not very different for the argument that the cashless payment system reduces the interest rate and avoids the money shortage at the end of every quarter. At this point, we leave it open whether or not a reduction in the interest rate is a desirable aim in itself and also if and

[26] One of the most peculiar and rather intangible suggestions is to replace banknotes with 'guaranteed cheques'. As if this proposal would have even the slightest benefit. Cf. 'unknown title', Plutus, no. 35/36, 1918.

how it would be affected by interventions into the financial system. In this context, if a change to the cashless payment system is useful because it can avoid the money shortage at the end of the quarter, then it is certainly the case that the same would be attained by increasing the number of notes in circulation. Propaganda aimed at the quarterly money shortages should thus promote a higher note issuing towards the end of quarters rather than a cashless payment system. The avoidance of quarterly money shortages by switching to a cashless payment system is (once more) nothing other than the expression of a self-deceiving monetary policy.

The transaction costs should be the only decisive factor in the decision whether to settle payments by banknotes or by a cashless system. For small everyday payments the use of banknotes may always be preferable; to heavily expand the cashless payment system for these transactions would mean to tie up valuable labour: a clerk can execute a hundred cashless transactions (debits, credits, notifications) a day, in addition to all the work at clearing houses, the post, and at stationery producers. The cashless payment system reduces the number of walks not (as is often said) banknotes. This is also its historical root.

Consequently the banknote will usually be seen as the best payment instrument if there are no large risks, for example, of losing the notes. The costs of cashless payments should be passed on to the customer and not spread to other accounts, which would ensure that labour-intensive cashless payments are only used when there is a particular economic advantage. In addition, the Reichsbank's promotion of cashless payments is also myopic because, as we have shown above, less reliance on banknotes reduces its influence on the money market. It also seems myopic from a fiscal viewpoint. As is generally known, issuing banknotes is the most lucrative of all bank business and there is no reason to pass on this business to cheque-issuing credit banks. This also explains why the accumulation of banknotes, as begun during the war, is not at all disadvantageous for the general public aside from the risk associated with the suddenness of the movement. If the habit of accumulating notes instead of holding savings accounts or war time bonds had become widespread, then the Reichsbank and the Reich respectively would only need to repay the interest-free banknotes and not the interest-bearing debt with banks or bond-holders. Any economic disadvantages would not have occurred, in particular it would not be expected that note-holders change their lifestyle and instead of saving, increase their consumption and thereby bring the notes into circulation.[27]

4. Economic liquidity (the credit crisis)

The previous section showed that cash liquidity is irrelevant to the determination of credit supply. Our hypothesis that the extent of the credit supply is determined by the bank's liquidity appears therefore incorrect. However, the withdrawal of cash from a bank account is a special case in the modern economy. Usually the 'disbursement' of 'deposits' takes the form of transferring deposits between banks or the giro centre. If the bank's customers claim all deposits, that is, all loans to the bank are withdrawn or transferred to another bank, then this situation is called *liquidation*. This shows clearly the bank's creditors' motive when withdrawing their deposits.

If all credit is withdrawn from a bank then it has to sell its assets, or for collectible but not marketable assets it forces its debtors to sell assets by cancelling their credit. Through the sale of assets the bank or its debtor receives a credit in the economic clearing process and the process of credit closure as explained takes place.

The bank's assets classify as 'economically liquid' if the bank or its terminable debtor can sell their assets at the right time and price in the case of a withdrawal of credit: the bank or its debtor needs to be able to 'inject products' into the economy with social and economic value.[28]

We shall not explain in any detail the plethora of liquidity rules developed in practice because they are only of interest when analysing banks from a private business perspective. We point only to the following which is relevant from an economic viewpoint. All banks in modern developed countries are in principle illiquid. In contrast to earlier historical stages: in the past banks only granted credit insofar as they received dispensable 'money'. The longer cancellation period

[27] It is therefore incorrect when Alfred Lansburgh, 'unknown title', *Die Bank*, 1918, p. 794 [this is cited as Landsburg, 1918 in the first edition] explains: 'Das Notenthesaurieren bringe die Gefahr, daß ein größerer, als der bisherige Teil der Noten zirkuliere.' [The note accumulation brings the danger that a share of notes, larger than before, is in circulation.]

[28] Cf. Joseph Schumpeter, *Theorie der wirtschaftlichen Entwicklung [The Theory of Economic Development]* (Leipzig: Duncker & Humblot, 1912), p. 9.

for these savings enabled banks to adhere to the old banking rule of a matching term structure on both asset and liabilities sides. This is fundamentally different for modern bank credit: as explained in detail previously, a credit means that the bank receives a long-term claim from the debtor and, in exchange, the debtor receives a short-term claim from the bank to buy the desired goods and services. What we called credit consolidation, that is, the transformation of short-term balances into long-term savings is a phenomenon of second order. From this it follows that inevitably a certain proportion of assets is illiquid because a certain amount of short-term liabilities is matched with long-term claims.

It is interesting to observe how the progressing development gave rise to a certain technique to grant credit and mitigate the dangers associated with the inevitable illiquidity of the asset. This technique artificially confers what we call 'indirect liquidity' onto the illiquid assets. The indirect liquidity is of the following nature: assume that a bank granted an operating credit and created cheque deposits. On the face of it, the bank has experienced a loss in liquidity. The bank claiming back the debt would mean that the business has to sell those goods which were bought with the short-term claims. The bank cannot do so for two reasons. First, the bank does not possess such an early termination right. Second, the firm has used the goods as an input into its production process and could not sell the produced goods in a semi-finished state. This illiquidity of the asset disappears at the moment that the bank does not have to 'claim back' but can sell the asset to someone else. The liquidity is then not based on the debtor's sales but, seemingly on a level higher, by the bank's sales of the claim against the debtor.

Indirect liquidity is generated by a formal-legal particularity in the technique of granting the credit such that the bank's assets are fungible and can be sold at any time.

The main example of such an indirectly liquid asset is the common *trade bill.* During its three-month term the asset is very illiquid in terms of direct liquidity because the debtor can only be forced after three months to sell the goods in the production process and settle the debt. The reason for calling a bill of exchange a highly liquid asset lies in its indirect liquidity: the debt cannot be collected before its term end, but the bank itself is in a position to sell the claim either on the market or in particular to the central bank, which always accepts them. Further examples for the creation of 'indirect liquidity' are the transformations of a stake in a company into tradeable shares, or of direct loans to the government, which are highly illiquid due to their long duration, into certified bonds. In general, any transaction transforming a debt into a tradeable paper shows the creation of 'indirect liquidity'.

The discussion also helps to explain an otherwise unintelligible process in the modern credit economy: under certain circumstances, banks grant their customers credit by allowing them to 'draw' a draft on the bank, that is, a bill of exchange is created showing the customer as the issuer and payee and the bank as the drawee. The bill is accepted by the bank, discounted with a third bank and the discount value credited to the customer's account.

The advantage for the customer is that the loan is much cheaper (usually at the discount rate plus provisions) than taken out from the bank directly. From the viewpoint of the discounting bank, it grants a credit to a customer of another bank at a lower rate than it would grant a credit to its own customer, even though the purpose could be the same, for example, an operating credit.

The phenomenon is explained simply by the following: an operating credit to an industrial company brings a substantial illiquidity to the bank because the raw materials bought with the credit are in the production process and cannot be sold easily. On the one hand, the bank has many creditors (i.e. the holders of the cheques) who can demand the settlement of their claims without notice. On the other hand, the operating credit cannot be cancelled because the goods in possession of the debtor do not have any value to others and usually operating credits cannot be cancelled at short notice from a legal viewpoint.

Using an acceptance credit to another bank, that is, granting the credit to the customer not directly but indirectly, has the advantage that the bankers' acceptance can easily be sold. This turns the actually illiquid asset into a highly liquid one by the virtue of 'indirect liquidity'. The structure of the goods market is not affected by the form of the credit and the liquidity advantage of the legal structure of credit justifies the different terms and conditions. It is noteworthy that nothing 'illegitimate' can be found in generating 'indirect liquidity'. Contrary to a raft of different contestable opinions a bankers' acceptance is as much or little profiteering as any other bank business.

It is of utmost importance to understand that higher liquidity offers protection in case of a credit crisis, the most severe test of the modern credit economy. This is particularly necessary in order to be in a position to critically comment on the suggestions to improve so-called 'economic liquidity'[29] which were widespread before the war.

The credit crisis expresses itself in a marked increase in interest rates; the cause of which is subject to a plethora of opinions. Whilst the practitioner tends to link the cause with a lack of 'capital' (even though this cannot be the case in times of stockpiling goods), others speak of a money shortage. In accordance with our own theory of bank credit we see the nature of the credit crisis in the following way: in a credit crisis some goods become unsaleable for some (yet to be explained) reason; their demand decreases below the usually expected level. This prevents some indebted sellers from setting their debts on time. The potential losses cause concerns to banks and they do not judge their own liquidity as sufficient any more. In the hope of reducing their outstanding claims, the bank will reject the prolongation of credits to reduce their 'liquidity requirement'[30] and try to improve their liquidity. Even if not refusing the prolongation outright, the bank will at least ask for a risk premium and therefore particularly high interest rates. This is the true cause of rising interest rates and not a lack of 'capital', goods, or money (leaving aside the case of a money crisis in the narrowest sense, which will always be subject to central bank intervention). If any 'lack of' should be made responsible then it is the lack of *trust* in their own liquidity, which also confirms that money and capital markets are in fact markets of trust.

In the case of a credit crisis, usually all the banks of country (not only a single bank) show the tendency to liquidate credits. In this case the liquidity of a single bank is of no advantage. It is easy to show that liquidity is a private business aspect in a modern economy, that is, that it collapses and becomes meaningless as soon as some reason requires the liquidation of not only one but many banks and hence of the whole economy.

If only one bank needs to be liquidated, then usually other banks take on its assets or they grant a credit to a customer to acquire goods

[29] Cf. von Schulze-Gaevernitz, *Die moderne Kreditbank*, p. 181 ff. and Carl Heiligenstadt, 'Der deutsche Geldmarkt' [The German Money Market], *Schmollers Jahrbuch für Gesetzgebung, Verwaltung und Volkswirtschaft*, vol 31, no 4 (1907): pp. 1539–73.

[30] See chapter [1.]A, section 5 'The essence of bank credit'.

and machines of a debtor of the liquidated bank. With the credit, the second bank takes over the service of the bank previously granting credit. Obviously, this cannot be the case if *all* banks want to liquidate. This would be analogous to the situation of a country with only a single bank being liquidated for some reason. The liquidation of such a single bank would only be possible by a general and complete 'closure' of all 'economic debt relations'. All debtors in the country would have to sell their goods simultaneously, whilst at the same time the 'economic creditors' (i.e. everyone with a positive bank balance) would be forced to buy goods. The debtors can only meet their obligations if they receive all bank deposits; only when all debts are repaid can the bank cancel out all liabilities and exit the nexus of debt.

It does not require any explanation that in a modern economy such a liquidation is simply not possible. 'Economic debtors' would only possess machines or intermediate goods which would not have any value to others without the machines; hence, they could not be bought by the 'economic creditors' at an appropriate price. In general, deflation in its worst sense and a collapse of the economy would be the consequence of such a liquidation. Even the liquidity of certain banks does not halt this collapse. To demand that banks discount more bills of exchange and grant less other credit in order to increase the 'economic liquidity' does not appear to be a well-founded claim. A change in the legal form of credit cannot fundamentally affect the composition and allocation of the nation's stock of goods or the decisive factor for economic liquidity: the balance of easily marketable and hard-to-sell goods. The stock of readily marketable goods like coffee is not increased; the stock of goods which are hard to sell like machines and plant is not reduced. Both are in certain stages of economic development in a constant relation which is solely determined by the desires of the consumers.[31] A certain shift can be

[31] David Ricardo, *Grundsätze der Volkswirtschaft und Besteuerung*, chapter 19 [Hahn mistakenly quotes chapter 14] correctly says about the problems associated with a large stock of plants, etc.: 'Dies is übrigens ein Übelstand, dem ein reiches Volk sich unterwerfen muß und man würde nicht mehr Grund haben sich zu beklagen als ein reicher Handelsmann, wenn er darüber jammern wollte, daß sein Schiff den Seegefahren ausgesetzt, während seines Nachbars Hütte von aller solcher Gefahr frei sei.'[Ricardo, *On the Principles of Political Economy and Taxation*, p. 266: 'This, however, is an evil to which a rich nation must submit; and it would not be more reasonable to complain of it, than it would be in a rich merchant to lament that his ship was exposed to the dangers of the sea, whilst his poor neighbour's cottage was safe from all such hazard.']

accomplished by establishing a cheaper and freer credit policy to a certain production sector and a more expensive and constrictive credit policy to another, but the change will be so minuscule that it will not be an essential factor for liquidity. Furthermore, a change in the legal form of the credit will barely cause this shift because there is a danger that debtors once accustomed to a certain production method continue to prefer (inadequate) shorter-term liquidity.

This situation cannot be altered in any way. It is ultimately caused by the fact that in the modern economy (and to a certain extent in every economy) goods require a certain time to be ready for consumption and cannot be transferred from the debtor to the creditors before then. After all, this is the consequence of the prevailing principle of the division of labour, which requires goods to flow from one sector to another to be finally ready for consumption. It also follows from the nature of the credit business which shows a split between the proprietor of the good and the eventual owner of the good.

Despite all efforts of liquidity improvers, a modern credit economy is always economically illiquid. Analogous to the cash liquidity above, this latent illiquidity means in practice that the constant economic liquidity can be and is assumed. Hence, banks only need to be concerned about their own economic liquidity. The case of a simultaneous liquidation of all banks is never feasible and will never be demanded in practice. In all cases of credit crises, a general moratorium will need to be established or particularly strong banks would need to expand their credit business to compensate for all liquidated banks. During the war, such institutions in Germany were the loan societies with their far-reaching privilege of accepting and collateralizing all kinds of assets.

The safest way to prevent a credit crisis or at least to dampen its effect is an agreement of all banks to continue existing credits; in general, banks should commit to a continuing credit business instead of competing for liquidity by withdrawing and withholding credits. Such an agreement would effectively merge all banks of a country into a single bank. In a country with a single bank there cannot be a credit crisis (as long as it is not desired and induced) and, similarly, it cannot be the case as long as a coordinated credit policy is guaranteed by agreements.

The ever-increasing concentration of the banking sector in England and Germany illustrates its economic significance particularly in this context. The formidable advantage of a concentrated banking sector in the case of a credit crisis will lead almost necessarily to a continuous increase in the concentration; this will persist until the sector mirrors the development of note-issuing institutions and eventually consolidates all non-note-issuing institutions into a single bank.

IV. INTEREST AS PRICE FOR LOST LIQUIDITY

If the extent of credits granted by banks depends on the condition of private economic liquidity, then the interest rate (i.e. the price of the credit) represents the fee for the liquidity loss due to the credit. From the viewpoint of the bank, the interest rate is also a risk premium; it is not only in parts a risk premium, as the prevailing opinion assumes, but is in its entirety a risk premium:[32] the discussed historical development from real and physical cash to an abstract means of payment has also altered the role of interest. It developed from the price for lending cash to the price for lending trust and, therefore, became the price for the assumption of risk.

Banks are private businesses and work to maximize their profits. This implies that the price of their service is determined the same way as it is for all other goods and services. According to the marginalist theory of value and price, the interest rate is formed in the following manner: every bank has a certain stock of available liquidity and, hence, credit. This stock is composed of different tranches, for example, each of one million marks. The bank may be ready to grant the first tranche at, say, 1 per cent interest rate and subsequent tranches at, say, 2 per cent, 3 per cent, 4 per cent, or 5 per cent because the bank is only willing to accept the loss in liquidity in exchange for a higher compensation. The significance of the marginal tranche for the entire stock[33] means that the required compensation of the highest relevant tranche determines the required interest rate for all of the bank's credits.

[32] That the interest payments cover banking fees and interest payments to others does not change anything in its role as risk premium in the relationship between bank and debtor.

[33] A detailed exposition of the price determination process cannot be given here. It is referred to in the well-known sections in Eugen von Böhm-Bawerk, *Positive Theorie des Kapitals [The Positive Theory of Capital]* (Jena: Gustav Fischer, 1889).

The credit supply of banks confronts the credit demand, which itself is composed of tranches of one million marks. The credit-seekers of the first tranche are willing to pay an interest rate of, say, 8 per cent. The credit-seekers of the following higher tranches have less acute needs or expect a lower return on the financed investment and accordingly offer only, say, 7 per cent, 6 per cent, or 5 per cent. Under conditions of perfect competition (nowadays more or less acceptable),[34] the interest rate would stabilize itself at roughly 4 per cent to 5 per cent. At this level, credit supply and credit demand are equalised: at a higher interest rate banks would compete for unabsorbed credit demand and exert downward pressure on the interest rate; at a lower interest rate credit-seekers with unmet demand would compete for credit and exert upward pressure on the interest rate.

This explains the interest payments to banks but not the interest payments to the creditors of banks. How are the interest payments to the banks' creditors interpreted in our framework?

We have to differentiate between whether the bank's creditor holds deposits as 'cash', that is, on cheque or current accounts or as deposits on savings accounts. The holder of *cheque and current accounts* owe their interest payments to historical chance, rather than to economic necessity. Unlike any other payment in economic life, the interest payment does not provide an incentive to deliver goods or services. The holders of a cheque and current account would also 'leave' their deposits if they did not receive any interest payments, as the example of England shows. At best, the interest payment induces a change in the use of payment means towards the use of cashless payment and low private cash reserves. Consequently the banks receive notes which they would otherwise have to source expensively from the central bank. Even if this case was true: a discontinuation of the average 1.5 per cent interest rate which has to be traded off against security concerns and tax evasion motives, would not reverse the habitual use of cashless payments.[35]

[34] If one attaches enough importance to the 'Konditionenkartell' such that these conditions need to be negated, then one would need to assume that the interest rate is determined under the conditions of a monopoly.

[35] The overestimation of the psychological effect of interest payments is also responsible for the recommendation at the end of the war to increase interest payments on cheque accounts in order to counter the accumulation of notes for tax evasion motives. As if a 3 per cent interest payment would appear to the tax evaders to be equivalent to a 50 per cent wealth tax.

The holders of long-term saving deposits enjoy their interest payment because they could use short-term deposits to grant credit themselves instead of converting them into long-term saving deposits. This represents competition for banks and also a threat to the latter's liquidity; it also has the effect that the interest rates charged and paid by banks do not diverge too far and that bank deposit-holders enjoy a substantial interest payment. We can also show that potential competition is the only reason for banks to pay interest on savings by assuming an uncompetitive situation: a credit-granting monopoly of banks (which is theoretically possible) would mean that banks do not have to pay interest on savings. The discontinuation of interest payments on savings would not have any consequences for the credit supply.

The material reason for interest payments on savings therefore depends on the fact that holders of savings are also in possession of purchasing power which is otherwise primarily created by banks; they also temporarily abstain from using their purchasing power, which they received for previous services. Our conception of the interest rate only meets the prevailing opinion that views the interest rate as the price for saved and lent cash, via this detour.

Part Two

Credit and the Goods Market

[2.]A. The Prevailing Opinion on the Relationship between Credit and Capital Goods (the Influence of Capital on Credit)

Hitherto, it was the purpose and duty of the discussion to analyse credit transactions of modern banks from an accounting and banking perspective. To this effect, it was necessary to introduce a number of new categories and distinctions: credit creation, credit prolongation, credit closure, credit consolidation, primary and secondary banks, money and economic, direct and indirect liquidity to name the most important.

With the help of this (as we believe unique) systematization from the economic viewpoint, it is now possible to explore how credit affects the direction, quantity, and distribution of goods produced in the economy. Because of their fundamental relevance for the supply and satisfaction of the population's needs these questions are the ultimate and highest goal for any economic study in general and in particular of the credit business.

The relationship between credit and what is commonly called the capital stock of a nation is treated first because it is decisive for questions of production and distribution. We will have to discuss, therefore, the term and nature of *capital* (a term we have so far avoided as far as possible due to its lack of clarity). This shall be done with brevity and avoids the infinite array of disputes which were raised by economic doctrines in this area in particular. This will seem more plausible and acceptable, as we will show that the best and most perceptive writings suppose long-passed economic states and, hence, their results are of no use for the current economic situation. Nevertheless, it will be necessary to set out the problem in question, to treat it briefly, and to add our critical observations. This also makes it easier to precisely position our views, which are already partly developed and partly remain to be explained, and to explain their deviations from the prevailing views.

Capital in the economic sense (and we will only treat this perspective) is 'the part of the economy's wealth, which is used to produce. It encompasses food and clothing, tools, raw materials, machines, and so on, which are necessary to successfully add labour to. This old definition by Ricardo is still the prevailing view nowadays. It is usually found in textbooks as 'Kapital sind die produzierten Produktionsmittel' ['Capital is that part of the wealth of a country which is employed in production, and consists of food, clothing, tools, raw materials, machinery, and so on, necessary to give effect to labour'].[1]

Already at the point of framing the question, our view fundamentally differs from the prevailing view. The question of the effect of credit on capital does not exist for the prevailing opinion; it is simply not raised. Contemporary theory occupies itself with the reverse problem, namely the effect of capital on the amount of available credit. As we have shown and refuted in Part One, in the prevailing opinion, the quantity of credit is a dependent variable and its dependence on the amount of capital needs to be examined. On the other hand, we acknowledge the fundamental independence of the quantity of credit from other factors than the existing trust; accordingly, only the impact of credit on the goods sphere can remain as a problem. In order to clarify the problem, we disregard the insights of our discussion so far and treat the problems posed by the contemporary theory. Hence, our question shall be: 'How does the quantity of available capital goods affect the quantity of available credit?'

An investigation of the literature reveals the rather profound confusion when treating this question. One cannot find a coherent view of a single author or even a clear and coherent exposition of the constituent trains of thought. The great complexity of the issue means that no clear account of the technical mechanism linking the quantity of capital goods with the quantity of credit and therefore interest rates

[1] David Ricardo, *Grundsätze der Volkswirtschaft und Besteuerung*, trans. Edward Baumstark (Leipzig: Verlag von Wilhelm Engelmann, 1837) or 2nd edition (Leipzig: Verlag von Wilhelm Engelmann, 1877), chapter 5 [David Ricardo, *On the Principles of Political Economy and Taxation*, i: *The Works and Correspondences of David Ricardo*, ed. Pierro Sraffa and Maurice Dobb (London: Cambridge University Press, 1951) p. 95].

has been stated until today. Vague explanations are pervasive in some areas of banking theory, but the explanations in this narrow sub-field are particularly vague.

The attempt to draw a coherent picture of the usual views and to systematise them as far as possible shows broadly two main themes with plenty of variations (despite many contradictions and some crudities). We will call the views of the first kind the *barter perspective* and of the second kind the *monetary perspective.* We do not express with these terms that the authors lived in the respective stages in the economic development or that they wanted to write about them. The views are rather the scientific residues of these development stages because the authors are caught in pictures of earlier ages as the basis of their deliberations. Thus, one can still find barter and very early monetary perspectives on capital in the current literature.

Both perspectives share the understanding that the amount of available credit and therefore the interest rate is truly dependent on the stock of goods. This stock originates from previous production periods. It grows by an increase in production or through reduced consumption in the sense of a primary and independent decision of the 'saving' individual. The main task of the following section is to set out the errors of this view on 'capital' supply.

I. THE BARTER PERSPECTIVE

In the economic development stage, commonly called the *barter economy*, goods are traded for other goods not for money. Accordingly in such an environment, the entrepreneur or whoever else requires tools, raw materials, 'sustenance goods for the production period', generally 'capital goods', can only obtain them in the following way: he needs to borrow the goods from another individual who produced and did not consume them, that is, who kept them in stock. The method of granting credit is eventually only the expression and consequence of the prevailing method of payment. In general, this will take the form of *rent*, in particular for durable goods, and for some special cases, for example, seed in the form of the *depositum irregulare*, where the good itself is not returned but is replaced on a like-for-like basis. The compensation for 'using' the borrowed capital (regardless of the form of payment, e.g. as a proportion of the harvested wheat) corresponds to the compensation in the modern economy of *rental and tenancy fees*. In contrast, they do not show any relation to the *interest on credit and money* in the modern economy. If one wants to avoid the concise description of 'rental and tenancy fees' then one should use the term '*interest on goods*' to avoid any confusion with interest on credit and money which is particularly important to avoid any wrong conclusions.

The barter perspective's concept of a transfer of 'capital' can be found in different contexts and for different reasons in the literature. Some authors do not presuppose the barter stage of economic development in their treatment but have the modern credit economy in mind. Nevertheless, they utilize the barter perspective in their theoretical formulation (often in the form of one or several Robinson Crusoes) because they do not perceive the fundamental differences between the two development stages as relevant.[2] The barter view can also be found in authors who think that borrowing real goods (coordinated by borrowing money) is actually a relevant phenomenon for the modern economy; the interest rate on money and credit is seen as of equal importance to the interest rate paid on goods.[3] Occasionally, some even go as far to claim that borrowing goods is the only or decisive form of borrowing capital.[4]

[2] In this category are writings like Emil Sax, *Der Kapitalzins [The Interest Rate on Capital]* (Berlin and Heidelberg: Springer, 1916) and to a certain degree also Eugen von Böhm-Bawerk, *Positive Theorie des Kapitals [The Positive Theory of Capital]* (Jena: Gustav Fischer, 1889).

[3] See e.g. Knut Wicksell, *Theoretischer Teil*, i: *Vorlesungen über Nationalökonomie*, trans. Margarethe Langfeldt (Jena: Gustav Fischer, 1913) [Knut Wicksell, *General Theory*, i: *Lectures on Political Economy*, trans. E. Classen, ed. Lionel Robbins (London: Routledge, 1934)].

[4] It appears to me that Ricardo, *Grundsätze der Volkswirtschaft und Besteuerung*, chapters 4–5 [Ricardo, *On the Principles of Political Economy and Taxation*, chapters 4–5] contain some passages to that effect; in those passage, he obviously has the rural tenancies in mind and thinks of the interest paid on capital as a form of a rental fee rather than an interest rate on money. The following quote is interesting: 'In allen reichen Ländern gibt es eine Anzahl von Menschen, welche man Geldkapitalistenklasse nennt. Sie treiben kein Gewerbe, sondern leben von den Zinsen ihres Geldes, welches in Wechselgeschäften oder Darlehen an den gewerb- und betriebsameren Teil des Gemeinwesens angelegt ist. Auch die Banken wenden große Kapitalien auf diese Weise an. Dieses so angelegete Kapital bildet ein umlaufendes Kapital von hohem Belaufe.' (Ricardo, *Grundsätze der Volkswirtschaft und Besteuerung*, p. 62) [Ricardo, *On the Principles of Political Economy and Taxation*, p. 89: 'In all rich countries, there is a number of men forming what is called the monied class; These men are engaged in no trade, but live on the interest of their money, which is employed in discounting bills, or in loans to the more industrious part of the community. The bankers too

Admittedly, the barter perspective is logically correct and when its conditions are satisfied gives some theoretical grounding for the common opinion that the amount of capital goods affects the amount of available credit. In fact, the structure of the supply of 'capital' is identical with the supply of capital goods in the described economy; the goods were produced and not consumed by a third person and as a consequence lent to someone. The more goods this person produces and the more he saves (out of private business motives), the higher is the supply of capital.[5] Thus, the quantity of available capital goods determines the supply of the capital market and is the basic determinant of the interest rate (as far as we can speak of a single interest rate). The barter view also offers an explanation as to why capital goods are priced at the interest rate and not at the relative prices of the goods in the market (which is not self-evident); the goods used as 'capital' are not offered for barter on the general goods market but for rent on a special market, the capital market. Finally the barter perspective on capital, further explains the classical view that the amount of capital determines the number and size distribution of firms[6] and subsequently the distribution of revenue between the labour and capitalist class.

Despite being logically coherent the barter view on capital is not useful to explain the relation between the quantity of capital goods and available credit in the modern economy. The most important

employ a large capital on the same objects. The capital so employed forms a circulating capital of a large amount.'] Since he defines 'circulating capital' in terms of goods, money seems to be a commodity itself (not as the usual antithesis to commodities), for which one has to pay compensation for its usage. This stands in stark contrast to the treatment of banks (particularly in chapter 27) in which Ricardo thinks completely in 'monetary' terms.

[5] 'Kapitalbildung oder [des] Sparen[s]—Produktion ohne entsprechende Konsumtion', says Wicksell, *Theoretische Grundlagen*, p. 8 [Wicksell, *General Theory*, p. 7: '*accumulation of capital*—which is equivalent to production without corresponding consumption'].

[6] Compare e.g. Ricardo, *Grundsätze der Volkswirtschaft und Besteuerung*, chapter 4: 'Die Menge der Kapitalien kann wachsen . . . dann wird der Marktsatz des Arbeitslohnes in die Höhe gehen, denn die Zunahme der Nachfrage nach Arbeit steht in geradem Verhältnis zur Vermehrung des Kapitals.' [Ricardo, *On the Principles of Political Economy and Taxation*, p. 95: 'Capital may increase in quantity . . . the market rate of wages will rise, for in proportion to the increase of capital will be the increase in the demand for labour; in proportion to the work to be done will be the demand for those who are to do it.']. In every conception other than the barter view, an increase in the quantity of capital goods will exert downward pressure on the wage rate, which needs to be compensated by the price for capital goods.

condition is not met: nowadays there is no special rental market for capital goods (apart from very few exceptions like houses). The goods used as 'capital' are rather bought, not rented, on the *general goods market.* An increase in capital goods therefore exerts some pressure on the goods' prices, but cannot be part of a special capital market and affect the special price of 'capital', that is, the 'interest rate'. On these special markets something other than the saved goods (which are already traded on the goods market) constitute the supply; but what?

The prevailing opinion, in as far as it is based on the barter perspective, faces a dilemma when applying considerations from the barter to the modern economy. It cannot be argued that 'money' and 'credit' constitute the supply of 'capital', because money is only seen as representing produced and saved goods (like the 'veil of the Maya') and its quantity is fully determined by the amount of available capital goods. At the same time, it is acknowledged that these capital goods are only traded on the goods not on the capital market and, hence, their supply can only affect the former. The dilemma is resolved by using the vague term 'goods of higher order' instead of the identical 'capital' at the critical passages; the neutral term 'capital' which has a less clear relation with the goods market is postulated as the determinant of capital supply. The assertion that something other than goods is traded on the capital market, hence determining the interest rate and consequently the distribution between the capitalist and labour class,[7] would only be meaningful if it explained how capital and goods differ. This is usually not done and the capital remains to

[7] Compare the following passage from Ricardo, *Grundsätze der Volkswirtschaft und Besteuerung,* chapter 1, section 3: 'Unter verschiedenen Verhältnissen von Überfluss und Mangel an Kapital im Vergleich mit der Arbeit, dürften diejenigen, welche ... Kapital ... geliefert haben, die Hälfte, einen vierten oder einen achten Teil des Erzeugnisses in Beschlag nehmen, der Rest würde als Arbeitslohn an diejenigen bezahlt, welche Arbeit geleistet haben.' [Ricardo, *On the Principles of Political Economy and Taxation,* p. 24: 'Under different circumstances of plenty or scarcity of capital, as compared with labour, ... those who furnished an equal value of capital for either one employment or for the other, might have a half, a fourth, or an eighth of the produce obtained, the remainder being paid as wages to those who furnished the labour.'] He previously defines capital in terms of goods, he even calls a typical capital good the 'weapon': 'Ohne eine Waffe kann weder Biber noch der Hirsch getötet werden.' ['Without a weapon neither the beaver nor the stag can be killed.'] A change in the relative quantities of labour and capital goods will only affect the distribution between owners of goods of lower or higher order and labourers respectively through changes in goods prices and wages. There will be no effect on the interest rate and the capitalist will not be affected.

be defined as goods.[8] Under these circumstances, the substitution of the term 'capital goods' with 'capital' is nothing else than a rhetorical trick, which is used at the weakest spot of the whole capital theory. It goes even further than that, namely it exposes a grave logical error: seeing capital goods as 'goods' and at the same time as 'capital' on the capital market leads to double counting. It is logically impossible to allow certain attributes of the good, different to its characteristic as a good, to be called 'capital' in their own right in order to make them the subject of supply and demand; it would be the same as saying colour is a separate entity to the coloured item and as such part of a different supply. As soon as the barter economy (in which special 'capital' goods have a special market) ceases to exist *supply and demand can only consist of either goods or money and credit, but never of the curious thing called 'capital'*. Theory has created this term and to operate it as if it was real (as is usually the case) is like the fakir who throws a rope in the air and then uses it to climb up.

Of course, the question of what is traded on the 'capital' markets remains unanswered by the view characterised here. It is certain that capital goods cannot be considered, as they are actually only traded on the goods markets. Hence, they cannot constitute part of the supply of capital markets as the application of the barter view to the modern economy suggests.

II. THE MONETARY PERSPECTIVE

In a monetary economy, goods are not *traded for goods* but *sold for money*. In this economic development stage, one needs money to buy

[8] It is interesting how Wicksell, *Theoretische Grundlagen*, p. 214 deals with the obviously appreciated difficulty. He defines capital as 'als eine einzige zusammenhängende, obwohl auf gewisse Weise nach Jahrgängen abgelagerte Masse ersparter (aufgespeicherter) Arbeitskraft einerseits und ersparter Bodenkraft andererseits' [Wicksell, *General Theory*, p. 150: 'a single coherent mass of saved-up labour and saved-up land, which is accumulated in the course of years'] and has the fundamental conception that capital is vintage goods. Further, 'Doch dieser Unterschied genügt, um das Aufstellen einer besonderen Produktionsmittelkategorie neben der Arbeit und dem Boden unter dem Namen Kapital zu rechtfertigen.' (Wicksell, *Theoretische Grundlagen*, p. 214) [Wicksell, *General Theory*, p. 150: 'But this difference is sufficient to justify the establishment of a special production factor category of means of production, side by side with labour and land, under the name of capital.'] This in particular has to be rejected; goods can only appear as goods, regardless of their age. These passages also show the vague and illogical terminology of an otherwise clear author, when treating the problem of capital.

capital goods, tools, and raw materials. Money has to be borrowed if it is not possessed and the demand for capital is expressed in the demand for money.

We find the monetary view in all those writings assuming this basic position about the relation of capital goods and available credit. It can be found remarkably often in the classics,[9] although often next to the barter perspective, and in particular in the more recent banking literature.

The monetary perspective has three major advantages over the barter perspective (also for the understanding of the modern economy). First, it draws a much more realistic picture of the transfer of capital goods in the modern economy; the credit seeker borrows (apart from exceptional cases) purchasing power rather than goods. The monetary perspective enables a distinction to be made between 'capital' and the goods market, even though goods are only offered on the goods market. Money as something particular and distinct to goods is offered on capital markets. Finally, only the monetary perspective captures the importance of *interest on money* for the modern economy.[10] From a barter perspective there is only an *interest on goods*, which, as discussed, has no relevance for the modern economy.

[9] Cf. Ricardo, *Grundsätze der Volkswirtschaft und Besteuerung*, chapter 27 [Ricardo, *On the Principles of Political Economy and Taxation*, chapter 27] and John Stuart Mill, *Grundsätze der politischen Ökonomie [Principles of Political Economy]*, trans. Adolph Soetbeer, 2nd ed. (Hamburg: Perthes-Besser und Mauke, 1864), chapter 23 and see chapter [1.]A, section 1.1 on 'The prevailing view of banking activities'.

[10] The barter perspective was particularly damaging for the theory of interest rates, because it tempted many writers to explain interest rates on money through interest rates on goods. It probably shows the excellence of Joseph Schumpeter, *Theorie der wirtschaftlichen Entwicklung [The Theory of Economic Development]* (Leipzig: Dunker & Humblot, 1912), in which he shows this conception of interest rates to be wrong. He further shows that the cause for the interest rate lies in the renting and particularities of money. The practitioner will barely doubt the relations, he knows that the rents on capital goods are oriented towards the interest rate on money and not that the rent on money is determined by the interest rate on goods. The price of rental property increases, if the interest rate on money decreases, but the interest rate on money does not increase if the rents increase. Contrary to the views of authors in the barter perspective, quality and quantity of capital goods do not affect the interest rate: if the capital good has a higher rent, then its price increases, but not the interest rate on money. A scarcity of capital goods does not actually increase the interest rate in a modern economy, but increases the prices on the goods market. Compare this with an interesting article, 'Geldflüssigkeit und Geldknappheit' [Money Liquidity and Money Scarcity], *Frankfurter Zeitung*, Abendblatt, 15 November 1919. The author of the article asserts the simultaneous abundance of money and scarcity of capital goods during and after the war. He believes this situation requires an explanation, but from our perspective this phenomenon is neither surprising nor requires a particular explanation.

The central question on the amount and source of the supply of capital markets is answered in the same way from the monetary as well as from the barter perspective: the amount of capital supplied is composed of the stock of goods from earlier production periods, which is increased by increased production or decreased consumption in the sense of a primary and independent decision of the capital-accumulating individual. The barter perspective views saver A as saving the actual good earmarked as a capital good, whilst in the monetary perspective saver A produces, sells, saves the revenues, lends to credit seeker B, who buys some capital good produced from C.[11]

This view that savings are the origin and determinant for the capital stock of an economy[12] is the largely unchallenged contemporary view. This section shall show that this view is untenable for the modern economy, particularly because the modern economy cannot be seen as a monetary economy any more. It does not require an

[11] Wicksell, *Theoretische Grundlagen*, p. 290 explains this process the following way: 'Die Nutzgegenstände, auf welche der Sparer durch Einschränken oder Aufschieben seiner Konsumation verzichet oder richtiger: die Arbeitskraft und Bodenkraft, welche sonst diese Nutzgegenstände hergestellt hätten, stellt er nun direkt oder durch die Vermittlung des Geldes, des Kredites und der Kreditinstitute einem Unternehmer zur Verfügung, und dieser verwandelt sie nach und nach, wie die Ersparungen stattfinden, in mehr oder weniger feste Kapitalgegenstände, also in Realkapital.' [Wicksell, *General Theory*, pp. 217–18: 'The commodities which a person foregoes by saving, and by restricting or postponing his consumption—or rather the labour and land which would otherwise have gone to the production of those commodities—he places directly (or by means of money, credit or credit institutions) at the disposal of an entrepreneur who converts them gradually, as the savings are effected, into more or less fixed capital goods, that is, real capital.'] Similarly, Adam Smith, *Untersuchungen über das Wesen und die Ursachen des Nationalreichtums [Adam Smith, An Inquiry into the Nature and Causes of the Wealth of Nations, 2 vols, ed. R. H. Campbell, A. S. Skinner and W. B. Todd (Oxford: Clarendon Press, 1976)]*, book 2, chapter 4, paragraph 6. [There were numerous German translations available at the time of Hahn and it was not possible to ascertain which one he actually used. An overview of German editions can be found in Adam Smith, *Untersuchung über Wesen und Ursachen des Reichtums der Völker*, trans. Monika Streissler, ed. Erich Streissler (Düsseldorf: Verlag Wirtschaft und Finanzen, 1999), p. 898].

[12] Cf. Adam Smith, *Untersuchungen über das Wesen und die Ursachen des Nationalreichtums*, book 2, chapter 3: 'Sparsamkeit, nicht Fleiß ist die unmittelbare Ursache der Kapitalvermehung' [Adam Smith, *An Inquiry into the Nature and Causes of the Wealth of Nations*, book 2, chapter 4, paragraph 16, p. 336: 'Parsimony, and not industry, is the immediate cause of the increase of capital']. In our opinion, industry not parsimony is the decisive factor.

additional explanation to grasp the utmost importance of this task, as most economic and fiscal policy recommendations are made on its basis.

The view that the savings of A are directly responsible for the purchase of B's capital good is dependent on the fundamental assumption that A's savings are necessary under all circumstances to endow B with purchasing power. It was shown in Part One that this assumption does not hold for a modern banking system. Granting credit based on savings is the exception nowadays and ad hoc credit creation the rule. Generally, B can be endowed with purchasing power, even if A has not saved any money but expends the revenue himself.

But, one will argue, 'creating money' does not mean to 'create goods'. If A does not save, but both A and B want to buy, then they have to share C's products. His production does not increase simply because there is more money or purchasing power available in the country. The increase in money or credit creation does not increase goods, but only raises prices.

This argument brings us to the core of the entire problem: Is the production of C, or of all producers in an economy, a constant that does not react to increases in money-induced demand and is independent of the product A sold previously? The question also touches on the weakest point in the modern literature on banking: the *inflation problem*. It can be seen as the crux of monetary theory.

The view, that the creation of purchasing power (or money) in order to grant credit generally only increases the price level has already been voiced by the followers of the quantity theory. Time and time again, it is stressed that an increase in money cannot increase capital. The converse view, which draws on reductions in the discount rate, is rejected as a laymen's opinion.

On the other hand, the practitioners in the real economy talk eloquently about the effects of credit, also primarily created by banks, on the production of a country. The authors studying and describing the banking sector and the modern credit business recognize the effects of credit. But they struggle to explain it theoretically and try to unify it with their views that any primary creation of purchasing power is nothing other than 'profiteering'. The solution to this dilemma is usually to argue that credit does not increase the production of goods but ensures their efficient economic allocation. This explanation is not useful from a scientific perspective, because it is too vague.[13] It is also wrong: credit and money creation respectively increase the amount of goods, as we will see later. The assertion that credit-seeking B could be endowed with purchasing power without any consideration for any savings of A cannot be countered with the argument that this creation of purchasing power does not increase 'capital' and is only inflationary. If a credit can be granted to whoever seeks it without using savings of another individual, then the monetary view is untenable, because it explicitly only allows credits to be transfers of savings to the credit-seeker.

That credit and money creation induces an increase in production is obvious, when considering that credit creation means increased demand as it is seen at the onset of *business cycles*. To our knowledge, these connections have only experienced sparse treatment in the literature. Even though the business cycle is extensively covered in the literature, no one seems to have explained the problem of capital accumulation and money creation.[14] No one has connected the concept of the business cycle with capital theory. Making this connection will be attempted in the following chapter.

[13] Unclear also Edgar Jaffé, *Das English-Amerikanische und das Französische Bankwesen [The English-American and the French banking system]* (Tübingen: J. C. B Mohr (Paul Siebeck), 1915), p. 220: The note issuance cannot build up new capital from nowhere, but can enable new production and therefore indirectly create new capital. The first part of the sentence is in our opinion untenable and is in direct contradiction to the second part of the sentence, which is quite close to our opinion.

[14] Pointers to this notion can only be found in David Hume, *Essays, Moral and Political* (Edinburgh: A. Kingaid, 1740/41), essay 'Of money'. His successors, in particular Mill, returned to a strict quantity theory. In this respect, their writings are a regression from Hume.

[2.]B. The Influence of Credit on Capital

I. THE PRIORITY OF CREDIT OVER CAPITAL GOODS CREATION

Capital accumulation is not the consequence of savings, but of granting credit; granting credit logically precedes capital accumulation.

This statement is fundamentally equal to the statement above on the consequences of granting credit on banking; the only difference is that this time we treat the effects of credit on the sphere of goods. Credit precedes deposits and can be granted without any consideration of savings or credit consolidation; similarly, granting credit is also the primary event to accumulating capital; hence, the accumulation of capital is not affected by savings.

The truth of this statement becomes apparent as soon as one examines the economic categories the terms 'capital accumulation' and 'capital creation' describe. 'Capital', that is, the part of a nation's wealth used in production, is obviously nothing other than a subset of all goods; the production of capital goods is nothing other than a subcategory of goods production in general. 'Credit creation' on the other hand refers to the creation of purchasing power. The entrepreneur obtaining credit is in a position to buy machines, and so forth, and pay wages or, in other words, to create demand for means of production. Credit creation therefore creates demand.

Demand (as well as the consumption it enables) logically precedes production.[1] This is often not recognised because temporally the

[1] Knut Wicksell, *Theoretischer Teil [General Theory]*, i: *Vorlesungen über Nationalökonomie*, trans. Margarethe Langfeldt (Jena: Gustav Fischer, 1913), p. 6 is right in

order is reversed. First, production takes place and only then the product is demanded and used or consumed. Nevertheless, demand is the precedent in an economic assessment. Each production presupposes sufficient demand, no production is tackled without demand; demand drags production and every production process started anticipates demand. Adam Smith said: 'Wenn nicht konsumiert wird, kann nicht produziert werden'['*Consumption* is the sole end and purpose of all *production*'].

If demand logically precedes production, then credit creation logically precedes capital accumulation. Without credit creation no capital goods can be produced and, hence, no capital accumulated in the sense of amassing a stockpile of means of production. It is credit creation causing capital creation as a secondary effect, like demand causes the satisfaction of itself through production.[2]

Credit creation is not only the cause of capital stock but also determines its composition, size, and even its distribution across the subjects of an economy. These extraordinarily interlinked relationships

saying, that 'die Lehre von den menschlichen Bedürfnissen, in quantitativer und qualitativer Beziehung, d.h. die allgemeine Lehre der Konsumation, da sie ja der Zweck der ganzen wirtschaftlichen Tätigkeit ist, logischerweise unbestreitbar an die erste Stelle gesetzt werden muss, wenn sie auch im wirklichen Leben der Zeitfolge nach als letzte auftritt.' [Knut Wicksell, *General Theory*, i: *Lectures on Political Economy*, trans. E. Classen, ed. Lionel Robbins (London: Routledge, 1934), pp. 5–6: 'the theory of *human wants*, quantitative and qualitative, i.e. the general theory of *consumption*, which, since it is the purpose of all economic activity, should logically be placed first, even though in actual life it comes last in point of time.'] Accordingly (and contrary to the usual arrangement) Wicksell treats demand before production. However, he does not draw any consequences for the capital theory.

[2] Herbert von Beckerath, *Kapitalmarkt und Geldmarkt [Capital and Money Markets]* (Jena: Gustav Fischer, 1916), p. 89 seems to misunderstand these relations and bases his argument on circular reasoning, when he says that the extent of credit markets are dependent on the stock of saleable goods. The existence of saleable goods is only the consequence of a demand for them. Similarly, Friedrich Benedixen, *Das Wesen des Geldes [The Nature of Money]* (Munich: Duncker & Humblot, 1908), p. 31 and Friedrich Benedixen. *Das Inflationsproblem [The Inflation Problem]* (Stuttgart: Ferdinand Enke, 1917), p. 33 see the discounting of bills of exchange as unproblematic for monetary policy because of their guarantee for a profit, this view appears untenable after what has been said above. The production and the sale of the goods is only conducted because it is expected and anticipated that the bill of exchange is discounted, which makes the acceptor of a bill a viable buyer of the goods. Logically, the sequence of events is as follows: discounting, sales against acceptance, production, and not vice versa in the timing sequence. Benedixen's notion would therefore mean that a bill of exchange needs to be discounted, once the producer and buyer expect it to happen—obviously a circular argument.

can only be analysed clearly by examining the effect of credit on the goods sphere in general and also every single consequence of credit creation in isolation. This will be undertaken in the next section.

II. THE EFFECT OF CREDIT ON THE COMPOSITION OF GOODS

It is useful to show the effect of credit creation on the composition and structure of the economy's goods market using a comparison. The best comparator for the quantity of available goods is the volume of water in a river,[3] as it is almost a perfect analogy. The water particle becomes part of the river at the source and leaves it at the estuary after a certain time. Analogously, the good becomes part of the goods stock of a nation at the beginning of production, matures, and is eventually fully consumed, thus exiting the goods sphere. In any given moment, new water particles enter the river and the ones which have spent the longest time in the river exit at the estuary. The river therefore carries water particles of different ages at all times; similarly, the flow of goods is augmented at any moment by production and diminished by consumption, such that goods of different maturity exist at any time. The entirety of all the water particles in the river give the impression of a coherent, flowing stream; analogously, the entirety of all the goods available in an economy forms what is usually called the nation's stock of goods.

Natural rivers are of different length and if all of them carry water at the same time, at a constant speed, the water particles in each will need a different amount of time to travel from the source to the estuary. Analogously, the streams of goods in an economy differ in length and different goods form part of the nation's stock for different durations. The shortest flow of goods consists of those goods with a very short time span between the start of the production and the end in consumption, as is the case with most daily needs products. The longest flow of goods consists of goods with a fairly long time between production and consumption (e.g. houses, machines).

[3] Cf. Joseph Schumpeter, *Theorie der wirtschaftlichen Entwicklung [The Theory of Economic Development]* (Leipzig: Dunker & Humblot, 1912), p. 70 on exchanging the image of a 'stock of goods' with the image of a 'flow' of goods.

The shorter flow of goods generally contains goods which are usually called consumption goods in the narrow sense, or goods of low order. The longer flows of goods generally consist of goods usually called goods of higher order because consumption is only satisfied through their products but not directly as it is the case with machines and factories. When goods have the characteristic of consumption goods (accordingly counted as goods of lower order) but have a long durability, they should nevertheless be part of the longest flows of goods. This is the case for durable goods (in particular houses) which are consumed directly, not only through their products, but for which consumption only ceases after a very long time.[4]

The labour of a nation casts itself in the riverbed of the goods flow, as labour is the origin of all goods and therefore the source of any flow of goods.

Has credit the power to alter the course of the nation's labour and how would that happen? It depends; credit can have different effects on production depending on the interest rate: assume that a production process has to be financed entirely by credit from the moment an entrepreneur commands its labourers to start the production process (or he buys the intermediate product in a finishing industry) until it is sold either to another firm or to the consumer. This would mean that the goods representing the product of the national labour is not owned by the entrepreneur but made available by way of credit. In practical terms the entrepreneur could use an open credit line with the bank to pay wages and the cost of raw materials or intermediate goods using cheques or withdrawn bank notes.

Assume further that the loan to the entrepreneur is interest free for the time of the production, that is, he only has to return the principal and no interest to the bank once he has sold all (intermediate) goods. In this case the entrepreneur would only have to charge the cost of wages, the proportional depreciation of machinery and raw materials to break even. The price of the product would not need to cover any interest payments;[5] only the value of labour would be paid by the final product.

[4] It is one-sided to follow Böhm-Bawerk and to talk only of 'roundabout methods of production'. 'Roundabout methods of consumption' are also a characteristic of the capitalist economy (e.g. durable buildings instead of shacks, with their differences in financing and construction).

[5] We will assume henceforth that rents on land and profits do not constitute a part of the production costs, such that only labour is considered as a factor cost in

The production of certain goods is dependent on the specific demand at higher or lower prices and to what extent demand can be met at prevailing prices. Assuming interest-free credit, the demand for all goods for which consumers are ready to pay at least the wage costs of production can be met. All these goods could be produced and would include a relatively large number of durable goods. In particular blocks of flats would be built in large numbers as the rent would only need to cover the amortised construction costs and no interest on the mortgage.

How would this change if banks ask for a positive interest rate, say 5 per cent, instead of zero per cent? Then the demand can only be satisfied for goods, for which the consumers are ready to pay the wage costs plus interest payments. Only those goods can be produced, in particular, only those blocks of flats can be built for which the tenants are ready to pay the amortised construction costs and the interest payments. This can only be the case for a smaller number of tenants with a stronger desire for housing. All others would forbear from renting a flat or would restrict the number of rooms rented. From this follows, that the production of durable goods (i.e. goods which take a long time from the start of production to the ending in consumption) will decrease with higher interest rates on credits to the firm or the owner of the good. This effect becomes more pronounced the more durable the good is.

The level of the interest rate is also crucial for deciding on which method of production is utilised. Each good can obviously be produced by different methods. The production technique can be more or less capital intensive, that is, capital can be invested for shorter or longer periods. Capital will be utilised longer if the production does not yield the product directly but in a more roundabout way[6] whereby the means of production are manufactured first and only then the final product. The final product, therefore, includes labour used directly to produce the final product and indirectly to produce intermediate products and machines. Assume the quantity of 1m shoes can be produced by either 10,000 craftsmen in one year or 5,000 workers could produce machines in the first year and use them to produce 1m shoes in the second year. In both cases 1m shoes are

production. For the argument in the text, it is sufficient to only consider the wages to be paid by the product.

[6] A term introduced by Böhm-Bawerk.

produced and 10,000 labourers have to be paid for 1 year, but in the second case the shoes are only produced in the second year. The entrepreneur has to wait two years to get reimbursed for his advanced 'capital'.

The peculiarity of the second method (more capital intensive) is that it can produce 25,000 pairs of shoes more than the first method, such that 1m pairs of shoes only contains the work of 9,750 workers. This means that the second method saves the cost of 250 workers and the shoes are produced 2.5 per cent cheaper. Hence, the entrepreneur will choose this method as it will grant him an extra profit (until competition catches up).[7]

This only holds if interest rates are zero. The picture changes if we assume that the bank charges 5 per cent interest on the credit; the second (more roundabout) method is only possible and profitable, if its additional profits are greater than the additional interest payments for using the capital longer in the production process. For the first method in our example the wages for 10,000 workers will remain in the firm for one year, whilst for the second method the wages of the 5,000 workers building the machines would remain in the firm for

[7] As some experts will have recognised, the analysis is based on a theory of capital and interest, as is advocated by proponents of an abstract capital theory. The old productivity theory thinks of every single capital good as a production factor. In contrast, the characteristic of an abstract capital theory is only to see the roundabout method of production as a factor, based on the fact that capital goods realize a profit and therefore its price features no expected premium over consumption goods. If one considers abstract capital theories to be correct in principle, then one should consequently avoid the term 'capital' in listings of production factors, as it has a connotation of the specific good, and use the term 'capitalist method of production' instead. Likewise the term 'interest on capital' should be replaced by 'interest on credit', in order to point out that interest is paid not because of a particular feature of the capital good but because of the credit-enabled change in the flow of goods. Schumpeter, *Theorie der wirtschaftlichen Entwicklung* comes quite close to our notion. However, Schumpeter's theory seems insufficient in one main respect. Schumpeter assumes that competition drives down the extra profit of a capitalistic method of production to zero and denies the existence of an interest rate in the static economy. In reality, profits can only be reduced to a level sufficient to pay interest on the bank credit, because otherwise credits would be closed and less capital-intensive production methods would need to be utilised. In such an environment the credit-financed capital-intensive production method would grant profits, sufficient for its continuation and to cover interest payments. Schumpeter's view is therefore only tenable if one believes in interest-free credits from banks. The fees caused by the administration of credits and also the risk assumed with granting credit would make this impossible, even if one assumes that deposits remain with the bank when no interest is paid on them (which is probably the case).

two years. Hence, the additional costs are 5 per cent of the annual pay of 5,000 workers, that is, the equivalent of the annual pay of 250 workers. If the technical advantage of the second method is less than the annual wages of 250 workers, then it could only be utilised at a lower interest rate, for example, at 4 per cent; if it is larger, then it could be even utilised at a an interest rate of, for example, 6 per cent or even higher.

From this follows the answer to the question of which production technique is utilised: the higher the interest rates the less often utilising a long production method is possible. The rarity of capitalist production methods increases with the level of interest rates.

Thus the interest and credit policy of banks has the following effects on composition of the stock of goods: if the interest rates remain unchanged then this will, *ceteris paribus*, neither change the length or relative width of the flow of goods. As soon as banks decrease their interest rates, the goods sphere will be affected in ways contrary to the ones described above for when interest rates increase.[8] The longer flows of goods, which now experience lower resistance, will grow in width at the cost of shorter flows of goods. This effect will be stronger the larger the decrease in the interest rate. But how does the development take place in detail?

A lower interest rate makes some firms profitable, and the additional credit makes bank balances and banknotes available to increase the firm's demand for, say, raw materials and intermediate goods. Consequently, the prices for these goods[9] will rise[10] and cause an expansion of the related industries. This will stimulate the producers of those raw materials and intermediate goods to expand their production in subsequent periods. The expansion will require an increase in their workforce, drawing away labourers from producing in the consumer goods industries which do not benefit from the additional profit and hence cannot increase wages. Therefore the

[8] The same effect will take place if a new invention alters the production processes with higher labour or other cost savings. The extra profit is therefore equivalent to a decrease in interest rates. On the other hand, a rise in the interest rate does not have any effect if it is compensated by cost-saving improvements in the production method.

[9] Cf. Ludwig von Mises, *Theorie des Geldes und der Umlaufmittel [The Theory of Money and Credit]* (Munich and Leipzig: Duncker & Humblot, 1912), p. 431.

[10] More detail will be given in this chapter, section III on 'The effect of credit on prices'.

country's labour force is more focused on more 'roundabout' methods of production and durable goods. The decrease in credit costs reduces the cost of production of raw materials and intermediate goods and the situation will prevail even after competitive pressures force prices and wages to adjust. In summary, a decrease in interest rate changes the composition of goods towards more durable, more intermediate and capital goods. The most pronounced effect will be the increase of the housing stock.

The decrease of interest rates causes a further effect, which could be called the *intertemporal effect.* Its nature is temporary and only becomes apparent in the transition phase, but has serious effects on the support of the population. In the static period, the product of labour entering production equals the product of labour available for consumption irrespective of the composition of the nation's flow of goods: as much water as enters a stream leaves it at the same time even for the longest streams. This is different for the transitory period when a shorter stream is diverted to a longer river bed, in which every water particle remains *x* weeks longer until it reaches the estuary. Once the first water particle reaches the estuary, the same amount of water enters and leaves the stream as before the diversion. However, there is a deficit in the outflow of the river during the *x* weeks the first water particle requires to reach the estuary. The same is true for the economy. The shift towards more roundabout methods of production causes a fundamentally transient (but long lasting e.g. months, years, or decades) and marked shortage of consumption goods the benefits of which only accrue in the future. The neutral countries during the war experienced how noticeable this effect was. Substantial amounts of consumption goods were exported to countries at war but only repaid years later (i.e. leading to an import of goods). This caused a situation in which subsistence of the population was seriously threatened by this scarcity. Limiting credit to nations at war were the most popular and reasonable interventions by neutral governments.

III. THE EFFECT OF CREDIT ON PRICES

Lowering interest rates not only reduces the production costs of durable goods, but also the production costs of firms in general (if the firm has outstanding loans). The decrease of the interest rate from

5 per cent to 4 per cent in the above example not only means a reduction of production costs of 1 per cent of the annual wages of 5,000 workers for the second, more capital-intensive firm but also a reduction of the annual wages of 10,000 workers by 1 per cent for *both* production methods.

The reduction in interest rates[11] leads to a reduction in production costs enjoyed by all firms and will tempt firms to increase their production: previously unprofitable production methods will benefit from the reduction in credit costs and become profitable. Consequently banks will generally grant more credit (*ceteris paribus*). A credit expansion will take place as long as it is not preceded by a particularly high number of 'credit closures' or 'credit consolidations'. A credit expansion means that more credits are granted than 'closed' or 'consolidated'; hence, the number of existing credits and in particular the amount of nominal purchasing power in the economy increases.

How does the multiplication of credit relations, the credit expansion, affect the prices of goods? It is the old question of the effect of monetary expansion on the prices of goods which appears here in a newer, modern and appropriate form for a cash-saving economy.

The effect of an increase in money on the goods prices, or the purchasing power of money as it is occasionally called, has been described often enough. We can restrict ourselves to stating that the increased purchasing power of the firm (competing with other firms) will cause first an increase in wages and then in prices for raw materials. Every stage of the supply chain will then 'recover' the increase in costs[12] by raising their own prices and this eventually leads to an increase in all prices (including consumption goods) in the economy.

In general, a credit expansion only takes place after a decrease in the interest rate, which means that there is a peculiar interdependency between the interest rate on money and goods prices:[13] interest rate

[11] Maintaining the same interest rate when expected profits increase has the same effect as a decrease in interest rate.

[12] See the discussion towards the end of chapter [1.]A in the first part, section II, subsection A on 'Credit creation'.

[13] Cf. Knut Wicksell, *Geldzins und Güterpreise* (Jena: Gustav Fischer, 1898) [Knut Wicksell, *Interest and Prices*, trans. Richard F. Kahn (London: Macmillan, 1936)] which certainly assumes a different cause to reach similar conclusions.

reductions[14] and price increases run in parallel. The interrelationship is fundamentally caused by the role of interest rates and the prices of goods (wages should also be included in the price of goods in a wider sense) as production cost coefficients for the firm. Every reduction in interest rates reduces the cost of credit and, hence, enables the firm to pay higher wages and prices for raw materials; increased purchasing will induce competition for the initially unchanged quantity of labour and raw materials and both prices will rise. The frequent claim that interest rate reductions (as far as they aim at increasing the quantity of money) do not have a long-run benefit for industry is in this respect true. However, it would be wrong to assume that the credit expansion accompanying a decrease in interest rates has no effect on the economy at all. Even if industry does not benefit, the income of the dependent circles (especially labourers) increases in line with prices. They also obtain a relative advantage over those with fixed incomes, that is, pensioners and fixed-wage earners. Hence, the class of individuals with fixed incomes has to bear the cost of the decreasing interest rate. Nevertheless, it remains to be shown that there will consequently be an increase in production. The argument, particularly used by quantity theorists, that the increase in the quantity of money accompanying a decrease in interest rate can never increase a country's industrial activity because the higher quantity of money can only buy the same amount of capital goods since prices increase, is erroneous.

The rise in prices due to an expansion of credit will be stronger the longer the credit term is and therefore the longer the credit closure is postponed. Credits enabling and inducing more roundabout methods of production do not only affect prices through the generation of bank money, that is, an increase in the quantity of money. They also exert upward pressure on goods' prices by retaining goods in the flow of production for a longer period of time. Over time, the goods' supply readjusts its composition, but a credit expansion can cause a drastic, temporary rise in the relative price of current and future consumption goods. The marked and durable effect of consumption credit (with war credits as its main component) on prices has its theoretic reason in the uncertainty about when the credit is going to be closed.[15]

[14] Under certain circumstances high prices run in parallel with high interest rates. This is caused by absolutely high interest rates, which are low compared to expected profits and therefore relatively low. Cf. footnote 11 in this chapter.

[15] The price rise during the war in connection with the amount of notes in circulation generated a plethora of comments on inflation, in particular in daily and

IV. THE EFFECT OF CREDIT ON THE QUANTITY OF GOODS

The chapter so far could give the impression that the quantity theory is correct. According to the quantity theory an increase in the quantity of money or credit expansion can have no other than an inflationary effect. Thereby any such expansion exhausts its potential and has no power left to increase the amount of capital goods.

The increase of money and credit expansion has another effect other than being inflationary. It has been barely observed and, to our knowledge, received insufficient theoretical analysis of its consequences: a credit expansion increases the amount of produced goods. Hence, it not only alters the length and the *relative* width of the flow of goods in an economy, but also causes an increase in the *absolute* width of the flow.

This fact has been generally denied because theoretical considerations are usually underpinned by an economic state as the classics describe it rather than the modern economy. As a consequence, almost all of the relevant literature explicitly denies the positive effect of an increase in the quantity of money on the amount of capital and

financial newspapers. However, it did not unearth any new perspectives or arguments. Mostly it was a repetition of quantity theoretic (occasionally banking theoretic) views. The writing of Robert Liefmann, *Geld und Gold [Money and Gold]* (Stuttgart and Berlin: Deutsche Verlagsanstalt, 1916) and *Die Geldvermehrung im Weltkriege und die Beseitigung ihrer Folgen [The Growth of Money during the World War and the Remediation of its Consequences]* (Stuttgart and Berlin: Deutsche Verlagsanstalt, 1918) contain virtually nothing on the inflation problem, i.e. under what conditions the increase of money in circulation increases prices. The few remarks which can be found (*Geldvermehrung im Weltkriege und die Beseitigung ihrer Folgen* p. 74), are subject to the same criticism as von Beckerath (cf. footnote 2 in this chapter), from whom the remarks are borrowed. The quantity theory as an explanation of the price level is only a first approximation and rough reflection of the real conditions, even if it is expanded to be based on the quantity of purchasing power (which seems a fitting expression in this context). As is generally known, the quantity theory states that an increase in the quantity of money causes an increase of all prices, because the higher amount of money is used to buy an unchanged amount of goods. It is therefore only correct if an increase in the quantity of money does not change the quantity of goods and, vice versa, an increase in the quantity of goods does not change the amount of money in circulation. But this is not the case. Neither the amount of goods is fixed or independent of the quantity of money nor is the quantity of money independent of developments in the goods market. For the first part compare the following section and for the second part of the statement compare n. 34 of this chapter and n. 1 of chapter [2.]C. in the second part on 'the effect of credit on savings'.

goods. The idea is called amateurish, inflationist, or even a regression to the ideas of John Law. In the economy of the classics the statement of the purely inflationary effect of an increase of money is correct. The production technology available, which can almost be called primitive compared to modern times, could only meet increased demand if an increase in the labour force preceded it. The much lower wealth of nations in those times meant that labour was virtually fully utilised; hence, an increase in money could only lead to higher prices and not increase the quantity of goods in an economy already operating at full capacity. The problem of booms, that is, demand increases inducing production increases, which was so characteristic of the economy during the last decade, did not feature in the economy of the classics and, thus, did not play any role in their theoretical deductions.[16]

In the modern economy, credit expansion grants additional purchasing power to firms and induces higher demand for goods and workers, thereby causing both a rise in production and prices. A real and absolute increase in production, not just of individual industries, but of all industries in their entirety manifests itself. That this is possible in a modern and not in a classical economy is due to two reasons. First, the increased utilization of machines in the production process has progressed astonishingly since classical times. For example, increasing the production of mass-produced goods in a factory from 1,000 to 2,000 pieces does not require doubling the number of workers, but only an increase of perhaps 10 per cent or 20 per cent. In earlier times with a much stronger focus on manual labour, the number of workers would need to be increased by at least 80 per cent or 90 per cent if not 100 per cent. Second, technological progress caused a much higher level of wealth in the modern economy. This caused a vast reserve of un- or underutilised labour (pensioners, woman, and labourers ready to work overtime) which can easily meet increased labour demand. Both elements could be characterised as the 'elasticity' of the economy. Apart from the industrial booms in the pre-war period, the enormous potential of this elasticity has been shown especially by the war-time boom. Production was increased to levels deemed impossible and this happened during a time in which most parties normally involved in the

[16] There is virtually no mention of the existence of booms in Adam Smith.

production process were conscripted into the army and therefore not available as productive labour.[17]

How can credit expansion force individual workers into the service of production? A country's reserve of labour (i.e. all those who are not active in production) is not employed, according to the subjective value theory, because they attach a higher value to their 'leisure' than the wage rate they expect from working. The pensioner does not work because the pension payments ensure already his subsistence and because the marginal utility from consuming non-elementary commodities is lower than the amenity of leisure. The vast majority of women do not work for the same reason. The worker not doing overtime does not do so because he values the calm of the ninth hour higher than the wage expected from working overtime. The typical unemployed person does not work because he prefers not to work rather than working for a wage that does not guarantee subsistence.

As explained earlier, competitive firms expand production as a reaction to lower interest rates (i.e. a credit expansion) which therefore leads to higher wages. The wages increase relative to the currently prevailing market rate or in the case of the unemployed only exceed zero. This will alter the decision problem of those currently not ready to work. The value of working is now preferred to not working; they become the 'marginal worker' instead of being the 'marginal non-worker'. The offered wage increases in real terms and the behavioural change is not due to self-deception caused by some kind of nominal illusion. Certainly the rise in wages will cause a rise in the prices of consumption goods, because they are faced with higher demand, but the wage increase is real not only nominal. Competition will force prices to equal costs but only the wage share of production costs will increase, not the expenditures on capital. Thus, the goods prices will rise by less than the increase in wages. Therefore it is a real increase in wages, which is a real wage increase. The increased wage carries a higher wage weight in the decision problem of the labourer because other fixed-income elements remain notionally constant (i.e. they devalue in real terms).

[17] Therefore the war did not show the impracticality of the capitalist production system but, on the contrary, its enormous potential. The purpose of the production, not the process itself, was wrong. If the financial resources (using the same financing arrangements) were used to build houses, means of transport and labour-saving machines, then the satisfaction of all needs would have brought the golden age, even for the expropriated.

The credit expansion caused the following changes in the economy: a *change in the distribution* causes an *increase in production*. The increase in production takes place because more people in the economy work. The distribution changes, such that workers receive a higher share of the national product than before. This share does not only reflect the value added by labour; in addition, through inflation they also receive a certain share of the national income previously accruing to fixed-income earners (capitalist, pensioners, and fixed-wage earners). A shift of real income towards workers and away from capitalists causes an increase in production. It also confirms that distribution, like consumption, logically precedes production even though it only occurs after it.[18]

It is, nevertheless, possible that pensioners and capitalists do not incur a loss of capital due to the credit expansion, despite the inflation-induced shift in the distribution. However, in agricultural production a loss will be unavoidable as a consequence of credit expansion. The technical law of decreasing yields at the extensive margin will always mean an increase in the price of agricultural produce. In industrial production a credit expansion can even take place without an increase in price and in some cases a price reduction is even possible. In these industries it is possible that a law of increasing returns to scale prevails; the increase in production caused by credit expansion could contribute to attaining technical perfection of the production method and consequently to a decrease in prices. It is therefore possible, that because of better production methods the prices do not rise as expected but in fact decrease; in these cases, not only the wage labourers benefit from the credit expansion but also capitalists and fixed-wage earners, albeit on a smaller scale.

The main relevance of credit expansion lies not so much in the sheer increase of produced goods or employment, but rather that it counteracts the underutilization of labour that can so easily occur in the modern economy. In the modern economy, every year a certain amount of labourers are made redundant by the continuing switch to less labour-intensive production methods, unless credit expansion is used. Furthermore, modern industrial countries are still experiencing a strong move to urbanization. However, the demand for labour does not increase in line with population growth and, therefore, a certain

[18] Similar to consumption, distribution should be treated before not after production in a systematic treatment.

proportion of this population increase remains unemployed. The resulting oversupply of labour exerts pressure on the wage rate (and therefore goods' prices) until the wage rate decreases sufficiently to make new production possibilities profitable and reduce the attractiveness of work to convert some 'marginal workers' to 'marginal non-workers'. Hence, a modern economy tends to experience distributional changes in favour of capitalists, who have a nominally fixed income and benefit from a decrease in prices, and away from labourers, whose wages decrease more than prices. In other words, all effects of the classical theory of the reserve army of labour with constant capital will come into force.[19] This is where credit expansion enters the picture as a corrective force and as an important social factor.[20] Credit expansion increases the demand for labour and groups of labourers who were not part of the production process as a consequence of the static credit structure and they re-join the productive labour force; it prevents the reduction of goods prices and the consequent increase in the rent for capital. In short, all effects of the classical theory of the reserve army of labour with increasing 'capital'[21] will come into force. This does not, however, constitute a causal relation for the increase in capital, that is, capital goods. An increase in capital goods can only occur with reduced capital prices and, hence, wage rates, but not in situations with increasing prices and wages. The high level of prices and wages is not maintained by more abundant 'capital' but by *credit*.

[19] Usually it is assumed, however, that the shift in distribution is caused by increasing interest rates. It remains doubtful whether increasing interest rates are realistic in this case because the marginal entrepreneur needs to pay for the employment of the superfluous workers using a less capital-intensive production technology out of the gains from declining wage rates and hence cannot bear any increased interest payments. It is falling prices, not increasing interest rates, which shift the distribution in favour of the capitalists.

[20] Credit expansion will not be inflationary in this case. The central question to the 'inflation problem' is whether a reserve army of labour has been built up in the economy. If goods were stockpiled or if the new purchasing power was generated through trading, which is seen by some as crucial, is not relevant. Cf. the beginning of this chapter and footnotes 52 and 53 in my essay Albert Hahn, 'Der Gegenstand des Geld- und Kapitalmarktes' [The nature of the money and capital market], *Archiv für Sozialwissenschaft und Sozialpolitik* 46, (1919).

[21] Also here it is usually assumed that the change in distribution is mediated by a change in interest rate (a decrease in this case). A decrease in interest rate does not need to occur necessarily in the situation described above. More credits will be sought even if the interest rate does not decrease because the decrease in wages causes a decrease in production costs and therefore offers an incentive to expand production.

From all these consideration follows: the quantity theoretic view, which is incidentally shared by almost all money, credit, and capital theorists, that an increase in money or credit respectively does not increase the production of goods is not only inaccurate but outright wrong.[22] Every credit expansion causes a shift in distribution and therefore an increase in production. Credit draws the goods from a nirvana, in which they would remain without the credit expansion. Whether or not a credit expansion is always beneficial to a country remains unanswered. It is beyond economics to judge whether or not production should be increased at the cost of capitalists, pensioners, and fixed-wage earners. It seems to be a theoretical problem but is in fact a political decision.

V. THE EFFECT OF CREDIT ON CAPITAL AND THE WEALTH OF NATIONS

Our analysis of the effect of credit on the goods sphere also answers the question of how credit affects capital goods, that is, 'capital'. Capital goods are like all other goods influenced by credit in their quantity, price, and composition. Credit is the primary reason for their production and determines their properties as a capital good.

This statement is of utmost importance[23] as from it follows that establishing new companies or production routes are independent of a smaller or larger 'capital' stock. A lack of capital can never undermine such an establishment because credit can allocate the capital required.

It follows necessarily from the arguments above and is confirmed by practical experience that the establishment of an industry, which is in the interest of a country, never failed because of a lack of factories or tools. If no factories were already established then they would be

[22] The only correct statement is that the quantity of money is irrelevant in a static analysis. The prevailing opinion's critique of John Law, who identifies a wealth in capital with the quantity of money, is certainly supported by us.

[23] It is not only important for the theory of banking but for almost all assessments of general economic problems e.g. the assessment of socialism and plans towards it must be affected by our assessment. Exploitation as a result of monopolistic firms with a limited amount of capital goods is different from exploitation as a result of credit, which is accessible to every trustworthy entrepreneur.

built as soon as the need arose, which in the worst case could cause an increase in the prices of today's consumption goods and therefore impose a reduction in consumption on fixed-income earners and pensioners.[24] However, the factory could not be built if the means of sustenance for the workers for building the factory and tools were lacking. This can give rise to the argument that establishing a new industry, in fact, depends on a stock of 'goods dedicated for its establishment', but the argument is not tenable. The present stands on the shoulders of the past in as much as the individuals involved in production rely on the past to provide their sustenance and certain goods; otherwise, they would not have any food, clothes, housing, or tools to use in the production process. If this normal stock of goods is available, as is always the case in a regular modern economy, then the establishment of new industries is independent of the capital stock. The addition of firms is not dependent on a *larger* capital stock as the size of the capital stock is irrelevant for the degree to which labour is used: a fully employed population working intensively does not necessarily require more goods like food, clothes, and housing than a half-employed population.[25]

Accordingly, the importance of the stock of capital goods for the country's production is not as high as the prevailing opinion estimates. It is certainly of lesser importance than the topic we shall look at now: the significance of the level of the *wealth* of a nation, following Adam Smith, and how the credit-granting practices of banks affect it.

Without assessing the controversies surrounding the wealth of a nation, we define it as the stock of goods available for consumption. As an indicator of the size of an economy we use the amount of labour used in production. We do not consider land or raw materials as constituents of wealth in their own right, but as a factor augmenting labour productivity. The discovery of a very profitable (i.e. little labour time is needed in exploitation) coal mine causes an increase in

[24] See the discussion towards the end of section II 'The effect of credit on the composition of goods' in this chapter.

[25] This should also address the criticism of Siegfried Budge, 'Waren- oder Anweisungstheorie des Geldes?' [A commodity or credit theory of money?], *Archiv für Sozialwissenschaft und Sozialpolitik* 46, (1919) and of Schumpeter's similar thoughts in Joseph Schumpeter 'Das Sozialprodukt und die Rechenpfennige' [The social product and penny-pinchers], *Archiv für Sozialwissenschaft und Sozialpolitik* 44, (1917).

the wealth of the nation only because it improves the productivity of miners.

The wealth of a nation (i.e. the stock of available goods in an economy) can be increased in two ways. On the one hand, the flow of all goods can be widened to continue the metaphor, that is, the production of all goods increases. In this case, the wealth of a nation increases because the available stock of goods is enriched by the goods not yet consumed. On the other hand, the wealth of nation can increase if the flows of goods is lengthened, that is, more goods are produced which are consumed over a longer period. In this case, the goods will disappear from the economy at a later time and, therefore, the stock of goods at any time will increase: a long river carries more water than a shorter one.

To satisfy the demands of a certain generation it is generally better to increase wealth in the first way. There is no interest in maximizing the amount of all goods existing at the same time but to maximize the amount of available consumption goods. A nation consuming large amounts of goods is richer than a nation with lower but more durable stocks of goods. However, there is another reason outside economics for increasing wealth the second way: to increase the stock of goods, that is, to increase the stock of mobile goods and the existence of as many buildings as possible. Producing more durable goods is advantageous should war or other events reduce the productive capacity below the necessary level of consumption. In this case, the existence of many long goods flows is an extraordinary advantage because goods maturing for consumption and durable goods still allow for further consumption. As long as the river is long enough, water still leaves the river at its estuary even if its source begins to run dry.

The way in which credit expansion can affect the width and the relative length of a goods flow has been discussed extensively earlier; similarly, its consequent effect on the nation's wealth has already been extensively covered.[26] We want to add here that the increase in production (as a consequence of credit expansion) described above can only be sustained as long as the credit expansion also causes an increase in consumption as well. If goods, be it from shorter or longer goods flows, reach their maturity and do not meet any demand, then their production is impossible over the long term. No matter how

[26] See sections II 'The effect of credit on the composition of goods' and IV 'The effect of credit on the quantity of goods'.

strong a river is, it will stagnate if its water cannot run off at the estuary: 'Wenn nicht konsumiert wird, kann nicht produziert werden' ['*Consumption* is the sole end and purpose of all *production*'].

Credit expansion usually induces enough consumption to meet the increase in production. The workers' newly acquired purchasing power (either as cheques or banknotes) induces demand and enables the producer to sell the increased production, thereby, enabling him to pay back the credit or in other words to 'close' it. As discussed above,[27] *the increase in production is possible in particular because higher wages are offered and the labour force expanded, that is, labourers receive a higher share of the national income for consumption. Generally, the increase in production is met by an increase in consumption.*

How far can production be increased by credit expansion? The theoretically and practically important question would be answered by: the positive effect on production should be there as long as credit expansion is able to recruit new workers for production, that is, until wage increases have attracted the last worker in the reserve army of labour.[28] The experience with credit and money expansion, which accompanied the large economic fluctuations in the last decades before the War shows, however, that this theoretical boundary of increased production and consumption is not reached. Production stagnates, which is caused by a stagnation of sales and consumption.

What is the reason for the stagnation in sales? It is the central question of any business cycle and crisis theory: what is the cause for a general stagnation of sales during the course of the boom period?

Over the course of centuries this question has often[29] been answered in the following way: the general stagnation of sales is a situation in which those who produce lack the purchasing power to consume in times of crisis and those who hold the purchasing power choose not to consume and build up savings. Equally often this notion was countered by the argument that all production either by entrepreneurs or workers induces consumption by them; the revenue generated by this consumption has the effect that the new production is met by the required

[27] See the discussion in section IV 'The effect of credit on the quantity of goods' in this chapter.

[28] One can assume that this was really the case in Germany at the end of the war. Even very high wage rates were not able to recruit new workers for industry, which suffered more and more as a result of this lack of labour.

[29] In particular by Malthus and his followers.

demand (which is the quintessence of the famous Say's law).[30] It is well known that the argument was so powerful that, despite practical experience, many writers refused to acknowledge the possibility of an oversupply, or reasoned that it is only a summation of oversupplies on individual markets.

We believe that our analysis of the banking processes associated with granting credit can edify the theory that production and consumption reaches equilibrium autonomously. Particularly useful is the insight that banks can freely create money and that as consequence the demand for money in the economy fluctuates. The argument that supply necessarily creates demands seems incorrect if the producers of the previously consumed goods save and do not consume. The lost purchasing power is not necessarily compensated by credit expansion by the banks.

This counterargument seems to warrant a return to a train of thought by Malthus'[31] who when he was analysing the cause of changes in the business cycle and the crisis believed: The stagnation of demand at the height of a boom is caused by working individuals saving instead of consuming. The usually circulating bank balances are consolidated into savings[32] and are not used to express demand on the goods markets any more. Demand does not meet production anymore and the flow of goods starts to cease. The decrease in demand causes a fall in prices and industry cannot afford to pay high wages. Wages begin to fall and workers, who picked up employment in the light of

[30] Cf. Jean-Baptiste Say, *Lettres a M. Malthus [Letters to Malthus]*, (1820), letter II.

[31] The clarity of Malthus insights is astounding. His critics claimed that all savings automatically increase the demand for goods and Malthus countered with the following argument: 'ihr Hauptirrtum in der Annahme liege, dass aus der Ansammlung von selbst Nachfrage hervorgehe' [their main error is to assume that any accumulation generates demand by itself]. This argument is also true nowadays, in particular for those believers of the prevailing opinion asserting an absolute dependence of credit on the amount of savings. Despite this congruence, our notion differs from Malthus's in one important aspect. Malthus locates the reason for increased savings in the income distribution which is disadvantageous for workers, whereas we see the credit-induced increase in production and the consequential psychological attitude as the reason.

[32] On the importance of savings in this context cf. John A. Hobsen *The Evolution of Modern Capitalism*' (London: The Walter Scott Publishing Company, 1902), chapter 11, paragraph 7 and following. The *Amtsblatt des deutschen Sparkassenverbandes* [*Gazette of the German Association of Mutual Savings Banks*] shows in April 1920, the month when demand stagnation set in, a massive increase in savings by 1bn marks, which provides interesting evidence of the relation between savings and demand stagnation.

higher wages, exit the productive processes. Production falls and in short, all those positive effects at the start of the credit expansion reverse. The unused labour time causes a great and permanent loss for the wealth of a nation. It is permanent because the time without production is lost forever. The saying 'time is money', usually only thought of in the context of the individual, also holds for the economy as a whole.

The final question of why working individuals suddenly spend less than they earn remains. The reasons for this phenomenon cannot lie solely in the domain of economics but are sociological and psychological in nature. Underconsumption has its reason in the psyche of the working man: a worker, an industrialist, a merchant does not simply want to spend more just because of higher income. The conservatism inherent in humans in all their social life, but particularly in their lifestyle, means that consumption remains within certain boundaries. People do not consume more simply because more is produced. People do not relinquish payment for their services[33] but demand it in a different form, namely in the form of investable means. Instead of satisfying current consumption wants, individuals satisfy their need for savings and investable means[34] to secure future consumption. As soon as their demand for consumption is satisfied to a certain degree, people start to feel, so to speak, in a mercantile not physiocratic fashion.[35]

[33] The crucial point is that he also does not stop working, as supporters of the barter-inspired doctrine of self-equilibrating supply and demand suppose. Compare e.g. J.-C.-L. Simonde de Sismondi, *Etudes sur les sciences sociales [Studies in the Social Sciences]* (Paris: Treuttel & Würtz, 1837), chapter 1: 'Es macht ihm (scl. Dem wirtschaftenden Menschen) mehr Freude, sich auszuruhen, als Dinge zu erzeugen, die er niemals brauchen wird.' [It gives him (the economic man) more pleasure to rest himself rather than producing things he will never use.] This has to be contested in particular for modern, capitalistic man.

[34] Unless some special legal actions (e.g. lifting the bank secrecy) or a collapse in the monetary system reinstates 'saving' in the form of goods.

[35] This adds to the reasons why the quantity theory of money can only be a rough explanation of the relations between the quantity of money and goods prices and why the core of the banking theory, which assumes an automatic elimination of additional, superfluous money, is correct. If the multiplication of money also brings a reduction in its 'velocity', then the increase in money cannot, or at least not necessarily, lead to an increase in prices. The possibility of a change in the velocity is usually granted in the theory through so-called 'hoarding', but the determinants of these 'hoards' are usually not assessed. In particular, the relation with the satisfaction of consumer's demands and therefore with the productivity of the economy is not made. That this relation is not only theoretical is also confirmed by certain experiences over the last

This gives rise to a problem of theoretical interest rather than of practical relevance: during a credit expansion, is there a possibility of preventing potential stagnation and its consequential loss in terms of a nation's welfare? As the stagnation of production occurs as a consequence of the stagnation of demand, this question is identical to: Is there a possibility of influencing the economy such that producers maintain production even though sales decrease and therefore goods are produced on stock rather than for consumption?

Such possibilities exist at least in theory. One possibility is to encourage firms to maintain production, adding and especially lowering the price for credit as soon as consumption begins to stagnate. That this policy really has such an effect is shown by the following thought: The entrepreneur is usually constrained from producing on stock, which is to begin production without being confident of selling it in the foreseeable future, by the interest payments due from the start of the production until the sale of the product. This forces the entrepreneur to aim for 'credit closure', that is, to sell the product, attracting purchasing power, and to pay off the credit. It is clear that a reduction in the interest rate reduces motivation to pay off credit quickly. The lower the bank's interest rate, the lower is the firm's incentive to sell goods. Theoretically if the interest rate approaches zero per cent then a firm is indifferent between selling and keeping on stock, whether or not they are consumed. Reducing the interest rate to zero could therefore lead to a continuous[36] production of goods regardless of their sales[37] but would also reduce the value of money. Certainly, this is only true if the entrepreneur does not need to worry about any further storage costs. Otherwise reducing the interest to zero

few years. At the beginning of the war, when the economy's productivity was high and consumer demand could be largely met, prices increased only slightly despite a large credit expansion. At the end of the war and after the revolution, when productivity was severely depressed and demand was often not satisfied, price rises occurred disproportionally faster. In the following time of redevelopment, when productivity rose again, the price rise was comparatively modest despite a continuing issuance of state debt. The analysis in the text also reveals how invalid Liefmann's assumption is, according to which the level of income, hence the receipts, is crucial for the level of prices. One should rather say that the level of expenditure is the crucial variable.

[36] Even the prospect of a potential cancellation of the granted credits, which grow into gigantic sums, cannot frighten the entrepreneurs. They are always able to obtain credit from someone else because credit without cost is seemingly a free good.

[37] In the case of durable goods, whether the received rent payments exceeds the amortization costs.

per cent would not be sufficient to induce continued production. It would require a negative interest rate, that is, interest is paid to the debtor, to ensure the profitability of production and motivate production to continue regardless of consumption. This would mean that the debtor receives interest payments from the creditor and not that the creditor receives interest payments from the debtor. In practice, the possibility of 'negative interest rates' would fail because anyone holding deposits could simply withdraw them as cash to relieve them from the interest burden.

The other possibility of continuing production despite a slack in consumption would happen if someone bought all surplus production to stockpile goods. This of course would be only viable if that someone had access to huge amounts of interest-free loans. Otherwise he would not be in a position to 'hold' these stocks. The government is such a privileged debtor. Despite paying interest on its bonds, it could always pass them on to citizens and hence enjoy practically interest-free loans. Moreover, the government would not need to take these interest payments into account when making decisions (unlike any other economic subject). Therefore, if the government aims to have a huge stock of goods for non-economic, particularly political or military reasons, it could act as the buyer of surplus production. It could start buying as soon as consumption begins to stagnate, secure the stocks of goods it deems necessary and keep production going.[38] The taxes necessary to serve the interest payments should be (at least theoretically)[39] easy to raise: the same amount owed by the government as debt is available in the economy as money and bank balances; it is also easily taxable because it is accrued by individuals as payments for services which are only demanded because government does so and are therefore boom profits.

[38] Malthus already made the suggestion that government should build roads, buildings, and should even spend on entirely unproductive activities to avoid the stagnation of sales. Cf. Thomas Robert Malthus, *Principles of Political Economy*, 2nd ed. (London: W. Pickering, 1836), chapter 7, section 3.

[39] Unfortunately only theoretically, as the limited success of the taxing efforts to meet war debts shows. The only difference to the situation mentioned in the text was that the acquired stocks were consumed immediately.

[2.]C. The Effect of Credit on Savings

To further complete the analysis of the effect of credit on the economy, we need to investigate the effect of credit on the accumulation of savings. The importance we attach to this question may seem in contradiction to the importance we attach to savings elsewhere. In fact, and contrary to the general belief, we do not think that savings are a precondition of credit or determine its amount. Nevertheless, the problem is of sufficient interest to us because the amount of savings in the economy determines whether a new credit increases the number of granted credits at a given time and therefore contributes to the expansion of credit. Only if a new credit is not simultaneously met with increased savings does it have the full effect on quantity, composition, and prices of goods described earlier. Hence, this negative effect of new savings warrants our attention on the factors affecting savings.

As pointed out above in the first section, no genuinely new deposits can be made without a preceding credit creation at the same or another bank. Hence, no savings can be accumulated without credit creation preceding it. As no general deposits can be created without credit creation, then obviously no savings can be created: in the end all savings are necessarily the consolidation of ordinary deposits. From this also follows that the more credit is expanded, the more savings are created in the economy.

This assertion is not surprising in itself, because it is only the reverse of our main insight that credit creation precedes the creation of deposits. However, we do also claim that an expansion of credit not only increases the absolute amount of savings proportionally, but also the accumulation of savings will take place much faster. For example: if we double the amount of ongoing credit in an economy from x billion to two times x billions, then savings will increase from x billion to two times x billion; the accumulation of the second billion of savings will take place much faster, say twice as fast as for the first billion. Credit expansion does not only increase but also accelerate savings. This is confirmed by the effects of the enormous credit expansion during the war on the accumulation of savings.[1] This credit creation not only caused the accumulation of an extraordinary amount of savings, but also the fact that it was built up in an astonishingly short time. It is well known that the accumulation of savings was so fast that war-time bonds could be issued every six months, that is, savings were transformed into bonds.[2] If this had not been the case, that is, if savings had not been consolidated with such speed, then the floating war debt of the Reich would have increased even more than it did and the successful financing of the war would have been uncertain.[3]

How can the accelerating accumulation of savings after a credit expansion be explained? The explanation lies in the peculiar psychological state of economic man who is inclined to save rather than consume additional income. He who produces more, does not necessarily consume more, but saves the amount not required for consumption.

[1] The prevailing theory has a fundamentally different view of the cause and determinants of the accumulation of savings. It identifies the level of interest rate as the crucial determinant. Most often, most recently and in detail by Gustav Cassel in his *The Nature and Necessity of Interest* (London: Macmillan, 1903) it is assumed that the lower the interest rate, the lower is the propensity or opportunity to save and therefore savings are lower. At the same time, Wicksell claims that savings do not decrease even with low interest rates, because individuals need to maintain savings in order to ensure the same level of consumption for themselves or their children. An observer of the practice will conclude that no other determinant is of lesser importance than the interest rate. An investigation into the laws of savings accumulation would need to test how an increase in income at a constant consumption rate changes the propensity to save and similarly how a decrease in income threatens the usual level of consumption and destroys savings. The effect of certain frictions in the economic gearbox would need to be investigated in this context. It seems that savings increase so strongly in the beginning stages of an increase in the quantity of money because workers in the earlier stages of the supply chain ask for too low wages; they are unaware of the true situation in the market and could demand higher wages without forcing marginal workers into unemployment. This seems to be an important factor in explaining certain fluctuations in the accumulation of savings during the war and after the revolution.

[2] The issuing of war time bonds is a typical case of 'credit closure'. See chapter [1.] B, section II, subsection 1 on 'The extent of means of primary banks'.

[3] We do not even consider the deposits which were a consequence of emptying the warehouses, etc. and which were de-consolidated later.

The fact that credit expansion can stimulate savings, that is, that the economy has higher levels of savings[4] after a credit expansion, is also used in practice when placing obligations and stocks. This is certainly guided by intuition rather than by theoretical considerations. We believe that the habit of selling certain options to banks first and placing it with the public only after enough savings are accumulated (using 'credit elimination') can largely be explained by the phenomenon mentioned above. One wants to allow time for the savings-generating force of the purchasing power granted by banks before calling on the public to absorb the assets issued.[5]

[4] If in this time the status of the banks becomes more strained, then this is because of the demand for credit increasing even more than credit consolidation.

[5] It seems obvious to use the sum of annual savings to estimate the increase in the nation's wealth. In fact, there is a large amount of statistics departing from this assumption. The best known is probably by Karl Theodor Helfferich, *Deutschlands Volkswohlstand 1888–1913 [The Wealth of the German People 1888–1913]*, 2nd ed. (Berlin: Verlag von Georg Stilke, 1914), page 115. We do not think that the amount of savings can lead to estimates of the level of the nation's wealth. Firstly, one would need to consider all deposits not only savings deposits to judge the available assets in the economy. A factory increases the nation's wealth, even if the purchasing power created for its erection has not been consolidated. Secondly, the quantity of available assets cannot be reflected by monetary values, which also makes all estimations of the nation's wealth problematic. The nominal prices, which are used to value assets on the balance sheet, are only comparing units in nature. To add these units up to reach the nation's wealth is as illogical as any attempt to add up numbers of unknown dimensions to reach a result of a known dimension. Also: Any such method would need to think of a country as richer if a shortage of water causes a positive price for the usually free water. Cf. the introduction to John Stuart Mill, *Grundsätze der politischen Ökonomie [Principles of Political Economy]*, trans. Adolph Soetbeer, 2nd ed. (Hamburg: Perthes-Besser und Mauke, 1864) for an argument against this assumption.

[2.]D. Credit and Business Cycles

All effects of credit on the production and distribution of goods were essentially deduced from the statement that credit can stimulate the economy.[1] It seems therefore only logical to ask if and to what extent the large periodic business cycles of the last decades before the war were due to credit expansion or contraction.

This question, whether the business cycle can be explained by the prevailing credit relations, is usually negated by most business-cycle theorists. It is beyond the scope of this work to counter this opinion and develop a positive crisis and business-cycle theory. We shall only make the following remarks: The boom in a business cycle is typically characterised by the following: New companies are founded and new buildings (both for industry and as homes) are planned. Banks are registering a higher demand, the status of banks (in particular the central bank) deteriorates and the interest rate starts to climb moderately. Simultaneously, the surge in building activities and the new formation of companies causes a higher employment rate and therefore more purchasing power is available to the population. Wages and prices rise, production increases; in short everything is flourishing. Only fixed-wage earners and pensioners worry about inflation.

Over the course of the business cycle, production prepares to produce ever more. The older production facilities are producing at full speed and the newer facilities finally become productive and multiply the overall production of goods. However, this state does not persist for long and the downturn (or the crisis in abrupt cases) sets in soon. As sales start to stagnate and goods start to stockpile, firms are forced to decrease their prices, incur losses, and production

[1] Cf. the discussion towards the end of chapter [2.]A in the second part, section II on 'The monetary perspective'.

shrinks. At this time interest rates soar, as banks become anxious about their liquidity due to some defaults on loans. They try to ameliorate their position by increasing their interest rates and bringing credit to a closure. Some production and construction projects become unprofitable and come to a halt. The construction sector with the long gestation period for its projects is especially affected by these interest rate changes: new buildings remain unfinished, others are repossessed or auctioned as a consequence of the higher mortgage payments.

This short exposition of boom and bust shows how similar the respective developments are to the effects of a credit expansion. It suggests that business cycles in the modern economy are indeed a phenomenon induced by changes in the credit practices of banks or other creditors. If this conclusion is accepted, then it follows that the start of a boom is due to a credit expansion induced by low interest rates since low interest rates make new businesses seem profitable. As described above in more detail, the onset of stagnation can be explained by the growing tendency of consumers to save instead of consume over the course of a boom. Finally, the characteristics of a recession are caused by credit contractions,[2] which banks believe to be the necessary course of action once stagnation has taken its toll on a company's profitability.[3]

If the theory is correct, then the question of interest is whether or not a recession with its adverse consequences for the economy can be prevented by banks. We can think of two ways banks could do so. First, banks could require extremely high interest rates and prevent the business cycle. This would prevent the bust but also the boom and its associated search for new profitable production opportunities, the consequential creation of new production facilities and wealth, and the prosperity of the economy in general. Second, banks could avoid

[2] Some downturns seem not only to be aggravated but primarily caused by credit contraction. Cf. Joseph Esslen, *Konjunktur und Geldmarkt 1902–1908 [The Business Cycle and the Money Market 1902–1908]* (Stuttgart: J. G. Cotta, 1909), p. 28: 'Die Einschränkung der Bautätigkeit machte, wie meist, den Anfang. Denn hier wirkte die fortgesetzt wachsende Schwierigkeit Hypotheken und Baugelder zu schaffen, geradezu prohibitiv' [The contraction of the building industry made the start, as so often. Particularly in this area, the increasing difficulty of creating new mortgages and money to build is almost prohibitive.]

[3] The daily newspapers usually speak of a lack of capital when banks contract credit and interest rates rise. Of course, a lack of capital does not exist at a time when capital goods are stockpiled and await to be sold. What is lacking is credit and trust.

the bust by trying to perpetuate the boom; how this could be achieved (particularly through expanding credit and lowering interest rates) is shown in the analysis of the wealth of a nation above.[4] Whether or not this is a practical solution remains an open question. It is sufficient to state at this point that an everlasting boom is not just a utopia, at least in theory.[5,6]

[4] See the discussion towards the end of chapter [2.]B. in the second part, section V on 'The effect of credit on capital and the wealth of nations'.

[5] The experiences of the war showed that it is also practically possible to prolong a boom. During that time, the Reich created credit and used the purchasing power to demand goods and maintain an intensive boom period over many years.

[6] Mikhail Tugan-Baranowsky in his critique of the Marxian crisis theory arrives at a similar result (Mikhail Tugan-Baranowsky, *Die theoretischen Grundlagen des Marxismus [The Theoretical Foundations of Marxism]*, trans. unknown (Leipzig: Duncker & Humblot, 1905), p. 218 ff. We also want to refer to his assessment because if one would use our conception of capital as a starting point, one would arrive at the same position to the Marxian critique of capitalism as Tugan-Baranowsky.

Part Three

International Credit

[3.]A. Credit and Capital Export

Hardly any question has shown as many theoretical difficulties as the question of whether or not the export of 'capital' is advantageous to the nation. We believe that the results of our analysis can progress such an explanation substantially.

First and foremost, the object of a capital export needs to be clarified. It follows from our analysis of the object dealt on credit markets in general[1] that capital export does not mean (at least not necessarily) 'money' export; also 'claims' cannot be regarded as the object of capital exports, even if in some cases the 'capital' export is preceded by an export of a 'claim' (e.g. the transfer of a cheque issued by a domestic bank to a foreign debtor). This is because 'es ist ja klar, wenn das Ausland Kapital nötig hat, will es entweder konsumieren oder produzieren. Dazu dienen keine Papierstreifen, sondern real verwendbare Güter' [it is clear that if foreign countries require capital, they either want to consume or produce. This cannot be achieved by pieces of paper, but by real, usable goods].[2] On the other hand, goods (consumption or production goods) are not the object of capital export. If as many goods are imported as exported, then one cannot speak of a capital export: the export of goods does not equate to the export of capital.

Capital export only takes place when a nation exports goods or services without importing goods or services in return: goods exported without goods imported defines the nature of the capital export.[3,4]

[1] See chapter [1.]A in Part One, the section on the prevailing views of banking activities.

[2] August Sartorius von Waltershausen, *Das volkswirtschaftliche System der Kapitalanlage im Ausland [The economic system of investing capital abroad]* (Berlin: Georg Reimer, 1907), p. 64.

[3] This is analogous to credit markets in general which serve to postpone services in return. Cf. chapter [1.]A in the first part, section II, subsection 1 on 'Credit creation'.

[4] It is irrelevant whether 'capital' or 'consumption' goods are actually exported.

Capital exports will take place when the home country grants credit to a foreign country. Capital exports can actually only be effected in this way. This last claim is occasionally challenged, as some think that a large decrease in the prices of domestic goods can force goods upon foreign countries without any credit being granted.[5] This overlooks the fact that a unilateral export without an accompanying credit to the foreign country would increase the demand for domestic currency and prevent the trade. The currency of a country which only exports would necessarily appreciate relative to the foreign currency until the export was not profitable any more, even if the domestic price is low compared to the price abroad. The payment of goods and services can either be made by returning goods or services or needs to be deferred by granting credit.[6] A third way is notionally ruled out.[7]

Is therefore the export of capital little else than the consequence of granting credit to a foreign country and identical to it? Capital export has all the positive effects of a credit expansion; the capital export will increase domestic production, savings (owed by foreign debtors), and prices. The consequences of capital exports are fundamentally the same as for a credit expansion in general. Thus, whether exporting capital is desirable is analogous to credit expansion in general, and has to be decided on political rather than economic grounds. Whenever an answer is sought to this question it will need to be tested as to whether it is desirable to increase overall production and pay with a loss in the real value of money and all its consequent effects on society. The analysis will also need to consider the following aspect which differs for credit expansion at home or abroad. A credit expansion at home induces an increase in production which will sooner or later be consumed and generate utility. This may not be true for credits granted to a foreign country: it could be the case that the expected unmatched import of goods is not desirable or possible because of tariffs. In this case the credit granted to the foreign country is in fact a gift and the associated savings can never fulfil its purpose: financing the import of goods. As a result, the domestic population loses the increase in production forever. These relations need to be

[5] Cf. Sartorius von Watershausen, *Das volkswirtschaftliche System der Kapitalanlage im Ausland*, p. 82.

[6] This is why claiming at the same time to promote goods exports and to curtail capital exports is ludicrous.

[7] The submission of precious metals is theoretically unimportant in this context.

considered as well when judging the advantages of capital export. Mercantile thoughts, which place more importance on having financial claims abroad than on domestic consumption, need to be dismissed.[8] A few months after the war broke out the Scandinavian states took the right decision to ban any capital exports, that is, to prohibit the granting of credit to states at war, or make it subject to certain conditions.

[8] Mercantile instincts played an important role in France which pursued a policy of promoting capital exports before the war. It is true, when Satorius von Waltershausen says about France: 'Seine Bürger sind befriedigt in dem Gedanken, gespart zu haben. Die Milliarden in der Fremde . . . sind ein papierner Luxus eigener Art.' [Its citizens are satisfied with the thought of having saved. The billions abroad . . . are a paper-made luxury on its own.]

[3.]B. Credit and Foreign Currency

We do not want to extensively consider the difficult exchange rate problem. However, the effects of credit described need to be adjusted when taking exchange rates into account. We therefore only make a few remarks about the effect of credit on exchange rates.

What are the determinants for exchange rates to be this or that value? The view of classical monetary theorists (in particular Ricardo)[1] is that exchange rates are determined by the ratio of domestic and foreign goods' prices.[2] This view is certainly correct, but not precise enough to attain a quantitative not only a qualitative solution to the exchange rate problem as it does not specify whether all or only certain prices, and in the latter case which prices, are considered.

The analysis did not experience any refinement by the classics' successors despite this weakness and even the analyses by modern authors are not making progress in this direction. In the latter one can often find the assertion that the exchange rate is determined by the ratio of 'average prices' or the 'price level', which is fundamentally identical to the classical formulation and certainly not more precise.

It is not surprising that the classics could not quantitatively fix the relation between the goods' prices and the exchange rate; because they appear to associate the market price with an average price of all offered and demanded goods. The solution of the problem should be easy for current authors as they can apply the theory of marginal

[1] In particular see David Ricardo, *The High Price of Bullion* (London: James Murray, 1810) [It was not possible to ascertain which edition Hahn used].

[2] It is a great achievement of classical monetary theory to identify the primary determinant of the exchange rate, as it is its great weakness to ignore secondary determinants like international credit relations.

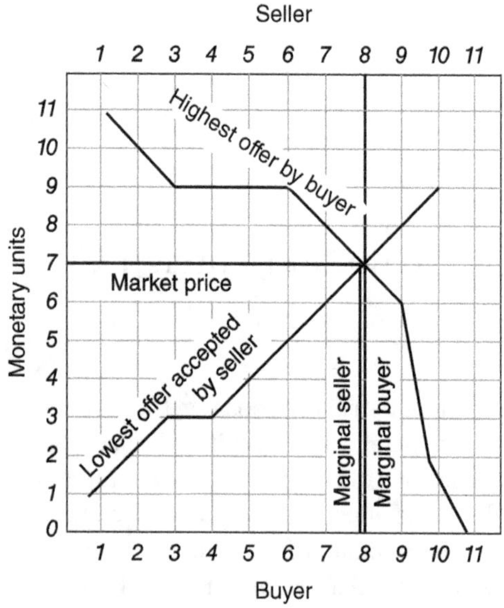

Figure 1

value and price to the market for foreign currencies. It is astonishing that no one (as far as we are aware) has undertaken this application.

The modern theory of prices states: the price is determined by the offer of the lowest bidder which is satisfied by the available supply and by the highest asking price which is accommodated by the demand.

It is well known that this allows determining the precise price graphically. As can be seen in Figure 1, one only needs to draw the bids of the buyers and the asking prices of the sellers for any amount of the good such that the buyers and sellers most likely to trade are on the same side. Connecting the dots results in two curves; their intersection determines the marginal buyer–seller pair and therefore the level of the market price.

Exactly the same procedure can be used to determine the level of the exchange rate. One only needs to make the following considerations: assume that there are two completely isolated countries, each with its own, non-metal[3] currency. The prices for different goods will be

[3] Precious metal currencies complicate this relation. On the role of metallic currencies in foreign exchange markets cf. Lucien Albert Hahn, *Von der Kriegs- zur*

determined in each of those economies separately. It will be either the case that all prices are higher, all prices are lower, or that some prices are higher and some prices are lower than in the other country. If, at a certain date, one allowed goods to be traded between those countries, then one would try and export some goods and import others. Those who would like to import goods will try and obtain foreign currency and those who would like to export goods will try to sell the foreign currency they obtain because they want to convert the value of the exported goods into the currency used at home.

Importers and exporters will therefore be actors on the market for foreign currency and will reveal their highest bids and lowest asking prices. How is the level of those bids and asking prices determined? How much will the buyer be ready to pay and how much will the seller ask for? Obviously, they will be dependent on the price differential for a certain group of goods abroad and at home. For example, if the quantity x has a price of 120 at home and 100 abroad, then the importer is ready to pay for the foreign currency a maximum agio[4] of 20 per cent because the trade is only profitable if the price converted to domestic currency is less than 120. On the other hand, an exporter of the same good in the same quantity would require a minimum agio of 20 per cent because the trade needs to generate at least 120 in domestic currency to be profitable.

One only needs to consider how much of a certain group of goods can be purchased at a price of 100 in foreign currency and how much more or less the same quantity costs at home. This leads to the highest bid someone is willing to offer for foreign currency when importing a certain good. At the same time it also determines the lowest asking price for foreign currency required by someone exporting the group of goods. If this procedure is followed for many groups of goods, then we obtain a fuller picture on the bids and offers on the foreign currency market. Drawing the level of bids and offers in a coordinate system, as described above, leads to an intersection of the curves and therefore to the exchange rate.

Friedenswährung [From War to Peace Currency], vol. 14, *Archiv für Sozialwissenschaft und Sozialpolitik*, ed. Edgar Jaffé (Tübingen: J. C. B. Mohr (Paul Siebeck), 1914), p. 24 ff.

[4] Fees and profits, as well as any barriers to free trade, are not considered in the following. The exposition is only meant to be schematic. We also do not consider that in practice the purchase of goods is usually done before the purchase of foreign currency, such that speculation is used to obtain foreign currency when imports are too high and to make the intertemporal adjustment until the next purchasing period.

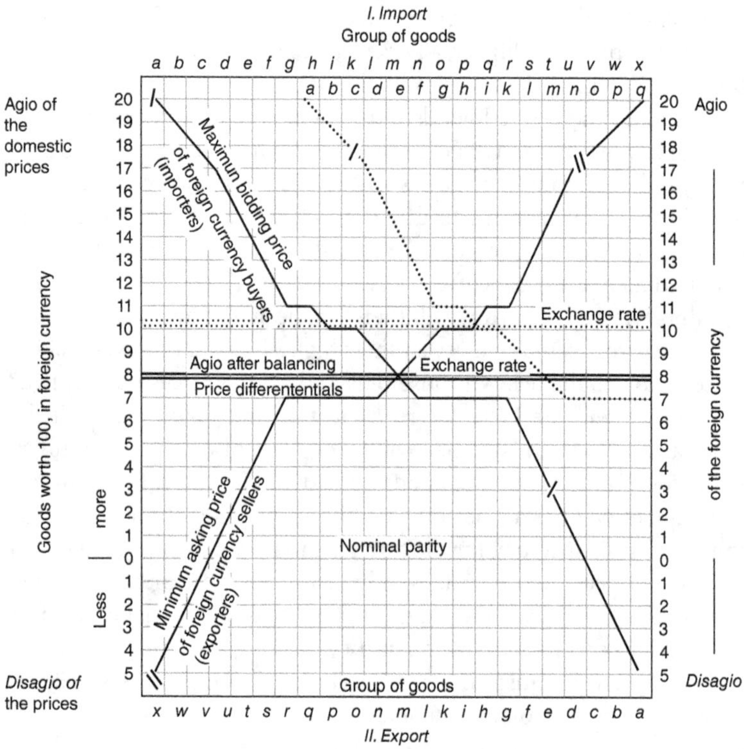

Figure 2

In the following account of the processes in more detail, we assume that in both economies all goods can be divided into 23 groups (*a*–*x*); each group has a different price at home and abroad. For example, group *a* carries a nominal price differential of 20 (foreign price 100, domestic price 120), group *m* shows a differential of 8 (foreign price 100, domestic price 108) and for group *x* the differential is 5, but in this case the domestic price is lower (foreign price 100, domestic price 95). For each group, the positive or negative difference between foreign and domestic price is drawn, such that group *a* with the highest domestic price (i.e. the most likely group to be imported) is to the left. Other groups with a lower difference are following to the right and finally follow the groups for which the foreign price is higher than the domestic price. Curve I connects all these points and, as discussed above, represents the level of all bids for foreign currency. It clearly shows that the buyer with the highest offer would be willing to pay an agio of 20 per cent for foreign currency, which is then followed by buyers only willing to pay less and finally by buyers who are only willing to buy foreign currency below parity.

Each group cannot only be considered for import, hence the purchase of foreign currency, but also for export and therefore for the sale of foreign currency. Thus, each group needs to be drawn into the coordinate system a second time. This time group *x* with a lower domestic than foreign price, and therefore most likely to be exported, is to the left. It is followed by the product groups which have a slightly higher domestic than foreign price and eventually arrives at those with the highest domestic agio. Curve II connects these points and represents the minimum asking price for foreign currency by exporters. It shows that the exporter would require an agio of at least 20 per cent for exporting product group *a*, whilst he would only require 8 per cent for group *m* and for group *x* he would even be satisfied with a disagio of less than 5 per cent.

In this configuration the goods most likely to be imported or exported are on the left of the co-ordinate system and the intersection of the curves shows which pairs are realised. Hence, the intersection of both curves determines the marginal buyer–seller pair. Only demand to the left of the intersection is satisfied by the supply and similarly only supply to the left of the intersection is actually demanded. In our example, groups *a* to *l* and parts of *m* are imported and groups *x* to *n* and parts of *m* are exported. The bid and asking price of the marginal buyer–seller pair determine the market price and therefore the exchange rate, that is, the value of the foreign currency in terms of domestic currency, is given. At the same time the exchange rate determined exerts feedback on the domestic prices: the prices for product groups *a* to *l* and parts of *m* will fall in the light of the import opportunities, such that they are only more expensive by the same proportion as the agio, in our case 8 per cent. On the other hand, prices of product groups *x* to *n* and parts of *m* will increase as a consequence of the export opportunities such that they are lower only by the same proportion as the agio.

This account is schematic and should only hint towards a theory of exchange rate formation. The value of foreign currency in a country is determined by the price difference of the marginally traded product group. The exchange rate does not change, as long as the price difference of this group remains constant.[5]

This results in the following important statement for the question of the possibility and desirability of a credit expansion: because each credit expansion has an inflationary tendency, that is, it can also raise the price of the marginal product group, it can lead (*ceteris paribus*) to a deterioration of the exchange rate. This also means: if and as long as a country attaches importance to an unchanged parity of its own currency with that of other leading countries,[6] then (domestic and foreign) credit expansion is only possible if these also expand their credit. Financial markets show some solidarity and simultaneous credit expansion could often be the case. Otherwise, credit expansion is prevented by large increases in interest rates.[7] The assertion that banks are unrestricted in their credit business is only correct under this modification. Hence, the fixing of interest rates is not entirely independent from foreign countries: A decrease of the interest rate below the usual foreign interest rates can only be effective if a lack of entrepreneurial appetite prevents a credit expansion,[8] which exceeds the credit expansion abroad, despite higher interest rates.

The credit business of a country's banks is also important for the exchange rate for a reason that does not immediately affect market prices. It is well known that the trade balance is only one part in determining the exchange rate: in addition to the demand and supply for foreign currency resulting from imports and exports of goods, some demand and supply for currency is due to other reasons. The most important and particularly interesting is the demand due to international credit relations; the demand side is especially affected when a new credit is granted to or when an old credit is paid back by the foreign country.

[5] Hence, 'the' prices or the 'average price' is irrelevant, and only the price difference of this particular product group is crucial, the price level of other product groups is only of indirect importance.

[6] In the case of a gold standard, that the export of gold is only negligible.

[7] The ability of the central bank to raise interest rates at commercial banks using their discount rate is somewhat different and can only be answered on a case-by-case basis. Cf. Chapter [1.]B in the first part, section b on 'ordinary money demand'.

[8] A low interest rate cannot be proof of the capital strength of a country because 'capital', as mentioned repeatedly, is only a consequence of credit creation. One could rather see low interest rates as a symbol of economic strength because it shows that the country has large labour reserves and uses technically complete production methods that can expand credit without risking increases in the price level or exchange rate.

The effect of demanding foreign currency to settle international credit relations can also be precisely solved by using the subjective value theory. One only needs to consider the effects of the additional demand on the exchange rate determined by the goods trade.

The solution to this last question follows clearly from the graphical exposition above, but more remarks are necessary: the dotted line in Figure 2 shows the seller curve II in relation to the buyer curve I when the demand is not only determined by importers but also by those who need foreign currency to settle international credit relations. It therefore shows the new position of the intersection and thus the level of the exchange rate. It also shows the consequences of the depreciation of the domestic currency: importing is curbed (groups *a* to *h* instead of groups *a* to *m* are imported), exporting is promoted (groups *x* to *i*, instead of groups *x* to *n* are exported) and domestic prices rise because of higher imports and more export opportunities.

Analogously, credit expansion can only be pursued with regard to a stable exchange rate if credit expansion is also pursued abroad (i.e. depreciating the foreign currency), or if there are deflationary tendencies at home which are able to compensate for the inflationary effects and the depreciating effects of credit expansion.

Economic Theory of Bank Credit
(Third Edition)

Part One

Credit and Banks

[1.*]A.II.3. Forms of Granting Credit

[Hahn introduces the graphical tools to analyse the effects of credit on the goods market in section A*.II.3 'Forms of granting credit'. Later parts of the book rely on this graphical analysis and therefore warrant its inclusion in this edition.]

Hitherto, we did not distinguish between different forms of credit; we now want to investigate these different natures and effects of credit. The term 'to grant credit' summarizes many different processes which need to be clearly distinguished from the viewpoint of banking and general economic theory. They differentiate themselves most importantly in their effect on the balance sheet and the money market, the intensity of the capitalistic structure of the economy, and their effect on the so-called 'general price level'.

The most important distinction is related to the question of whether or not granting credit multiplies the number of existing credit relations in the economy, which we shall call *credit expansion*. Otherwise, newly granted credit can also simply maintain the number of credit relations and substitute for credit relations which were paid off or somehow differently closed. We shall call this situation *credit accommodation*.

a) Credit accommodation

A very clear understanding of the nature and effects of credit *accommodation* in the narrow sense is a prerequisite for other cases. The easiest way to gain this understanding might be to use graphical illustrations. The reader shall also pay full attention to Figure 3 and subsequent figures because they show in an inevitably stylised and schematic way the complicated processes in the economy which are the basis of all further content in this book.

We explained earlier that a credit can be disbursed by creating a new deposit in the name of the debtor; this deposit can then be transferred to a seller in exchange for goods or services. As the reader already knows, the reason for the credit (from the economic and private business perspective) is to grant the debtor the productivity advantage of the so-called 'Wartendürfens'[1] [right to

[1] We borrow this term from Gustav Cassel, *Theoretische Sozialökonomik [The Theory of Social Economy]*, 3rd ed. (Leipzig: Deichert, 1923); also compare Adolf Weber, *Allgemeine Volkswirtschaftslehre [General Economics]* (München and Leipzig: Duncker & Humblot, 1928) p. 260 ff.

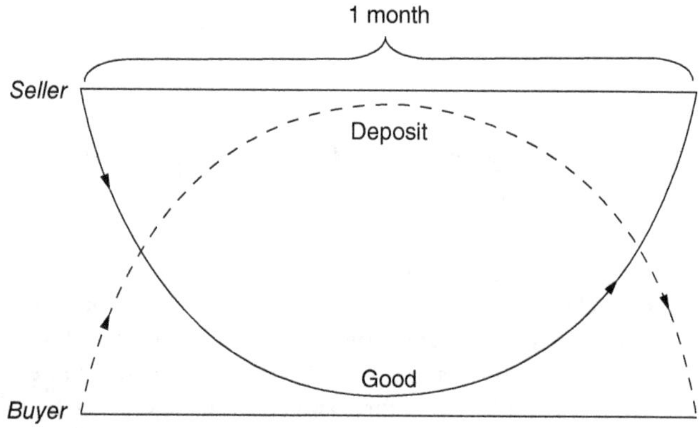

Figure 3

wait] as is the case for any usage of capital: the debtor does not need to deliver the purchased or processed good immediately for consumption but only after a certain time. He enjoys the cost reduction of the roundabout method of production and pays interest for it. We want to illustrate the process of granting credit in the following way which considers all the above mentioned interrelationships and particularly stresses the temporal sequence.

We assume that the roundabout method of production requires one month. Figure 3 shows how the good (which could also be labour) is transferred to the buyer in exchange for deposit created by credit at the beginning of the production period. The buyer makes the good available for consumption in exchange for the previously created deposit at the end of the production period. This closes both the good and money circuit: The good generally is made available for consumption to the one who borrowed it at the beginning of the production period; the deposit compensates the credit line and closes it.

It does not need to be stressed that this figure is a stark stylisation of the real processes. Certainly in the economy there are very short and very long production processes which do not begin on the same day, to mention only one discrepancy. The portfolio of existing roundabout methods of production in the economy could potentially be illustrated by the following Figure 4.

When illustrating the succession of several production periods we can draw the following Figure 5.

The figure shows an economy with a constant amount of credit, that is, no increase in credit takes place. It follows that the deposits created at the beginning of each production period are formally but not newly created; they are only a substitute for paying back credit in substance. Incidentally,

Figure 4

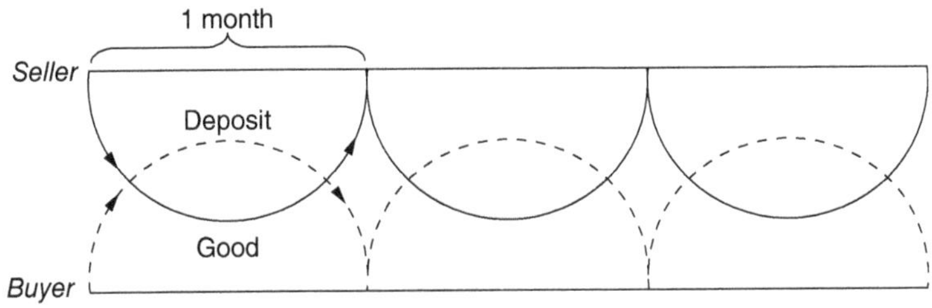

Figure 5

the creation of formally new deposits is also not necessary; instead of paying off the loan, the debtor could transfer the deposits to a separate account with the same or another bank to use it at the beginning of the next production period. This does not, however, change the nature of the entire process.

b) Credit expansion

A credit *expansion* occurs in an economy when the total amount of granted credit increases. A credit expansion generally means more roundabout methods of production and therefore the prolongation of granted credits, effects we illustrate in Figure 6 which is an extension of Figure 3 and 5. It does not picture the changes in the circulation of deposits but only the movements of goods. It shows how the goods, which would be ready for consumption at the end of the first production period, are diverted into longer production methods under the influence of credit expansion; it also shows how the flow of goods is prolonged and appears to double in number in the second production period.

Things are relatively simple up until here; they are only complicated because we have to distinguish two cases of credit expansion: inflationary and non-inflationary credit expansion.

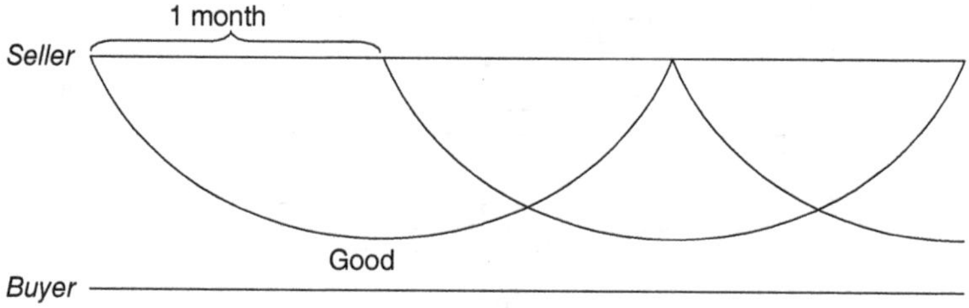

Figure 6

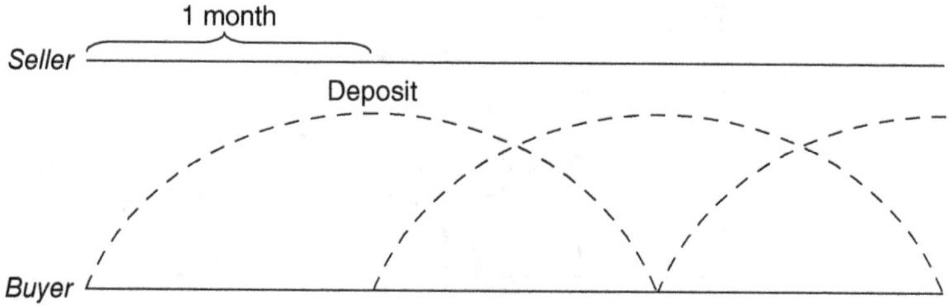

Figure 7

α) *Non-inflationary credit expansion*

Non-inflationary credit expansion occurs if a deposit matching the amount of credit expansion is retained as saving for another production period instead of being used as intended to buy goods on the market. This situation is clarified in Figure 7.

If a holder of a bank deposit can postpone spending (either for consumption or production) the deposits for one month, then he will be able to postpone the same amount at the end of the second production period. This is because the holder will not require under any circumstances any more than the original monthly expense. The goods enter consumption one month later as a consequence of delaying spending the deposits. This is illustrated in Figure 8.

β) *Inflationary credit expansion*

It is main the purpose of this book to highlight the relative independence of credit expansion from previous or current savings. Furthermore, it wants to show the important theoretical and practical consequences of a credit expansion exceeding simultaneous savings. Accordingly, inflationary credit expansion is the most relevant and important case in this book.

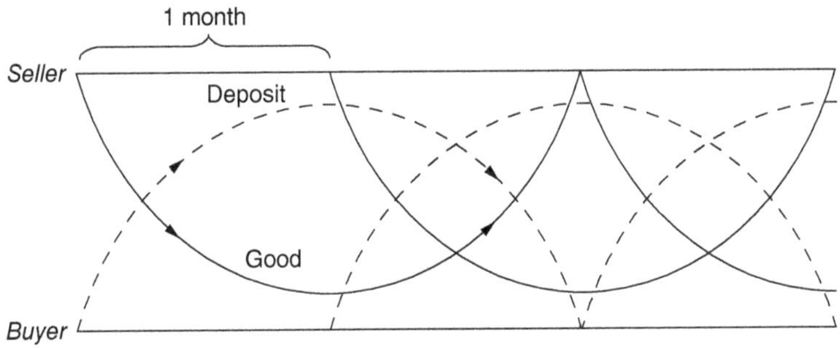

Figure 8

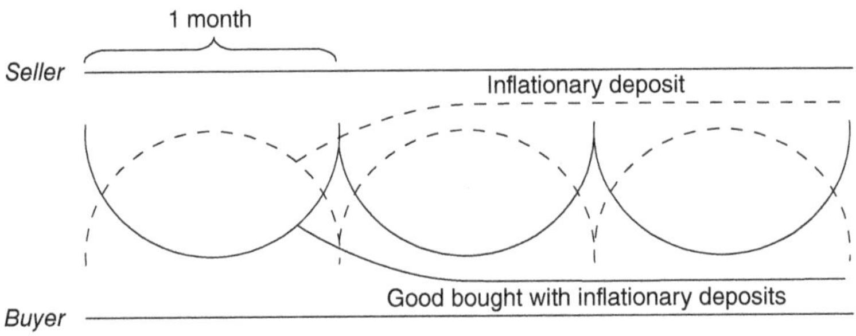

Figure 9

The movement of goods and the creation of debt occur the same way in the case of inflationary credit expansion as in the case of non-inflationary credit expansion. To this extent it is the same situation as in Figure 8, but the side of bank deposits requires an addition. The additional credit is granted in the second production period and the deposits from the first period are not saved. Hence, the buyers receive new deposits (materially not only formally) at the end of the first production period. In the non-inflationary case, deposits of the first production period are saved; in the inflationary case, the new deposits created by credit add to the available bank balances. As will be explained later in detail, these balances can have a substantial effect, namely affecting general price inflation. Assuming that the new deposits amount to the old deposits and considering that the old and new deposits have to share the social product (as will also be later explained in detail), then following picture is painted in Figure 9.

This illustration is unrealistic insofar as a virtually infinite production process cannot coexist with relatively shorter roundabout methods of

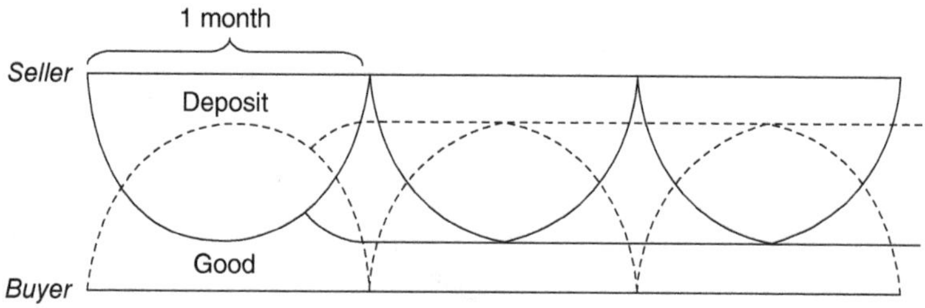

Figure 10

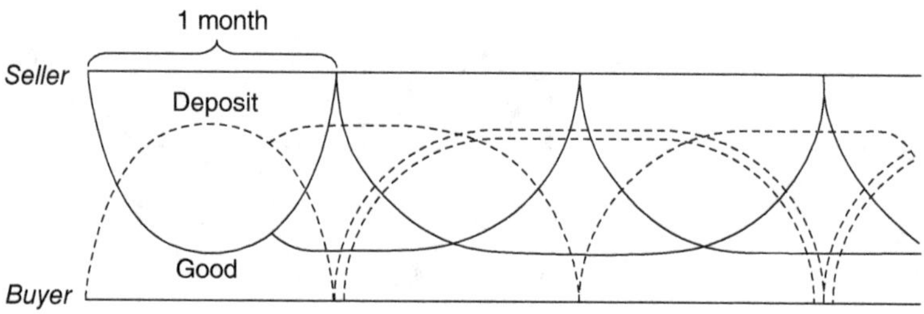

Figure 11

production. A re-balancing of all roundabout methods of production takes place across all sectors and then within the sector according to the profitability of the respective capital uses. Accounting for this fact leads to the sketch in Figure 10 which shows the shortening of the 'infinite' roundabout method of production and the increase of the short production processes.

The increase in prices (due to the creation of inflationary credit) also has consequences for the credit system. The regular credits experience an increase in order to maintain the amount of goods they can buy. The picture changes when accounting also for this fact (see Figure 11).

The last illustrations show an important conclusion regarding the effect of inflationary credit on the capitalistic structure of the economy, the money market, prices, and profits. We will later look at all of these effects in more detail. Here, we only want to briefly look at the accounting implications of inflationary credit for balance sheets.

Non-inflationary credit expansion shows a simultaneous increase in debtors and creditors of the bank, but it does not increase current accounts (neither in name nor nature). The increase in bank deposits leads to an increased transformation of earlier deposits into savings, hence leading to an increase of the latter and expresses the fact that the build-up of savings is the counterpart to credit expansion. Inflationary credit expansion shows a simultaneous increase in debt accounts, with newly created bank balances as their counterpart. It will be shown later[2] that those bank deposits transform into savings relatively quickly; the final result for the bank's accounts is therefore not very different for inflationary or non-inflationary credits. In the former case, the bank's balance sheet will experience a further increase in debt and credit because already existing credits rise. To illustrate this process schematically (therefore not realistic), let the original amount of loans be one billion Marks which is balanced by the same amount of deposits. If inflationary credit expansion creates another billion of loans, then the final result would have the following form. Loans and savings first increase by one billion and then as a secondary effect, loans and positive deposits grow by another billion. The final result shows loans worth three billion on the assets side and two billion on current accounts and one billion as savings on the liabilities side.

[2] Cf. chapter [2.*]B., section III on 'credit and savings'.

Part Two

Credit and the Goods Markets

[2.*]A. The Influence of Credit on Goods Production

Hitherto, it was the purpose and duty of the discussion to analyse credit transactions of modern banks from an accounting and banking perspective. To this effect, it was necessary to introduce a number of new categories and distinctions. To name the most important: inflationary and non-inflationary credit expansion; primary and secondary banks; money and economic, direct and indirect liquidity; technical and non-technical money demand.

With the help of this (as we believe unique) systematisation from the economic not the private business-legal perspective, it is now possible to make statements regarding the complex question about the effect of credit on type, quantity, and distribution of goods produced in the economy. These questions are the ultimate and highest goal for any economic study in general and in particular of the credit business.

Ahead of the analysis, we have to point out that goods production is dependent on the demand for goods under certain technical and economic conditions of production. Demand (as well as the consumption it enables) logically precedes production.[1] This is often not recognised because temporally the order is reversed. First, production takes place and only then the product is demanded and used or consumed. Nevertheless, demand is the precedent in an economic assessment. Each production presupposes sufficient demand, no production is tackled without demand; demand drags production and every production process started anticipates demand. As

[1] Knut Wicksell, *Theoretischer Teil*, i: Vorlesungen über Nationalökonomie, trans. Margarethe Langfeldt (Jena: Gustav Fischer, 1913), p. 6 is right in saying, that 'die Lehre von den menschlichen Bedürfnissen, in quantitativer und qualitativer Beziehung, d.h. die allgemeine Lehre der Konsumation, da sie ja der Zweck der ganzen wirtschaftlichen Tätigkeit ist, logischerweise unbestreitbar an die erste Stelle gesetzt werden muss, wenn sie auch im wirklichen Leben der Zeitfolge nach als letzte auftritt.' [Knut Wicksell, *General Theory*, i: *Lectures on Political Economy*, trans. E. Classen, ed. Lionel Robbins (London: Routledge, 1934), pp. 5–6: 'the theory of *human wants*, quantitative and qualitative, i.e. the general theory of *consumption*, which, since it is the purpose of all economic activity, should logically be placed first, even though in actual life it comes last in point of time.'] Accordingly (and contrary to the usual arrangement) Wicksell treats demand before production. However, he does not draw any consequences for the capital theory.

Adam Smith said 'Wenn nicht konsumiert wird, kann nicht produziert werden' [Consumption is the sole end and purpose of all production].

The question about the effect of granting credit is accordingly identical with the question about which changes the demand structure in the economy experiences due to granted credit.

I. The effect of credit expansion on the length of the goods flow

It is useful to show the effect of credit creation on the composition and structure of the economy's goods market using a comparison. The best comparator for the quantity of available goods is the volume of water in a river,[2] as it is almost a perfect analogy. The water particle becomes part of the river at the source and leaves it at the estuary after a certain time. Analogously, the good becomes part of the goods stock of a nation, beginning with production, maturing and is eventually fully consumed, thus, exiting the goods sphere. At any given moment, new water particles enter the river and the ones which have spent the longest time in the river exit at the estuary. The river therefore carries water particles of different ages at all times; similarly, the flow of goods is augmented at any moment by production and diminished by consumption, such that goods of different maturity exist at any time. The entirety of all water particles in the river give the impression of a coherent, flowing stream; analogously, the entirety of all goods available in an economy forms what is usually called the nation's stock of goods.

Natural rivers are of different length and if all of them carry water at the same, constant speed, the water particles in each will need a different amount of time to travel from the source to the estuary. Analogously, the streams of goods in an economy differ in length and different goods form part of the nation's stock for different durations. The shortest flow of goods consists of those goods with a very short time span between the starting of production and the ending by consumption, as it is the case with most daily needs products. The longest flow of goods consists of goods with a fairly long time between production and consumption (e.g. houses, machines).

The shorter flows of goods contain generally goods which are usually called consumption goods in the narrow sense or goods of low order. The longer flows of goods generally consist of goods usually called goods of higher order, because consumption is only satisfied through their products but not directly as is the case with machines and factories. When goods have the characteristic of consumption goods (accordingly counted as goods of

[2] Cf. Joseph Schumpeter, *Theorie der wirtschaftlichen Entwicklung [The Theory of Economic Development]* (Leipzig: Duncker & Humblot, 1912), p. 70 on exchanging the image of a 'stock of goods' with the image of a 'flow' of goods.

lower order) but have a long durability, then they should nevertheless be part of the longest flows of goods. This is the case for durable goods (in particular houses) which are consumed directly, not only through their products, but for which consumption only ceases after a very long time.[3]

The labour of a nation casts itself in the riverbed of the goods flow, as labour is the ultimate production factor for all goods and therefore the source of any flow of goods.

Has credit expansion the power to alter the course of the nation's labour and how would it happen? It depends; credit can have different effects on production depending on the interest rate: assuming a constant demand, each increase in the number of granted credits causes a decrease in the interest rate as the price of credit.

Interest is a premium which is paid because the good is only completely consumed (amortised) at a later point as a consequence of longer lasting production or consumption. The interest rate (owing its existence to the scarcity of credit) ensures that only finitely long consumption and production periods can be chosen. A decrease in the interest rate therefore loosens this constraint and the production and consumption periods in the economy increase.

This happens in detail in the following way: if the interest rate was relatively high, say 8 per cent, then certain consumption periods were excluded. One builds houses made of, for example, wood with a lifetime of twenty-five years instead of, for example, bricks with a lifetime of fifty years. The reason is that the capital used each year remains invested twice as long in the latter case than in the former, which would mean a higher cost of 8 per cent of the originally invested capital. A higher rent or price could only compensate for these higher costs in very few, specific cases. If the interest rate decreases, then the additional cost of choosing longer consumption periods decreases and these longer periods become more and more viable. Durable goods (i.e. the period from the start of the production until the end of the consumption is long) will therefore be produced in higher quantities the lower the interest rate charged to entrepreneurs or the owner of the goods.

The level of the interest rate also affects the *production* as each good can obviously be produced by different methods. The production technique can be more or less capital intensive, that is, capital can be invested for shorter or longer periods. Capital will be utilised longer if the production does not yield

[3] It is one-sided only to talk of 'roundabout methods of production'. 'Roundabout methods of consumption' are also a characteristic of the capitalist economy (e.g. durable buildings instead of shacks, with their differences in financing and construction). This is clearly exposed in Gustav Cassel, *Theoretische Sozialökonomik*, 3rd ed. (Leipzig: Deichert, 1923), p. 178 ff. [Gustav Cassel, *The Theory of Social Economy*, trans. Joseph McCabe, 2 vols (London: T. F. Unwin, 1923)].

the product directly but in a more roundabout way[4] whereby the means of production are manufactured first and only then the final product. The final product, therefore, includes labour used directly to produce the final product and indirectly to produce intermediate products and machines. Assume the quantity of one million pairs of shoes can be produced by either 10,000 craftsmen in one year or 5,000 workers could produce machines in the first year and use them to produce one million pairs of shoes in the second year. In both cases one million pairs of shoes are produced and 10,000 labourers have to be paid for one year, but in the second case the shoes are only produced in the second year. The entrepreneur has to wait two years to get reimbursed for the 'capital' he has advanced.

The peculiarity of the second method (more capital intensive) is that it can produce 25,000 pairs of shoes more than the first method, such that one million pairs of shoes only contains the work of 9,750 workers. This means that the second method saves the cost of 250 workers and the shoes are produced 2.5 per cent cheaper. Nevertheless, the entrepreneur will not choose the second method if the interest rate on credit is 8 per cent. For the first method in our example the wages for 10,000 workers will remain in the firm for one year, whilst for the second method the wages of the 5,000 workers building the machines would remain in the firm for two years. Hence, it would cause additional costs of 8 per cent of the annual wage of 5,000 workers or 4 per cent of the annual wage of 10,000 workers. If the interest rate decreases to 4 per cent then the costs of the longer production process are lower than its additional benefits and would accordingly be chosen.

In summary, the increase in credit causes a decrease in the interest rate and therefore the production and consumption periods increase. Credit expansion also means that more goods and services can be demanded on the markets and thus causes an increase in the length of the goods flow, which experiences now a lower resistance. This applies in equal absolute measure to all goods flows in the economy regardless of length (which means different relative changes).

The way in which the goods are diverted from a shorter to a longer flow of goods is illustrated in Figure 12.

We can draw two conclusions which are important for understanding the relevant processes. First, the so-called 'additional demand' for credit, which is a symptom of the long production period, is not really a demand for *more* credit but for *longer* credit (not necessarily from a private business perspective but from an economic perspective). Second, as long as the credit expansion expresses itself in an elongation of the flow of goods, it is certain to cause an increase in the amount of simultaneously available goods in the

[4] A term introduced by Böhm-Bawerk.

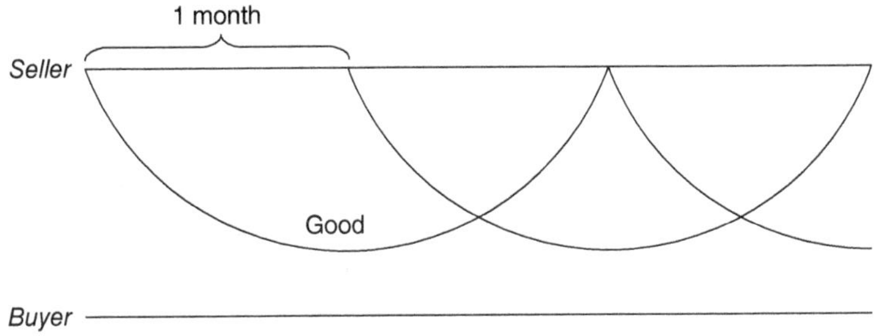

Figure 12

economy. However, this is *not* based on an increase in production (leaving potential productivity gains aside). Whether the worker produces in the first period shoes or a machine to produce shoes, which enter consumption at the end of the second period and help to amortize the machine, is not relevant for total production in the economy. The *amount of products* in the economy rather experiences an increase because goods dedicated for consumption are diverted into production. The coexistence of goods with different starting points in production gives the impression of an increase in production which is ultimately not true.

II. The effect of credit expansion on the width of the goods flow

Credit expansion not only causes an elongation of the flow of goods but also a widening.[5] More roundabout methods of production are used and already existing production is intensified: manual labour is substituted with machine labour and more of the existing manual and machine labour is used.

The reason for this phenomenon is that the credit expansion causes a decrease in the interest rate which in turn means a reduction in the cost of production. This cost reduction means that not only more roundabout methods of production become profitable but also new production processes which had been too expensive can be used. For example, a factory awkwardly situated for transportation and hence unprofitable can resume production and hire workers. The extent to which the factory can hire workers depends on the elasticity of the labour market. If a small increase in the demand for labour increases wages substantially, then the profit margin shrinks quickly;

[5] Cf. Richard Strigl, 'Die Produktion unter dem Einflusse einer Kreditexpansion' [Production under the Influence of a Credit Expansion]. *Schriften des Vereins für Sozialpolitik 173*, no. 2 (1928), p. 185 ff. and Hans Neisser, *Der Tauschwert des Geldes [The Exchange Value of Money]* (Jena: Gustav Fischer, 1928), chapter VI, section 1 'Der Einfluß der Gütermenge auf die Geldmenge' [The influence of the quantity of goods on the quantity of money].

an intensification of existing production does not happen and more roundabout production methods are used. The wage rate might not rise because, for example, wages are determined by tradition or collective wage agreements or a large army of unemployed weighs heavily on the market; in this case the intensified use of the already existing production technologies will be an important consequence and curtail the use of more roundabout methods of production. The extent to which the additional credits are used one way or another is ultimately decided by whether or not the decrease in the interest rate is used to produce more intensively or to implement more roundabout methods of production.

Theory and practice tend to neglect these consequences of the credit expansion because the inexpensiveness of the credit supply is relatively unimportant for the employment rate in normal times, in particular because workers could be laid off in the transition period. One only hears of the importance of cheap credit for the rationalisation of production methods, and so on. Large circles in Germany only became aware of the relevance of the credit supply for the employment rate after the experience of hyperinflation. During this period, it was rightly assumed that the capital supply and in particular the import of capital were decisive for the potential employment of the army of unemployed. Without any capital or with extraordinarily high rates for renting capital, one cannot employ anyone or only those who are so frugal that their work can be compensated by a production method without capital or overburdened with interest payments.

The decrease in credit costs naturally has its strongest impact on the most roundabout methods of production because interest payments are relatively more important compared to the investment in wages. A production method without any capital does not experience any increase because a decrease in the interest payments does not reduce the production costs.

Figure 13 illustrates the process of a widened flow of goods and contrasts it with an elongation of the flow of goods for comparison.

It shows that, for example, the result of the first production period does not extend as machines into the second, but as food for the additionally hired

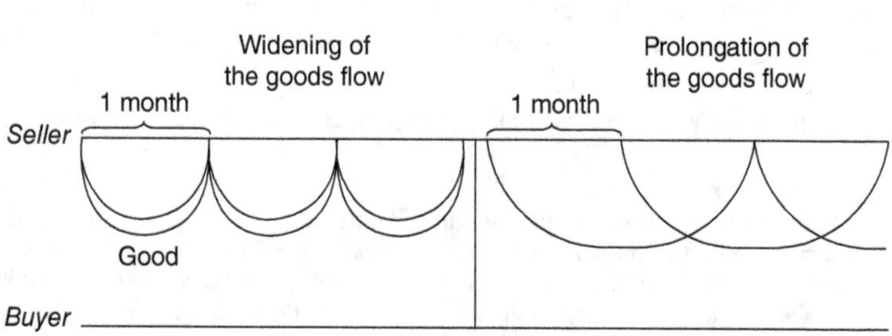

Figure 13

workers who do not own any additional subsistence means. The products of the first period are thus consumed to maintain the workers rather than invested in machines to expand the means of production.

We also want to point out here that the consequences of the credit expansion are the same for both inflationary and non-inflationary credit expansion.

III. The effect of credit expansion on prices and wages

I. *Non-inflationary* credit expansion does not change the general price level (using this term with all the necessary caveats) and the general wage level, apart from the previously described effects. It merely leads to a temporary change in relative prices and for certain wage rates; during the transition period, an increased demand for production factors and workers leads to a relative rise in prices and wages in those industries producing intermediate goods and other precursors compared to industries producing consumption goods. A general increase in prices (apart from the one set out in section II on 'The effect of credit expansion on the width of the goods flow') and wages does not occur. The main reason is that the increased demand for goods at the end of the first period of those firms receiving newly granted credit and newly hired workers, respectively, is counteracted by the saver's abstention from consumption (compare Figure 8 in section [1.*]A.II.3).

II. The situation is different at this (and only this) point for the *inflationary* credit expansion. We mentioned already in section [1.*]A.II.3 and showed in Figure 9 that the newly created demand adds to the previously existing demand and they compete against each other. The higher purchasing power on the market drives a price increase. This process (the fundamental process of any quantity theoretic consideration) has already been the subject of many publications such that it is unnecessary to consider it here.[6]

[6] The price rise during the war has sparked a number of statements on inflation, in particular in the daily and financial press but also in the economic literature. Gustav Cassel, *Deutschlands wirtschaftliche Widerstandskraft [Germany's Economic Resistance]* (Berlin: Ullstein, 1916), which applies his purchasing power parity theory to Germany, gave the impetus to the scientific discussion. In response Robert Liefmann tried to explain the inflation with a quantity theory embedded in his theory of income (Robert Liefmann, *Geld und Gold [Money and Gold]* (Stuttgart und Berlin: Deutsche Verlagsanstalt, 1916) and Robert Liefmann, *Die Geldvermehrung im Weltkriege und die Beseitigung ihrer Folgen [The Growth of Money in the First World War and the Remediation of its Consequences]* (Stuttgart and Berlin: Deutsche Verlagsanstalt, 1918)). Generally Liefmann bases his view on von Beckerath and von Schulze-Gaevernitz and accepts the price-increasing effect of credit inflation but deems it unimportant for the business cycle. A general analysis of the inflation problem is also given in Otto Heyn, 'Über Geldschöpfung und Inflation' [On Money Creation and Inflation], *Finanz- und volkswirtschatliche Fragen 73* (1921) which was preceded by a

III. The seller of the goods attracting additional demand uses the acquired purchasing power to pay off loans and, as far as they are inflation gains, to make bank deposits. In the new production period, banks will grant more loans (indeed have to, because all nominal prices, especially wages, increased) without generating more purchasing power. We have already alluded to this in section [1.*]A.II.3 and it can also be seen in Figure 11.

Credit expansion is a one-off complete process which does not have any inherent need to be progressed or reversed. It is particularly misguided to assume[7] that the larger amount of credit and the reduced interest rate can only be maintained by a continued injection of new doses of credit into the economy. This is also shown in the graphical exposition in section [1.*]A.II.3 (in particular Figure 10 and Figure 11).

IV. The previously described effect of inflationary credit on goods prices also has further consequences. At the end of the first production period, the firm faces a demand with a higher purchasing power relative to its initial prices. This rise in demand (induced by credit expansion in the second period) causes higher profits for the firm; this fuels the entrepreneur's hopes to maintain the increased profit in the third production period and he seeks new credit from the bank. Higher demand for credit causes further

number of articles (e.g. Otto Heyn, 'Probleme des Geldwesens' [Problems of the Finance Sector], *Weltwirtschaftliches Archiv 10*, no. 2 (1917)). Friedrich Bendixen, *Das Inflationsproblem [The Inflation Problem]* (Stuttgart: Ferdinand Enke, 1917) tries to explain inflation from a banking perspective. The quantity theory is the most common approach in the war literature; I have shown in my essays (Lucien Albert Hahn, 'Handelsbilanz—Zahlungsbilanz—Valuta—Güterpreis' [Trade Balance—Balance of Payment—Exchange Rate—Goods Price], *Archiv für Sozialwissenschaft und Sozialpolitik 48* (1920–1) and Lucien Albert Hahn, 'Statische und dynamische Wechselkurse' [Static and Dynamic Exchange Rates], *Archiv für Sozialwissenschaft und Sozialpolitik 49* (1922); both are re-published in Lucien Albert Hahn, *Geld und Kredit [Money and Credit]* (Tübingen; J. C. B Mohr (Paul Siebeck), 1929)) that the quantity theory cannot be readily applied to the case of inflation and the exchange rate. The quantity theory is only a first approximation to, and rather rough interpretation of, the real relationship. Apart from that not every increase in the quantity of money causes inflation (cf. p. 82–3) it is not correct to assume that a change in the quantity of money does not change the quantity of goods and vice versa. Neither the quantity of goods is constant or in a fixed relation with the quantity of money nor is the quantity of money independent of the amount of goods. If the quantity theory is modified in these respects, then it can also be used to explain inflationary phenomena and is also rightly used in the post-war monetary literature. We shall mention Hans Neisser, *Der Tauschwert des Geldes [The Exchange Value of Money]* as an example for the fruitful application of the quantity theory. An example from the foreign literature is D. H. Robertson. *Banking Policy and the Price Level* (London: P. S. King & Son, 1926).

[7] Cf. Lucien Albert Hahn, 'Kritik der Misesschen Theorie des Geldes und der Umlaufsmittel' [A Critique of Mises' Theory of Money and Means of Circulation], *Archiv für Sozialwissenschaft und Sozialpolitik 53*, no. 2 (1925), p. 515.

credit expansion. This leads to a well-known phenomenon in times of inflation or at the start of a boom: if banks do not increase interest rates to fend off new requests for credits, then this leads to ever more credit granted.

It needs to be made clear that the additional profit (which is already enjoyed and is hoped will last) is at the cost of those owning purchasing power during the production period (those who are commonly called the owners of money). These are mainly fixed wage earners, pensioners, and receivers of interest payments but also wage-earning labourers *insofar as their income is only spent during the production period.*

V. The renewed credit expansion causes the same effects on the length and width of the goods flow as described above. The incentives to expand production are driven by expected price increases and if they are exhausted then no further price increases take place towards the end of the third production period (which can last for a very long time); all those firms and roundabout methods of productions which only seemed profitable in the light of rising prices ultimately become unprofitable. This is when the so-called 'business cycle' swings and turns downwards.

The ever-increasing amount of loans, which are a consequence of the marked price increases caused by earlier credits, was the reason for the incredible expansion of investments and otherwise unprofitable production during the German inflation episode (apart from the last period). These developments are still vivid in our memories and are also hinted at in more common business cycles (which remain to be discussed).

IV. The effect of credit expansion on the employment rate

The phenomenon previously called the widening of the flow of goods means that goods which would have been consumed in the absence of a credit expansion are now used in production by labourers. *These labourers were not employed before and therefore one can say that credit expansion is increasing production.*

This fact has been generally denied because theoretical considerations are usually underpinned by an economic state as the classics describe it rather than the real modern economy. As a consequence, almost all of the relevant literature explicitly denies the positive effect of an increase in the quantity of money on the amount of capital and goods. It calls the idea amateurish, inflationist, or even a regression to the ideas of John Law. In classic economics the statement of the purely inflationary effect of an increase of money is correct. Production technology (which can almost be called primitive compared to modern times) could only meet increased demand if an increase in the labour force preceded it. The much lower wealth of nations then meant that labour was virtually fully utilised; hence, a credit expansion could only lead to higher prices and not to an increase in the quantity of goods in an economy already operating at full capacity. The problem of business cycle booms (which was such a characteristic of the economy of the last decade) did not feature in classic economics and, thus, did not play any role in their theoretical deductions.[8]

In the modern economy credit expansion grants additional purchasing power to firms and induces higher demand for goods and workers, thereby causing both a rise in production and prices. A real and absolute increase in production, not just of individual industries, but of all industries in their entirety manifests itself. That this is possible in a modern and not in a classical economy is due to two reasons. First, the increased utilization of machines in the production process has progressed astonishingly since classical times. For example, an increase in the production of mass-produced goods in a factory from 1,000 to 2,000 pieces does not require doubling the number of workers but only an increase of perhaps 10 per cent or 20 per cent. In earlier times with a much stronger focus on manual labour, the number of workers would need to be increased by at least 80 per cent or 90 per cent—if not 100 per cent.[9] Second, technological progress caused a much higher level of wealth in the modern economy. This caused a vast reserve of un- and underutilised labour (pensioners, women, and labourers ready to work overtime) which could easily meet increased demand for labour. Both elements could be characterised as the 'elasticity' of the economy. Apart from the industrial booms in the pre-war period, the enormous potential of this elasticity has been shown especially by the wartime boom. Production was increased to levels deemed impossible and this happened during a time in which most parties normally involved

[8] There is virtually no mention of the existence of booms in Adam Smith.

[9] This assertion attracted criticism by Adolf Lampe, *Zur Theorie des Sparprozesses und der Kreditschöpfung [On the Theory of Savings and Credit Creation]* (Jena: Gustav Fischer, 1926), p. 128, footnote 1 and p. 160, who suggests that one needs to assume an 'optimal combination of available production factors' when comparing the modern and the classical economy. Hence, a doubling of production would require a doubling of labourers. This critique is erroneous because it does not recognise the specific technical situation of modern industry. A furnace can only be used to produce a certain tonnage every day, not more or less. Cf. Otto von Zwiedineck-Südenhorst, 'Beiträge zur Erklärung der strukturellen Arbeitslosigkeit' [Contributions to the Explanation of Structural Unemployment], *Vierteljahreshefte zur Konjunkturforschung 2*, no. 2, supp. 1 (1927), p. 50: 'Mit der fortschreitenden Entfaltung und Vervollkommnung des technischen Apparates tritt die Tendenz zur größeren Stetigkeit des Arbeitsbedarfs in die Erscheinung. Der Arbeitsbedarf einer industriellen Unternehmung schwankt für einen kapitalintensiv ausgerüsteten Betrieb nicht und immer weniger proportional der Arbeitsaufgabe, wie sie der Markt stellt.' [Progress in the development and refinement of the technical apparatus shows a tendency towards more stability in labour demand. The labour demand of industrial firm does not fluctuate for capital-intensive factories. It also decreases proportionally with labour savings as the market requires.]

in the production process were conscripted into the army and therefore not available as productive labour.[10]

How can credit expansion force individual workers into the service of production? A country's reserve of labour (i.e. all those who are not active in production) is, according to the subjective value theory, not employed because they attach a higher value to their 'leisure' than the wage rate they expect from working. The pensioner does not work because the pension payments already ensure his subsistence and because the marginal utility from consuming non-elementary commodities is lower than the amenity of leisure. The vast majority of women do not work for the same reason. The worker *not* doing overtime does not do so because he values the calm of the ninth hour higher than the wage expected from working overtime. The typical unemployed person does not work because he prefers not to work instead of working at a wage rate that does not even guarantee subsistence.

Credit expansion causes firms to compete and leads to higher wages. Wages increase relative to the currently prevailing market rate or in the case of the unemployed exceed zero. This will alter the decision problem of those currently not ready to work. The value of working is now preferred to not working; they become the 'marginal worker' instead of being the 'marginal non-worker'. The wage offered rises. How can the increased wage be paid?

In the case of non-inflationary credit expansion the higher wage rate can be paid because interest rates on capital decrease. In the case of inflationary credit expansion, one also has to consider other factors: why certain costs (e.g. interest rates on long-term bonds, taxes) do not rise (at least initially) despite the general increase in prices, such that higher wages can be paid. However, one also needs to notice if the inflationary credit expansion is continued into the next production period, then wage increases might not be real but only nominal; the well-known phenomenon that wage increases lag price increases might even cause a real wage decrease.[11] Those workers who spend their wages during the production period give a part of their real purchasing power to the holder of the newly created purchasing power. However, this does not negatively affect the wage increase and the employment rate, as long as the population is under the illusion of a constant value of the money.

[10] Therefore the war did not show the impracticality of the capitalist production system but to the contrary its enormous potential. The purpose of production, not the process itself, was wrong. If the financial resources (using the same financing arrangements) were used to build houses, means of transport and labour-saving machines, then the satisfaction of all needs would have brought the golden age, even for the expropriated.

[11] Cf. Emil Lederer, *Konjunktur und Krisen [Business Cycles and Crises]*, Grundriss der Sozialökonomik IV 1, (Tübingen: J. C. B. Mohr (Paul Siebeck), 1925), p. 367.

Credit expansion causes the following changes in the economy: a *change in the distribution* causes an *increase in production.* The increase in production takes place because more people in the economy work. The distribution changes, such that those participating in the production process receive a higher share of the national product than before. This share does not only reflect the value added by labour; in the case of inflationary credit they also receive a certain share of the national income previously accruing to fixed income earners (capitalists, pensioners, and fixed-wage earners). A shift of real income towards the working class and away from capitalists causes an increase in production. It also confirms that distribution, like consumption, logically precedes production even though it only occurs after it.[12]

The main relevance of credit expansion lays not so much in the sheer increase of produced goods or employment, but rather that it counteracts the underutilisation of labour, which can so easily occur in the modern economy. In the modern economy, every year a certain amount of labourers are made redundant by the continuing switch to less labour-intensive production methods unless credit expansion is used. Furthermore, modern industrial countries are still experiencing a strong degree of urbanization. However, the demand for labour does not increase in line with population growth and, therefore, a certain proportion of this population increase remains unemployed.[13] The resulting oversupply of labour exerts pressure on the wage rate (and therefore goods prices) until the wage rate decreases sufficiently to make new production possibilities profitable and reduces the attractiveness of work to convert some 'marginal workers' to 'marginal non-workers'. Hence, a modern economy tends to experience distributional changes in favour of capitalists, who have a nominally fixed income and benefit from a decrease in prices, and away from labourers, whose wages decrease more than prices. In other words, all effects of the classical theory of the reserve army of labour with constant capital will come into force. This is where credit expansion enters the picture as a corrective force and as a pre-eminent social factor. Credit expansion increases the demand for labour and groups of labourers, who were not part of the production process as a consequence of the static credit structure, to re-join the productive labour force; it prevents the reduction of goods prices and its consequential increase in the rent for capital. In short, all effects of increasing 'capital' will come into force. This does not, however, constitute a causal relation for the increase in capital goods. An increase in capital *goods* can only occur with reduced capital prices and, hence, wage rates, but not in situations with increasing

[12] Similar to consumption, distribution should be treated before not after production in a systematic treatment.

[13] Cf. Zwiedineck-Südenhorst, 'Beiträge zur Erklärung der strukturellen Arbeitslosigkeit'.

prices and wages. The high level of prices and wages is not maintained by more abundant 'capital' but by *credit*.

From all these considerations follows: the quantity theoretic view, which is incidentally shared by almost all money, credit, and capital theorists, that an increase in money or credit respectively does not increase the production of goods is not only inaccurate but outright wrong.[14] *Every credit expansion causes an increase in production, as a consequence leads to a shift in distribution. Credit draws the goods from a nirvana, in which they would remain without the credit expansion.* Whether or not a credit expansion (also an inflationary credit expansion) is always beneficial to a country remains unanswered. It is beyond economics to judge whether or not production should be increased at the cost of capitalists, pensioners, and fixed-wage earners. It seems to be a theoretical problem but is in fact a political decision.

An increase in credit drives an increase in production but the described effect can only be maintained as long as more credits also lead to more consumption. Production is not viable in the long run if the goods (either from shorter or longer flows of goods) do not meet an appropriate demand at the instant they are ready for consumption. Even the strongest current in a river comes to a halt if the water cannot exit at the estuary: consumption is the sole end and purpose of all production.

In general, credit expansion usually creates the necessary consumption increase to match the production increase by itself. The purchasing power (in the form of cheques or banknotes) transferred to the new labourers creates demand and is transferred back to the producer; this enables them to sell the additional products and to pay back the new credits. In particular, the increase in production is made possible by offering higher wages, that is, a higher proportion of the social product is transferred for consumption. In any case, the additional production meets a higher demand.

From this it follows that it cannot be inferred that credit expansion is a reason for an economic crisis or depression. We do not see credit expansion as a cause but that various reasons can lead to its reversal. We shall treat this in more detail further below.

[14] The only correct statement is that the quantity of money is irrelevant in a static analysis. The critique of John Law's ideas, who identifies a wealth in capital with the quantity of money, by prevailing opinion is certainly supported by us.

[2.*]B. Credit and Capital

I. Does credit expansion equal capital expansion?

The central question of credit theory is: to what extent does the granting of new credits increase the debtor's (and therefore the economy's) stock of capital?

For now, we do not want to be more specific with the term 'capital' and simply consider it as the entrepreneur's ownership of productive means and the workers' means of consumption (that is the stock of so-called 'intermediate goods'). Then this question is answered depending on the type of credit in two ways.

If the credit does not create any new purchasing power (thus is only granted out of the economy's *savings*), then the credit increases capital goods insofar as the good is not consumed by the saving individual but used for production by the individual who receives the purchasing power through the credit. The question of whether or not the credit creates capital in the sense of new goods is already answered by the fact that the non-inflationary credit simply transfers the claim for a good to another individual.

It is more difficult to make a statement about the capital-creating force of inflationary credit (which is not granted out of the economy's savings). The question was answered very differently in different economic development stages. Times in which the capital-creating force of credit was overestimated alternated with times in which it was underestimated. Even nowadays, we are far from completely clarifying all theories and opinions.

The basic conception in pre-classical time was that new credit generates capital. The notion was not voiced in this way and also could not be expressed as such given the state of the capital theory. Its prevalence nevertheless shows in statements on the pressing problems of those times like a scarcity of capital and high interest rates. The view was that it is in the interest of commerce to solve both problems which could be simply addressed by a credit expansion and an increase in the quantity of money (e.g. through a higher issuance of notes by one or more note-issuing banks), respectively.

The classics (especially Ricardo) showed the untenability of this notion (which was lately adopted by vulgar economists), which is a great achievement and deed to monetary theory; as if high interest rates and a scarcity of capital goods could be eliminated without a problem by a growth in credit and the quantity of money. The classics recognised that a low interest rate can have clearly distinct reasons: a large amount of savings or a growing quantity of money. Through the lens of the quantity theory of money (according to which a growth in the quantity of money with a constant 'goods side' leads to a proportional increase in prices) they could see that non-inflationary credit expansion is irrelevant for prices and that an inflationary credit expansion always leads to a price rise. However, they went even further. They concluded from the price-increasing effect of credit and money growth that all its effects are *exhausted* in the increase in goods prices, that it does not have any other long-run effect. The classics therefore explicitly denied the capital-creating force of inflationary credit using the argument that 'making money' does not equate to 'making goods'.

We see ultimately the classical view only as a step towards the solution not as the solution itself, despite the recognition of the great progress of the classics compared to the pre-classical notions. The credit expansion (even if it is through the new creation of purchasing power, that is, an increase in the quantity of money) is never as irrelevant for capital creation as the classics thought. Daily experience already shows this . . . If credit (also *inflationary*) is granted and appropriately used, then it creates new production machines, factories, generally capital in the economic sense for the debtor.

How does the post-classical theory deal with this fact? We can broadly distinguish two strands.

1. This view approaches the pre-classical notion, according to which a credit expansion makes economic capital available. Macleod is the author which expresses this notion most concisely and equates 'credit' simply with 'capital'. His exposition is built on a correct idea but he could not express it in a correct theory. Nevertheless, one cannot simply discard his view on the grounds that he wrongly expanded an argument which is correct for capital in the 'private business sense' to capital in the 'economic sense'.

2. The more recent view maintains the classical assertion that no amount of new money can create capital because 'making money' does not equate to 'making goods'. They conclude that credit can create new means of production but only if these goods were already produced and effectively held on call.[1] If this condition is met, then credit generates capital. Credit does not have the power to create goods but it can allocate the goods in the right way. If the condition is not met, then credit does not generate capital because it is not production in itself.

[1] This notion was the dominant view until recently. It was particularly argued in W. Lexis, 'Kredit' [Credit], *Handwörterbuch der Staatswissenschaften*, vi: 3rd ed. (Jena: Gustav Fischer, 1910).

Also this notion, which was the dominant dogma until recently, is not satisfactory. A look at the actual processes in the economy shows that in reality, every time credit is granted it generates means of production (provided the debtor uses it to that effect) regardless of whether or not goods were on stock in the economy. The availability and amount of the goods stock is eventually only relevant for the question whether or not goods prices rise: the smaller the stock of goods, the stronger is the tendency of prices increasing. In any case, an existing stock of superfluous goods is not necessary for the creation of means of production. A machine has never not been used because it was not on stock, instead it would have simply been built.

One dilemma remains: on the one hand, it is theoretically undeniable that production can create goods and granting a credit is not production in itself; on the other hand, the capital-generating power of credit also cannot be denied in practice.

The dilemma cannot be resolved as long as one maintains the position that capital in the economic sense (i.e. the stock of means of production) can only be grown by increasing production. However, this position is wrong: capital creation is *not* a matter of goods *production, but* a matter of the *distribution*, in particular the *inter- and intratemporal* distribution of goods.

1. Each time a more roundabout method of production is used the economy's stock of capital grows which shows that the nation's stock of capital goods can also increase *without* an increase in the *scale of production* of a certain technology. The example above of shoe manufacturing illustrates this well: if the more capitalistic method of production is chosen instead of producing shoes manually, then a machine to produce shoes is built in the first period which produces shoes in the second period. Accordingly, the capital stock comprises the product in making (the shoes) and the machines at the beginning of the second period. In this case, the proceeds of labour reach from the first into the second period, the amount of simultaneously available goods in the economy increases. This is similar to the total amount of water in a lake increasing (assuming an unchanged inflow of water) if the outlet is blocked and the water needs to swell above a certain height to be eventually discharged (i.e. is retained for a while).

2. The usage of more roundabout methods of production is nothing other than a temporal shift in the consumption of the social product; hence, the increase in the nation's goods stock (caused by an elongated flow of goods) is not a consequence of increased production, but a consequence of changes in the *intertemporal distribution* of goods.

3. The change in production methods towards more roundaboutness (a shift of consumption into the future) also causes a change in the current distribution of goods; thus, the increase in the nation's goods stock is also a consequence of changes in the *intratemporal distribution* of goods. The

consumer does not use the goods produced in previous production periods (e.g. sewing machines in the household, coal for heating) but instead the firm uses them in production (e.g. sewing machines in a tailor's shop, coal used in a furnace) such that they become part of the goods finally consumed in the future.

4. The fact that there are very many goods (e.g. coal) which can be used not only for consumption or production but for both purposes corroborates that capital creation is only a matter of distribution not production. When those dual-purpose goods were produced in the past, it was not clear whether they were used to produce goods of higher or lower order. The usage of the goods in either way depends on the size of the economy's stock of the respective goods. For any theoretical analysis one needs to assume that there are no specific capital goods, which are clearly determined for the purposes of consumption or production when produced. The clear identification of this fact is the achievement of the proponents of the so-called 'abstract' and 'purchasing power' theories of capital.[2] The inter- and intratemporal distribution assigns the position of the good in the production process, that is, whether a good becomes a capital or consumption good, a good of higher or lower order.

5. It is logically impossible that credit, which is not a phenomenon of the production sphere, creates goods in itself. The fact that capital creation is a matter of distribution and not production resolves the dilemma mentioned above. It only remains to ask if and to what extent the granting of credit

[2] We use the term 'abstract' capital theories to signify those theories which do not identify capital with certain goods but an 'abstract productive power' or the power to use goods. An 'abstract' capital theory is the one of Clark, for which Schumpeter (Joseph Schumpeter, *Theorie der wirtschaftlichen Entwicklung [The Theory of Economic Development]* (Leipzig: Duncker & Humblot, 1912)) reserves the term 'abstract' capital theory in the narrow sense. The second form of an 'abstract' capital theory was recently suggested in Adolf Weber, *Allgemeine Volkswirtschaftslehre [General Economic Theory]* (Munich and Leipzig: Duncker & Humblot, 1928). As Weber acknowledges (p. 178), his theory is based on the notion that capital can be differentiated in 'produced means of production' and 'ownership of means of production', which has its roots in Rodbertus and was further elaborated by Adolf Wagner. The same notion is at the heart of Cassel's theory of capital disposition in Gustav Cassel, *Theoretische Sozialökonomik [The Theory of Social Economy]*, 3rd ed. (Leipzig: Deichert, 1923), p. 177 ff. Our criticism relating to the 'abstract' capital theories can be found in section II of this chapter. Closely related to the 'abstract' capital theory but different to the extent that they equate the power to use capital with purchasing power; these theories are called 'purchasing power' theory in Schumpeter, *Theorie der wirtschaftlichen Entwicklung*, p. 255. In the following we also adhere to this theory, which has its origin without doubt in Macleod. He did not draw any conclusions from this notion though and, according to Schumpeter, *Theorie der wirtschaftlichen Entwicklung*, pp. 254–5, the theory was further developed by Hawley, Davenport, Veblen, and in particular Schumpeter, *Theorie der wirtschaftlichen Entwicklung*.

causes the necessary changes in the inter- and intratemporal distribution to alter the methods of production. This question was already answered above in the affirmative.

One can summarise the discussion above as: capital creation does not belong to the production sphere but is purely a function of income distribution. Credit expansion (inflationary and non-inflationary) transfers goods to firms, which are now in a position to express demand, and capital is increased. On the other hand, capital decreases in the case of (deflationary or non-deflationary)[3] credit contraction. The granting of credits is primary to capital creation.

II. What is 'capital'?

I. It is not our intention to enter into a general analysis of the nature of capital, particularly because the problem has experienced a substantial clarification in recent years. Nevertheless, we do not regard it as superfluous to argue against a notion which hampered the development of a capital theory and appears in discussions time and time again. We call this notion the barter perspective.

With the term 'barter perspective' we do not mean that the authors lived in and wrote about this stage in economic development. The view is rather the scientific residue of that development stage because the authors are entangled in the conditions of an earlier age as the basis of their deliberations. Thus, one can still find barter and very early abstract perspectives on capital in the current literature.

Goods are traded for other goods and not for money in the economic development stage commonly called the *barter economy*. Accordingly in such an environment the entrepreneur (or whoever else) requires tools, raw materials, 'sustenance goods for the working period', generally 'capital goods', which can only be obtained in the following way: he needs to borrow the goods from another individual who produced and did not consume them, that is, who kept them on stock. The method of granting credit is eventually only the expression and consequence of the prevailing method of payment. In general, this will take the form of *rent*, in particular for durable goods, and for some special cases, for example, seed in the form of the

[3] The terms deflationary and non-deflationary credit contraction are used in symmetry with the terms inflationary and non-inflationary credit expansion. An inflationary credit expansion takes place if the newly granted credits exceed new 'savings'. Non-inflationary credit expansion takes place if new savings keep up with newly granted credits. Accordingly, a deflationary credit contraction takes place if new savings exceed newly granted credits. Non-deflationary credit contraction takes place if the reduction in savings matches the reduction in credits.

depositum irregulare, where the good itself is not returned but only replaced on a like-for-like basis. The compensation for 'using' the borrowed capital (regardless of the form of payment, e.g. as a proportion of the harvested wheat) corresponds to compensation in the modern economy like *rental and tenancy fees*. In contrast, they do not show any relation to the *interest on credit and money* in the modern economy. If one wants to avoid the concise description of 'rental and tenancy fees' then one should use the term '*interest on goods*' to avoid any confusion with interest on credit and money which is particularly important to avoid drawing any incorrect conclusions.

The barter perspective's concept of a transfer of 'capital' can be found in different contexts and for different reasons in the literature. Some authors do not presuppose the barter stage of economic development in their theory but have the modern credit economy in mind. Nevertheless, they utilize the barter perspective in their theoretical formulation (often in the form of one or several Robinson Crusoes) because they do not perceive the fundamental differences between the two development stages as relevant.[4] The barter view can also be found in authors who think that borrowing real goods (coordinated by borrowing money) is actually a relevant phenomenon for the modern economy; the interest rate on money and credit is seen as of equal importance to the interest rate paid on goods.[5] Occasionally, some even go as far as to claim that borrowing goods is the only or decisive form of borrowing capital.

Admittedly, the barter perspective is logically correct and when its conditions are satisfied it gives some theoretical grounding for the common opinion that the amount of capital goods affects the amount of available credit. In fact, the structure of the supply of 'capital' is identical with the supply of capital goods in the described economy; the goods were produced and not consumed by a third person and as a consequence lent to someone. The more goods this person produces and the more he saves (out of private business motives), the higher is the supply of capital. Thus, the quantity of available capital goods determines the supply of the capital market and is the basic determinant of the interest rate (as far as we can speak of a single interest rate). The barter view also offers an explanation as to why capital goods are priced at the interest rate and not at the relative prices on the goods market (which is not self-evident); the goods used as 'capital' are not offered

[4] In this category are writings like Emil Sax, *Der Kapitalzins [The interest rate on capital]* (Berlin and Heidelberg: Springer, 1916) and to a certain degree also Eugen von Böhm-Bawerk, *Positive Theorie des Kapitals [The Positive Theory of Capital]* (Jena: Gustav Fischer, 1889).

[5] See e.g. Knut Wicksell, *Theoretischer Teil*, i: *Vorlesungen über Nationalökonomie*, trans. Margarethe Langfeldt (Jena: Gustav Fischer, 1913) [Knut Wicksell, *General Theory*, i: *Lectures on Political Economy*, trans. E. Classen, ed. Lionel Robbins (London: Routledge, 1934)].

for barter on the general goods market but for rent on a special market, the capital market. Finally the barter perspective on capital, further explains the classical view that the amount of capital determines the number and size distribution of firms[6] and subsequently the distribution of revenue between the labour and capitalist classes.

The barter view on capital, however, is not useful for explaining the relation between the quantity of capital goods and the available credit in the modern economy. The most important condition is not met: nowadays there is no special rental market for capital goods (apart from very few exceptions, like houses). The goods used as 'capital' are rather bought, not rented, on the *general goods market*. On these special markets something other than the saved goods (which are already traded on the goods market) constitute the supply, but what?

Views based on the barter perspective, face a dilemma when applying conclusions from the barter to the modern economy. It cannot be argued that 'money' and 'credit' constitute the supply of 'capital', because money is only seen as representing produced and saved goods (like the 'veil of the Maya') and its quantity is fully determined by the amount of available capital goods. At the same time, it is acknowledged that these capital goods are only traded on the goods market and not on the capital market and, hence, their supply can only affect the former. The dilemma is resolved by using the vague term 'goods of higher order' instead of the identical 'capital' at the critical passages; the neutral term 'capital' which has a less clear relation with the goods market is postulated as the determinant of capital supply. The assertion that something other than goods is traded on the capital market would only be meaningful if it is explained how capital and goods differ. This is not usually done and capital remains defined as goods.[7]

[6] Compare e.g. David Ricardo, *Grundsätze der Volkswirtschaft und Besteuerung*, trans. Edward Baumstark (Leipzig: Verlag von Wilhelm Engelmann, 1837) or 2nd edition (Leipzig: Verlag von Wilhelm Engelmann, 1877), chapter 4: 'Die Menge der Kapitalien kann wachsen . . . dann wird der Marktsatz des Arbeitslohnes in die Höhe gehen, denn die Zunahme der Nachfrage nach Arbeit steht in geradem Verhältnis zur Vermehrung des Kapitals.' [David Ricardo, *On the Principles of Political Economy and Taxation*, i: *The Works and Correspondences of David Ricardo*, ed. Pierro Sraffa and Maurice Dobb (London: Cambridge University Press, 1951), p. 95: 'Capital may increase in quantity . . . the market rate of wages will rise, for in proportion to the increase of capital will be the increase in the demand for labour; in proportion to the work to be done will be the demand for those who are to do it.'] In every conception other than the barter view, an increase in the quantity of capital goods will exert downward pressure on the wage rate, which needs to be compensated by the price for capital goods.

[7] It is interesting how Wicksell, *Theoretische Grundlagen*, p. 214 deals with the obviously appreciated difficulty. He defines capital as 'als eine einzige zusammenhängende, obwohl auf gewisse Weise nach Jahrgängen abgelagerte Masse ersparter (aufgespeicherter) Arbeitskraft einerseits und ersparter Bodenkraft andererseits'

Under these circumstances, the substitution of the term 'capital goods' with 'capital' is nothing else than a rhetorical trick, which is used at the weakest point of the whole capital theory.[8] It goes even further than that, that is, it exposes a grave logical error: seeing capital goods as 'goods' and at the same time as 'capital' on the capital market leads to double counting. It is logically impossible to allow certain attributes of the good, different to its characteristic as a good, to be called 'capital' in their own right in order to make them the subject of supply and demand; it would be the same as saying colour is a separate entity to the coloured item and as such part of a different supply. As soon as the barter economy (in which special 'capital' goods have a special market) ceases to exist *supply and demand can only consist of either goods or money and credit, but never of* the curious thing called '*capital*'. Theory has created this term and to operate it as if it was real (as is usually the case) is to do it like the fakir who throws a rope in the air and then uses it to climb up.

II. We need to state what the term 'capital' refers to if we want to concisely explain our own notion of capital. We do not want to conduct a long philological analysis of the everyday usage of the term 'capital'; we rather restrict ourselves to the statement that if it said that someone requires 'capital' then he would like all those effects described above which are consequential to granting credit to take place. The desire for these effects is the cause of the demand for capital. The capital usage implements those effects. This constitutes what is commonly called the 'capitalistic method of production'.

Having said that, we claim that *capital is the abstract power to force goods and service into certain roundabout methods of production and to stay there for a certain time*. This power is embodied in the purchasing power which is allocated through credit and is generally transferred in the form of bank deposits. If capital is needed, then one needs purchasing power or, to put it

[Wicksell, *General Theory*, p. 150: 'a single coherent mass of saved-up labour and saved-up land, which is accumulated over the course of years'] and has the fundamental conception that capital is vintage goods. Further, 'Doch dieser Unterschied genügt, um das Aufstellen einer besonderen Produktionsmittelkategorie neben der Arbeit und dem Boden unter dem Namen Kapital zu rechtfertigen' (Wicksell, *Theoretische Grundlagen*, p. 214) [Wicksell, *General Theory*, p. 150: 'But this difference is sufficient to justify the establishment of a special production factor category of means of production, side by side with labour and land, under the name of capital']. This in particular has to be rejected; goods can only appear as goods, regardless of their age. These passages also show the vague and illogical terminology of an otherwise clear author, when treating the problem of capital.

[8] This criticism particularly applies to 'abstract' capital theories, especially in Clark's version which differentiates between the productive ability of capital goods and the capital goods themselves.

plainly, money. We do not want to propose that money and credit is lent on the credit market because it is simply a fact not part of a theoretical insight. This means furthermore that money is not just the means to satisfy capital demand but an end in itself. We use the same arguments as Schumpeter[9] when making this assertion because we are fully aware that money is only a means to an end and that producing money does not necessarily mean producing goods. We have, however, stated that the purchasing power allocated by the credit is the means by which goods are diverted for productive purposes. Schumpeter[10] says 'Es ist ein besonderes agens' [it is a special agent] and as such is the subject of demand and a market in its own right.

III. Credit and savings

The generation of savings (saved capital) is not involved in the generation of capital (in the sense we use it). We have mentioned several times already that capital (as we understand it) can be generated even if no savings are deposited, that is, if inflationary credit expansion takes place. Nevertheless, savings remain an important element in the understanding of credit because the amount of new savings in the economy determines whether a credit expansion is non-inflationary or inflationary (with all its consequences). Whether deposits are spent or saved depends on the individual's frugality (which require no further explanation). Savings activity and trends in its development in a way only explain the structural increase in savings. The restructuring of assets and income (which takes place constantly for a plethora of reasons) is in practice of almost higher importance for the generation of savings.[11] Inflationary credit expansion can also induce the

[9] Schumpeter, *Theorie der wirtschaftlichen Entwicklung*, p. 175 ff.

[10] Schumpeter, *Theorie der wirtschaftlichen Entwicklung*, p. 271.

[11] The prevailing theory has a fundamentally different idea of the reasons and determinants of the creation of savings. The interest rate is seen as the critical factor by those who see savings as a necessity of capital creation (cf. Ferdinande Homann, *Das 'Sparen' als ein Grundproblem der Theorie der kapitalistischen Wirtschaft ['Savings' as the Basic Problem of the Theory of Capitalistic Economy]* (Jena: Gustav Fischer, 1927) and the writings referenced therein). Cassel in particular put this hypothesis forward (see Gustav Cassel, *The Nature and Necessity of Interest* (London: Macmillan, 1903), p. 144 ff.). Cassel thinks mainly of the small merchant who intends to save a pension for himself and his children. The interest rate is the decisive factor: if the interest rate is low, then an exceedingly large amount of capital is required to finance the desired pension; a small income, however, does not enable the merchant to save enough. However, the interest rate is irrelevant for entrepreneurs and workers with higher wages according to Cassel. Wicksell, *Theoretische Grundlagen*, p. 282 [Wicksell, *General Theory*, p. 210] denies that the case considered by Cassel is representative and argues that the main savings motive is to ensure an adequate future income. The saving activity would also not decrease at lower interest rates because the individual would need to continue to save in order to reach the same pension that would cover the individual's own needs and

restructuring of assets, which is the most important reason in our context and shall be looked at here briefly.

Our explanations show that it is self-evident that an inflationary credit expansion creates new bank deposits. These deposits are in principle long-term (not short-term) savings as shown in Figure 9 and the subsequent discussion in section [2.*]A.II ('The effect of credit expansion on the width of the flow of goods'). The newly created purchasing power is the reason for the entrepreneur's inflation and boom profits. These profits can then be used productively which is nothing other than a simultaneous investment and generation of savings; alternatively the profits can be left as savings. In fact, each period of credit expansion leads in practice to strong growth in savings deposits (in addition to the short-term deposits). The necessary proportion of the respective types of savings has already been explained in [2.*]A.II.3, section b) β) Inflationary credit expansion.[12]

The fact that credit expansion can stimulate savings (i.e. that the economy has higher savings after a credit expansion) is also used in practice when offering obligations and stocks for the first time on the public market. This is certainly guided by intuition rather than theoretical considerations. We believe that this also explains the habit (pertinent to the beginning of the boom) of selling certain stocks to banks first and offering them publicly only after enough savings are accumulated. One wants to give time to the savings-generating force of the purchasing power granted by banks before calling the public for the absorption of the issued assets.[13]

to safeguard their children's future. A similar argument can be found in E. Lukas, 'Erwägungen über die Bestimmungsgründe und die innere Verbundenheit des Angebots und der Nachfrage, die den Kapitalzins begründen' [Assessment of the Determinants and Inner Consistency of Supply and Demand that Cause the Interest Rate], in *Eheberg-Festgabe* (Leipzig: Deichert, 1925), p. 61 ff. and Homan, *Das 'Sparen' als ein Grundproblem der Theorie der kapitalistischen Wirtschaft ['Savings' as the Basic Problem of the Theory of the Capitalistic Economy].*

[12] For a detailed explanation of these relations and in particular for their empirical validation, I would like to refer to Lucien Albert Hahn, 'Zur Frage des volkswirtschaftlichen Erkenntnisinhalts der Bankbilanzziffern' [On the economic explanatory power of the bank's balance sheet], in *Geld und Kredit* (Tübingen: J. C. B. Mohr (Paul Siebeck), 1924).

[13] We analyse the potential to estimate the so-called 'nation's wealth' using the annual increase in savings in Hahn, 'Zur Frage des volkswirtschaftlichen Erkenntnisinhalts der Bankbilanzziffern'.

[2.*]C. Credit and Business Cycles

We did not primarily have the vast credit expansions ordered by the government (e.g. the German inflationary period) in mind when we analysed the effects of inflationary credit expansion previously.[1] Most of the earlier results carry over to this situation; however, we have to reflect the unproductive use of a large amount of credit with its devastating effect for the currency, which we have already considered elsewhere.[2] Here we want to focus our attention on those inflationary credit relations which were granted to varying extent in the last decades (a period which never showed any stability in the flow of credit).

The so-called business cycles are, without a doubt, the most interesting consequences of the fluctuations in the credit business. In line with the monetary business cycle theory, we claim that those business cycles are nothing other than the effects of an inflationary and then deflationary credit policy of banks.

We do not want to present a detailed argument in favour of a monetary business cycle theory. Instead, we would like to point towards signs which seem to indicate it is correct:

[1] Hayek published an extraordinary book (Friedrich August von Hayek, *Geldtheorie und Konjunkturtheorie [Monetary Theory and the Trade Cycle]* (Vienna and Leipzig: Hölder-Pichler-Tempsky, 1929)) after we completed the revision for the 3rd edition of this book, which is the reason why we cannot treat his exposition in detail. Hayek's view is similar to ours because he also bases his theory on Wicksell. The only point of divergence is the position on the general price level. Hayek regards the assumption of a general price level as wrong, even useless, in developing the monetary business cycle theory (p. 55); this is a similar view to Ludwig von Mises, *Geldwertstabilisierung und Konjunkturpolitik* (Jena: Gustav Fischer, 1928) [A translation is published as 'Monetary Stabilization and Cyclical Policy' in *Mises on the Manipulation of Money and Credit*, ed. by Percy L. Greaves, trans. Bettina B. Greaves (Dobbs Ferry, New York: Free Market Books), p. 57–107]. In contrast, we continue to use the idea of a general price level; nevertheless, we believe that this difference does not weigh heavily in our general agreement with Hayek.

[2] Compare my essays from the inflation period, published in Lucien Albert Hahn, *Geld und Kredit, Gesammelte Aufsätze [Money and Credit: Collected Essays]* (Tübingen: J. C .B Mohr (Paul Siebeck), 1924).

I. What are the typical signs of a business cycle?

a) The most typical sign of an economic upswing is *demand growth in the goods markets.*
b) *Price increases* on the goods markets are key symptoms of the business cycle and are a consequence of the demand growth.
c) The third key indicator is the *rise* of the economy's *employment rate.*
d) The fourth sign is that capital investments show above average increases in bursts, that is, more roundabout methods of productions are used.

None of these four symptoms represents the nature of the business cycle by itself but the combination of all four perfectly defines the business cycle. Other economic phenomena may show one sign or another but the simultaneous appearance of all four symptoms only takes place in the business cycle.

A further characteristic of the business cycle is that the economic upswing is followed by an economic downturn. The economic downturn shows all symptoms of the economic upswing but with an inverted sign; the only difference is that the downturn takes place more abruptly, in particular the fall in demand for goods.

II. The four listed symptoms of the economic upswing are identical with the consequences of credit expansion which we deduced earlier. This implies that the credit expansion is a reason for the economic upswing. The following analysis reveals that it is actually the sole reason.

Many of the symptoms can have different causes: a higher employment rate can be caused, for example, by less expensive labour which in turn can be caused by a lower collective wage agreement or new technology with higher labour productivity; higher investment can be induced by a higher level of saving activity by the population. In contrast, demand growth and price rises (which are, of course, across the board and not limited to certain products or sectors) on the goods markets can only be explained by an increase in the quantity of money or in its velocity (as implied by the quantity theory of money). Furthermore, a decrease in demand (in particular, stagnation of sales) and prices on the goods market can only be caused by a decrease in the quantity of money or its velocity. Given a constant quantity of money and velocity, the phenomenon of sales stagnating is impossible in a monetary economy as much as in a barter economy (according to Say's law). Everyone participating in production receives money, which in total is sufficient to buy all goods without any reductions in prices.

In the modern economy there is only one cause of investment increasing at the same time as demand: the primarily purchasing-power-creating (inflationary) credit expansion of private banks in conjunction with a credit expansion of the central bank.

Credit expansion is necessary and sufficient to explain all the symptoms of the business cycle listed above. We can deduce that such a credit expansion causes the following:

a) Any credit expansion is financed by the creation of bank money by commercial banks and banknotes by the central bank. Therefore there is an increase in the quantity of money; this means additional purchasing power, which in turn means a notional increase in demand.
b) A notional increase in demand causes a rise in prices, given a constant supply of goods.
c) New credit (financed through the creation of money by commercial and the central bank) lowers the interest rate below the level which would prevail without this money creation (in Wicksell's terminology the 'natural interest rate'). This gives rise to extra profits, which enable previously unused labour and factories to be used productively. Firms also receive extra profits caused by actual or anticipated price increases during the production process. The result is an increase in the employment rate.
d) The increase in money is motivated by granting new credits and therefore increases investment i.e. using more roundabout methods of production.

As an aside, foreign credit only cause symptoms c) and d) (a rise in employment, lowering of the interest rate and an increase in investment) but does not cause symptoms a) and b) (a rise in demand and in prices). Whether or not the symptoms caused by foreign credit are called a business cycle is a matter of terminology, but they are certainly not business cycles as happened before the war.

This implies that only the increase in the quantity of money and velocity respectively *can* cause the symptoms of the business cycle. Empirical observation shows that business cycles are always accompanied by an increase in the quantity of money and very likely also its velocity.[3]

III. There was actually a lively debate surrounding the relation of the credit expansion and the business cycle. The debate covered issues like whether or not the credit expansion is actually the cause of the business cycle, whether or not it is coincidental to the business cycle or even if the credit expansion is a symptom caused by the business cycle. We want to concur with Mitchell[4]

[3] Cf. Lucien Albert Hahn, 'Zur Frage des volkswirtschaftlichen Erkenntnisinhalts der Bankbilanzziffern' [On the Economic Explanatory Power of the Bank's Balance Sheet], in *Geld und Kredit.*

[4] See Wesley Clair Mitchell, *Business Cycles: The Problem and its Setting* (New York: National Bureau of Economic Research, 1927), p. 54: 'When we have accounted

and think that the scientific significance of this debate is vastly overestimated. It is certainly the case that a business cycle without credit expansion is impossible. Thus, the credit expansion is at least a necessary condition for the business cycle. In practice this means, however, that the unfolding of the business cycle can be stopped by suppressing the credit expansion. The specific trigger for the credit expansion is theoretically and practically irrelevant for bringing the expansion to a halt, for example: if the gold stock increases and the central bank would usually decrease the interest rate, then it could simply maintain the interest rate; a second case could be that technological progress increases the industry's willingness to pay higher interest rates, then the central bank could simply increase the interest rates to eliminate the incentive for a credit expansion.

We have sketched a monetary business cycle and crisis theory which can explain the fluctuations in the four described economic data. It does not explain that these fluctuations are cyclical (i.e. the upswing is followed by a downturn, etc.), similar to a pendulum or wave motions. Following Wicksell[5] we think that the cycle has the following explanation.

Assume that a certain interest rate on capital investments prevails in the economy or is at least expected. If the central bank increases the discount rate absolutely but not relative to the expected surplus of the investment, then the effective interest rate decreases below its natural level.

1. This causes a credit expansion and the business cycle gathers momentum; the price increases during the upswing generate extra profits and are an incentive to expand credit further.

2. Credit is further expanded and the business cycle gathers further momentum unless the central bank eliminates this incentive at the right time.

3. Eventually the incentive is exhausted and the number of debtors does not rise at this stage; prices also do not increase any more.

4. The interest rates are set as if ever further increases in prices are expected; they act restrictively when these expected price rises do not materialise. The resulting credit contraction causes prices to decrease.

in casual terms for each stage in a lengthy series of actions and reactions, we find that our analysis deals with many causes, each one of which is logically indispensable to the theory we have elaborated. On reflection, we see the application to our work of the old contention that the idea of causation has pragmatic, rather than scientific, warrant. All the conditions which are indispensable to produce a certain result stand on much the same footing from the viewpoint of science.'

[5] Knut Wicksell, *Geldzins und Güterpreis* (Jena: Gustav Fischer, 1898) [Knut Wicksell, *Interest and Prices*, trans. Richard F. Kahn (London: Macmillan, 1936)].

5. Falling prices lead to a further contraction of credit which causes a further decrease in prices.
6. The depressing force of falling prices is exhausted at some point and the business cycle reaches its low. The economy recovers from this position again and a new cycle begins.

We have to add that the fall in prices does not occur instantly. At first some regular consumers lose purchasing power and sales stagnate (this happens earlier for those earlier in the supply chain). This induces a demand for so called 'bridging loans' which cause interest payments and at some point the bridging loans are not prolonged. This causes prices to fall and the liquidation of firms begins. The schematic overview in Table 3 shows the development of a business cycle.

IV. Since the pre-war period business cycles have experienced a change not only in numbers but also in quality. Before the war stabilising policy measures (in particular changes to the discount rate) were implemented in an attempt to curtail the excesses of the business cycle. However, these attempts were based on instinct rather than on theory. The policy was further hindered by attempts to consider other symptoms and by the insufficient state of the empirical research on business cycles. The empirical research and in particular business cycle statistics progressed substantially (the estimation of a general price index). The desire to prevent fluctuations of the general price level with monetary causes has grown stronger (see Irving Fisher, J. M. Keynes). This created a quite different situation: certain up- and downward fluctuations of the general price level will still occur. However, there is no doubt that the general public would not tolerate (at least) *substantial*, general *increases* in the price level. The central bank would need to suppress such developments through its open market policy. Fighting price increases in their early stages (if not suppressing them outright) alters price expectations. Removing the expectation that prices will rise from the mind of the economy's individuals removes a crucial factor in the business cycle: if no-one believes in a price increase, then a crucial driver for price increases is suppressed.

V. *It would certainly be a mistake to assume that any analysis of the business cycle and the effects of inflationary credit are rendered superfluous by a stabilised price level.* It has been shown that there are phenomena showing all symptoms of an economic upswing (higher demand, higher employment, more investment, also higher wages) apart from an increase in prices.[6]

[6] See Eugen Altschul, 'Konjunkturaufschwung bei sinkenden Preise' [Economic Upswing at Decreasing Prices], *Magazin der Wirtschaft*, 17 February 1927. Altschul

Table 3

Phase	a) Trigger	b) Credit volume	c) Impact on the price level
Phase 1: Recovery	Falling interest rate	Credit expansion	Increase in purchasing power and therefore the price level
Phase 2: Expansion	Increased price level (1c)	Further credit expansion	Further price increases
Phase 3: Boom	Increased price level, but does not act as an incentive any more (2c)	No further credit expansion	No further price increases because of no further credit expansion
Phase 4: Contraction	Absence of price level increase (3c)	Credit contraction	Price level decrease as a consequence of credit contraction
Phase 5: Recession	Decreased price level (4c)	Further credit contraction	Further price level decrease
Phase 6: Depression	Decreased price level, but does not act as an incentive for further depression	No further credit contraction	No further price level decrease

The economic upswing in the US that started in 1925 is accompanied by rising prices. The last economic upswing in Germany, starting in spring 1926, brought a general increase in the level of prices, but at a rather insignificant scale when compared to the pre-war period. The upswing has been rightly called a 'Mengenkonjunktur' which is signified by an increase in output at constant or decreasing prices. It is enabled by inflationary credit which causes changes in the technology used which in turn shows a deflationary effect and offsets the inflationary tendencies of credit.

VI. To what extent is the 'Mengenkonjunktur' part of the business cycle or is it simply the expression of structural change?

Structural change can be positively defined as an expression of the natural development of the economy. One can also define it negatively as all those changes which are not caused by the business cycle. The changes caused by the business cycle need to be identified by a business cycle theory in order to avoid a circular argument. Following the monetary theory of the business cycle, we identify all changes caused by changes in the volume of inflationary credit as due to the business cycle. All other changes in the economy are 'structural'.

The Mengenkonjunktur is a unique intermediate case between a symptom of the business cycle and structural development. On the one hand, credit expansion induces a permanent increase in purchasing power. The creation of purchasing power causes all the symptoms of the economic upswing apart from the increase in prices, because the higher demand meets a higher supply. On the other hand, this symptom can only occur because of the technical changes associated with economic development. Only this technological progress enabled expanding inflationary credit which would have otherwise not been done to maintain price stability. This is probably the reason why the Institut für Konjunkturforschung in Berlin occasionally interprets the American upswing as a structural upswing in connection with an economic downturn. This interpretation does not seem to be accurate: unlike a Mengenkonjunktur, a structural upswing in connection with a downturn of the business cycle does not (at least not necessarily) lead to price decreases at constant wages but leads to wage increases with no (at least not necessarily any) decrease in prices. The Mengenkonjunktur also leads to an increase in employment and investment

was the first to show that economic upswings can take place without any price increases or even with decreasing prices. He attempts a theoretical interpretation of the economic upswing taking place in the US since 1925 (which largely conforms with ours). He concluded that the price development is not a clear indicator for the business cycle and should only be used with caution in business cycle analysis. This has important implications for business cycle research, in particular as it is practised at the Harvard institute.

which exceeds the effects of a structural change on its own (i.e. without an expansion of inflationary credit).

It needs to be noted that there is no reason to assume the Mengenkonjunktur to be cyclical. No price increases occur and therefore no bullish expectation is built up. This removes the element that pushes the boom period over its peak and leads to the economic downturn. The Mengenkonjunktur is therefore unique; neither can it be seen as a reaction to something nor as causing any other reactions. It also does not need to show the well-known phases of the business cycle or affect the stock or money markets. Inflationary credit can and will be expanded without any price increases as long as technology continues to progress and decrease production costs. A pause in technical progress leads to a stop in expanding inflationary credit but it does not necessarily mean that it is contracted which would lead to a downturn.

An economy which only shows Mengenkonjunkturen but not any other business cycles might sound like utopia for some; it is however necessary under some circumstances to take prevailing tendencies into account and describe a *future* economy to identify the *present* economy, instead of fondly describing *past* economic ages to do justice to the present (as is usually done nowadays).

The practical consequence of our analysis and ideas is that any analysis of the business cycle solely relying (either explicitly or implicitly) on the schematic phases of the cycle needs to be treated with even greater care. Furthermore it also shows the spuriousness of pessimistic evaluations of the economic situation *solely* based on an assumption that the downturn is inevitable.

[2.*]D. The Limits for Inflationary Credit Expansion

This book looks at the delicate subject of inflationary credit expansion and as such is potentially more prone to misunderstandings. There is a danger that some think it overvalues the potential and practical relevance of credit inflation; some might also take the view that credit inflation is of such low importance in this 'credit theory' that it implicitly shows that a long-run expansion of inflationary credit is not possible. These arguments do not affect the scientific value of the book, however we shall make following counter arguments:

I. It is correct that a strong inflationary credit expansion cannot be prolonged ad infinitum. The depreciation of the domestic currency would already give a clear stop signal in an open economy. It cannot be undertaken for long even if the central banks of the trading countries expand inflationary credit in a coordinated manner. A moment is eventually reached when the ever-increasing prices cause mistrust in the purchasing power of the currency and long-term savings are used to consume. This causes either an immense scarcity of money, unless the central bank keeps the interest rate low, which leads to further inflation and eventually leads to the collapse of the economic system.

The recent period of inflation is a historical case of this development which showed the usage of long-term savings for consumption and the incomprehensible Reichsbank policy to maintain low interest rates in 1922.

II. It is also correct that the inflationary credit's stimulating effects on demand and prices cannot be maintained or escalated by further credit expansion. The central bank either does not lower the interest rate in which case the incentives to increase prices exhausts itself and credits are restricted, or the central bank succeeds in expanding credit further in which case the catastrophic consequences described in the paragraph above occur.

III. However this does not imply that any stimulating effects of inflationary credit are only transient and cannot cause further consequences. An economic upswing generally endures without ever-new doses of stimulation when it is caused by a reduction in the interest rate not by an increase in prices.

IV. To assume that inflationary credit expansion has only occurred exceptionally is a further error. We see the typical business cycle as the consequence of alternating credit inflations and deflations, but throughout history shorter or longer periods of inflationary credit expansion have occurred. The development of the German economy since 1870 should be seen as one long period of inflationary credit expansion (albeit at fluctuating strengths).[1]

V. It was finally argued that inflationary credit loses importance the more price-stabilizing policies are pursued. The objection is certainly valid but one should not lose sight of the fact that an economic upswing at constant prices is possible. This interesting possibility cannot be fully appreciated without a theory of inflationary credit because it is also a case of inflationary credit.

VI. To pre-empt any misunderstanding we also want to note that the so-called (particularly in the English literature) 'stabilisation of the business cycle at a high level of employment' is not a stabilisation of the business cycle. A stabilisation of the business cycle means preventing deviations from an average level of economic activity, that is, preventing a change of economic data which cannot be durable; in particular, this means avoiding an unsustainably low interest rate and price increases or decreases which will sooner or later be reversed. The stabilisation at a 'high level of employment' aims to fix the average economic activity at a high level of employment. However, the level of employment is something structural. It is dependent on the relation between the price of labour and its productivity. This relation changes throughout the business cycle causing fluctuations in the employment rate. The average level of employment, however, can only be changed through means beyond the business cycle.

[1] The credit volume has increased twelvefold in the period of 1870 to 1910 according to Eugen Altschul. The period between 1872 and 1900 shows a strong degree of credit expansion and the curve representing credit expansion rises steeply until 1910. Cf. Eugen Altschul, 'Bankbilanzen und Konjunkturverlauf' [Balance Sheets of Banks and Business Cycles], *Bankwissenschaft* 4, no 6, pp. 203–4.

Index

The manufacturer's authorised representative in the EU for product safety is Oxford University Press España S.A. of el Parque Empresarial San Fernando de Henares, Avenida de Castilla, 2 – 28830 Madrid (www.oup.es/en or product.safety@oup.com). OUP España S.A. also acts as importer into Spain of products made by the manufacturer.

www.ingramcontent.com/pod-product-compliance
Lightning Source LLC
LaVergne TN
LVHW011512200926
848484LV00001B/17
* 9 7 8 0 1 9 8 7 2 3 0 7 3 *